Markus Brameier and Wolfgang Banzhaf

Linear Genetic Programming

Genetic and Evolutionary Computation Series

Series Editors

David E. Goldberg
Consulting Editor
IlliGAL, Dept. of General Engineering
University of Illinois at Urbana-Champaign
Urbana, IL 61801 USA
Email: deg@uiuc.edu

John R. Koza
Consulting Editor
Medical Informatics
Stanford University
Stanford, CA 94305-5479 USA
Email: john@johnkoza.com

Selected titles from this series:

Nikolay Y. Nikolaev, Hitoshi Iba
Adaptive Learning of Polynomial Networks, 2006
ISBN 978-0-387-31239-2

Tetsuya Higuchi, Yong Liu, Xin Yao
Evolvable Hardware, 2006
ISBN 978-0-387-24386-3

David E. Goldberg
The Design of Innovation: Lessons from and for Competent Genetic Algorithms, 2002
ISBN 978-1-4020-7098-3

John R. Koza, Martin A. Keane, Matthew J. Streeter, William Mydlowec, Jessen Yu, Guido Lanza
Genetic Programming IV: Routine Human-Computer Machine Intelligence
ISBN: 978-1-4020-7446-2 (hardcover), 2003; ISBN: 978-0-387-25067-0 (softcover), 2005

Carlos A. Coello Coello, David A. Van Veldhuizen, Gary B. Lamont
Evolutionary Algorithms for Solving Multi-Objective Problems, 2002
ISBN: 978-0-306-46762-2

Lee Spector
Automatic Quantum Computer Programming: A Genetic Programming Approach
ISBN: 978-1-4020-7894-1 (hardcover), 2004; ISBN 978-0-387-36496-4 (softcover), 2007

William B. Langdon
Genetic Programming and Data Structures: Genetic Programming + Data Structures = Automatic Programming! 1998
ISBN: 978-0-7923-8135-8

For a complete listing of books in this series, go to http://www.springer.com

Markus Brameier
Wolfgang Banzhaf

Linear Genetic Programming

 Springer

Markus F. Brameier
Bioinformatics Research Center (BiRC)
University of Aarhus
Denmark
brameier@birc.au.dk

Wolfgang Banzhaf
Department of Computer Science
Memorial University of Newfoundland
St. John's, NL
Canada
banzhaf@cs.mun.ca

Library of Congress Control Number: 2006920909

ISBN-10: 0-387-31029-0   e-ISBN-10: 0-387-31030-4
ISBN-13: 978-0387-31029-9   e-ISBN-13: 978-0387-31030-5

Printed in the United States of America

9 8 7 6 5 4 3 2 1

springer.com

We dedicate this book
to our beloved parents.

Contents

Preface

This book is about linear genetic programming (LGP), a variant of GP that evolves computer programs as sequences of instructions of an imperative programming language. It is a comprehensive text with a strong experimental basis and an in-depth focus on structural aspects of the linear program representation.

The three major objectives of this book are:

☐ To discuss linear genetic programming in a broader context and to contrast it with tree-based genetic programming.

☐ To develop advanced methods and efficient genetic operators for the imperative representation to produce both better *and* shorter program solutions.

☐ To give a better understanding for the intricate effects of operators on evolutionary processes and emergent phenomena in linear GP.

Part I of the book is dedicated to laying a foundation for basic understanding as well as to providing methods for analysis. The first two chapters give an introduction to evolutionary computation, genetic programming, and linear GP.

Chapter 3 presents efficient algorithms for analyzing the imperative and functional structure of linear genetic programs during runtime. The special program representation used in this book can be transformed into *directed acyclic graphs* (DAGs). So-called *structurally* noneffective code can be identified that is disconnected from the effective data flow and independent of program semantics. Other important parameters of linear programs include the *number of effective registers* at a certain program position, the *dependence degree* of effective instructions, and the *effective dependence distance*.

Chapter 4 concludes Part I and is dedicated to a comparison of standard LGP with neural networks on medical diagnosis data. Both machine learning techniques turn out to be competitive in terms of generalization ability and learning speed, if certain efficiency considerations are taken into account.

Part II is concerned with methods for evolutionary search, and how they can be improved. In Chapters 5 and 6 we discuss and develop variation operators for the linear (imperative) representation. The most efficient solutions – concerning highest prediction accuracy and lowest complexity – are obtained if only one effective instruction is changed or created at a time. This demonstrates the high power of applying mutations exclusively in linear GP. Both chapters also investigate the influence of variation-specific parameters.

General parameter of linear GP are the subject of Chapter 7. For instance, the number of registers used by the imperative programs determines their functional structure, expressed in features like the maximum width of the DAG.

At this point the worth of LGP has been established beyond doubt, so it is time for another comparison on a wider range of benchmark problems. In Chapter 8 two advanced variants of linear GP clearly outperform tree-based GP, especially if the size of solutions is respected. This concludes Part II of the book.

Part III is dedicated to the analysis and control of different GP features. Chapter 9 will look at the diversity of code and the effective step size of operators. How can it be measured, how can it be controlled, and to what effect does this lead? Among other things, the efficiency of the evolutionary search is improved by a novel multi-objective selection method. Even without explicit control, the effective step size of mutations decreases over the generations due to an increasing robustness of effective code.

The phenomenon of code bloat is at the center of interest in Chapter 10. It is a well-known problem that genetic programs grow – mostly by non-effective code – without showing corresponding improvements in fitness. Neutral variations are identified as an indirect but major cause of code growth. It turns out that linear programs hardly grow without neutral variations if the step size is limited to one instruction. In general, code growth in linear GP occurs to be much more aggressive with recombination than with mutation.

Most results presented in this book refer to genetic programs as a single sequence of instructions. Program teams are investigated in Chapter 11 as a way to enlarge the complexity and dimension of LGP solutions.

All in all the book is an empirical investigation of considerable magnitude. Its detailed text is supported by 115 tables and 132 figures in total and describes an even higher number of different experiments, comprising ten thousands of documented GP runs.

We hope that readers will enjoy studying this book and that they get inspired by learning new arguments and aspects about this interesting branch of genetic programming and evolutionary computation. We are convinced that the text makes a valuable contribution to a more thorough and deeper understanding of what actually goes on in the evolution of imperative computer programs. It provides sufficient introductory material for learners and serves as a comprehensive resource of information for readers who are familiar with the field.

Markus Brameier and Wolfgang Banzhaf,

Aarhus and St. John's, June 2006

About the Authors

Markus Brameier received a PhD degree in Computer Science from the Department of Computer Science at University of Dortmund, Germany, in 2004. From 2003 to 2004 he was a postdoctoral fellow at the Stockholm Bioinformatics Center (SBC), a collaboration between Stockholm University, the Royal Institute of Technology, and Karolinska Institute, in Sweden. Currently he is Assistant Professor at the Bioinformatics Research Center (BiRC) of the University of Aarhus in Denmark. His primary research interests are in bioinformatics and genetic programming.

Wolfgang Banzhaf is a professor of Computer Science at the Department of Computer Science of Memorial University of Newfoundland, Canada, and head of the department since 2003. Prior to that, he served for 10 years as Associate Professor for Applied Computer Science in the Department of Computer Science at University of Dortmund, Germany. From 1989 to 1993 he was a researcher with Mitsubishi Electric Corp., first in MELCO's Central Research Lab in Japan, then in the United States at Mitsubishi Electric Research Labs Inc., Cambridge, MA. Between 1985 and 1989 he was a postdoc in the Department of Physics, University of Stuttgart, Germany. He holds a PhD in Physics from the University of Karlruhe in Germany. His research interests are in the field of artificial evolution and self-organization studies. He has recently become more involved with bioinformatics.

Chapter 1

INTRODUCTION

Natural evolution has always been a source of inspiration for science and engineering. "Endless forms, most beautiful", as Darwin put it. Who would not marvel at the unbelievable variety of life, who would not admire its complexity? A process that could bring about such wonders in nature, couldn't we glean from it some tricks that would be useful for our own activities? Couldn't we learn some methods for the design of other systems, for instance, machines and their behaviors? It is along these lines of thought that algorithms where conceived, able to catch aspects of natural evolution.

1.1 Evolutionary Algorithms

Evolutionary algorithms (EAs) mimic aspects of natural evolution for the purpose of optimizing a solution to a predefined problem. Following Darwin's principle of natural selection, differential fitness advantages are exploited in a population of solutions to gradually improve the state of that population. The application of these principles, often referred to as *artificial evolution*, led to different approaches, such as *genetic algorithms* (GAs), *evolution strategies* (ES), and *evolutionary programming* (EP). A comparatively young research area in this context is *genetic programming* (GP). Evolutionary algorithms as a whole, together with *neural networks* and *fuzzy logic*, are considered methods of *computational intelligence* [120].

A general evolutionary algorithm is a radical abstraction from its biological model and may be summarized as follows:

ALGORITHM 1.1 (*general evolutionary algorithm*)

1. Randomly initialize a population of individual solutions.

2. Select individuals from the population that are fitter than others by using a certain *selection method*. The *fitness* measure defines the problem the algorithm is expected to solve.

3. Generate new variants by applying the following *genetic operators* with certain probabilities:

   □ *Reproduction*: Copy an individual without change.

   □ *Recombination*: Randomly exchange substructures between individuals.

   □ *Mutation*: Randomly replace a substructure in an individual.

4. If the termination criterion is not met, → 2.

5. Stop. The best individual represents the best solution found.

While genetic algorithms [50, 41] started out with individuals represented as fixed-length binary strings, evolution strategies [110, 119] traditionally operated on real-valued vectors. Both techniques have developed over the years and borders are more blurred between them than they used to be, yet they are applied primarily to parameter optimization problems. Genetic programming [64, 9], on the other hand, varies individuals on a symbolic level as computer programs. That is, the representation is usually executable and of variable size and shape.

In a more general sense genetic programming may also be regarded as a method of *machine learning*, a field that studies computer algorithms able to learn from experience [84]. Especially some of the early machine learning approaches show clear resemblance to modern GP. Friedberg [39, 40] attempted to solve simple problems by teaching a computer to write computer programs. Due to his choice of search strategy, however, his results did not lead to a breakthrough. Later, evolutionary programming [37, 38] was introduced as a method using *finite state automata* (FSA) as representation of individuals. This work could arguably be called the first successful evolutionary algorithm for automatic program induction.[1] It was Cramer [30], however, who first applied EAs to more general programs. He experimented with linear structures and tree-based hierarchical program representations. The potential of this approach was only later uncovered

---

[1] Program in this case would be the set of state transitions of the FSA.

through the extensive work of Koza [63–67]. He and his coworkers could demonstrate the feasibility of this approach in well-known application areas. He also gave the method the name *genetic programming*.

1.2   Genetic Programming

Genetic programming (GP) may be defined generally as any direct evolution or breeding of computer programs for the purpose of inductive learning. In particular, this definition leaves GP independent of a special type of program representation. GP may, in principle, solve the same range of problems as other machine learning techniques, e.g., neural networks. Indeed, most of today's real-world applications of GP demonstrate its ability in *data mining*, as shown by the discovery of regularities within large data domains. For supervised learning tasks that means to create predictive models, i.e., classifiers or approximators, that learn a set of known and labeled data and generalize to a set of unknown and unlabeled data. Other application areas of GP comprise, for instance, control problems, time series prediction, signal processing and image processing.

Genetic programs may be regarded as prediction models that approximate an *objective function* $f : I^n \rightarrow O^m$ with I^n denoting the input data in a space of dimension n and O^m denoting the output data in an m-dimensional space. Most cases considered in this book will have an output space dimension of only $m = 1$. Genetic programs can also complete missing (unknown) parts of an existing model. Other evolutionary algorithms, like genetic algorithms or evolution strategies, minimize an existing objective function or model by searching for the optimum setting of its variables (model parameters).

Suppose, an objective function f represents the problem to be solved by GP. In practice this function is unknown and defined only incompletely by a relatively small set of input-output vectors $T = \{(\vec{i}, \vec{o}) \mid \vec{i} \in I' \subseteq I^n, \vec{o} \in O' \subseteq O^m, f(\vec{i}) = \vec{o}\}$. The evolutionary process searches for a program or algorithm that represents the best solution to this problem, i.e., that maps the given *training (data) set* T to a function in the best possible way. Training samples are also referred to as *fitness cases* in GP. GP models are not only expected to predict the outputs of all training inputs I' most precisely but also many inputs from $I^n \setminus I'$. That is, the genetic programs are required to generalize from training data to unknown data. The generalization ability is verified by means of input-output examples from the same data domain as (but different from) the training examples.

The *genotype space* $\mathcal{G}$ in GP includes all programs of a certain *representation (type)* that can be composed of elements from a *programming language*

$\mathcal{L}$. If we assume that programs do not induce side effects the _phenotype space_ $\mathcal{P}$ denotes the set of all mathematical functions $f_{gp} : I^n \to O^m$ with $f_{gp} \in \mathcal{P}$ that can be expressed by programs $gp \in \mathcal{G}$. The programming language $\mathcal{L}$ is defined by the user over an _instruction set_ (or _function set_) and a so-called _terminal set_. The latter may comprise input values, constants, and memory variables.

The _fitness function_ $\mathcal{F} : \mathcal{P} \to V$ measures the prediction quality, the _fitness_, of a phenotype $f_{gp} \in \mathcal{P}$. For this book we assume the range of fitness values to be $V = \mathbb{R}_0^+$ for continuous problems and $V = \mathbb{N}_0$ for discrete problems. Fitness is usually derived from a mapping error between the predicted model f_{gp} and the desired model f. Because fitness cases represent in general only a fraction of the problem data space, fitness may only partially reflect the phenotype behavior of a program.

In most situations, fitness evaluation of individuals is by far the most time-critical step of a GP algorithm since a genetic program has to be _executed_ at least once for each fitness case in the fitness function. Prior to that, the genotype representation gp has to be translated into the phenotype function f_{gp}. Such a genotype-phenotype mapping is usually deterministic and produced by an _interpreter_ $f_{int} : \mathcal{G} \to \mathcal{P}$ with $f_{int}(gp) = f_{gp}$ and $\mathcal{F}(gp) := \mathcal{F}(f_{gp})$, the fitness of a genotype being the same as the fitness of its phenotype. Neither function f_{int} nor $\mathcal{F}$ are bijective because a phenotype may be represented by more than one genotype and different phenotypes may have the same fitness.

Composition of the instruction set and the terminal set determines the expressiveness of programming language $\mathcal{L}$. On the one hand, this language must be powerful enough to represent the optimum solution of our problem or at least a good local optimum. On the other hand, finding a solution becomes more difficult if the _search space_ of programs $\mathcal{G}$ is increased unnecessarily by too large a set of program components. If $\mathcal{L}$ is _Turing-complete_, every computable function may be found in principle, provided that the maximum program size is sufficiently large to represent such a function. In practice, however, it is recommended to define a language as small as possible. In order to resolve this trade-off situation genetic programming requires knowledge from the user about the problem domain. Because Turing-completeness requires infinite loops and we cannot know beforehand whether a program will terminate or not, a maximum bound on execution time will be necessary. This can be implemented through a restriction on the maximum number of executed instructions.

There are many ways to represent a certain function by a program, mostly due to neutral code in genotypes that is not expressed in the phenotype.

The *complexity* of a genetic program is usually measured as the number of instructions it holds. A growing variable-length representation is important in GP since, in general, the minimum representation size of the optimum solution is unknown. Following the *principle of Occam's Razor*, among all solutions with equal fitness the shortest solution should be preferred. This solution is supposed to achieve the best generalization performance. In GP, how compact a program will be possible for a certain objective function depends on the expressiveness of the programming language used, and on the variability of the representation.

In reality, the maximum size of programs has to be restricted to prevent programs from growing without bound and consuming all system resources. If no maximum restriction is imposed on the representation size, then not only the generalization ability of solutions may be reduced, but also the efficiency of genetic operations. Additionally, a longer execution time of programs increases the time for fitness evaluation. Should one choose too small a maximum complexity, then the optimum solution may be altogether impossible to find due to insufficient space for a proper representation. Again it is up to the user to find a good trade-off between these conflicting goals. Yet, both the success of the evolutionary search and the growth of programs depend not only on the representation but on the variation operators, too.

Let $P(t) \subset \mathcal{G}$ denote the state of a *population* at time t. Training time or *runtime* of evolutionary algorithms is often measured in terms of *generations* or generation equivalents. From a random subpopulation $P' \subseteq P(t)$ of $n = |P'|$ individuals a *selection operator* $s : \mathcal{G}^n \times \mathcal{P}^n \to \mathcal{G}^\mu$ selects $\mu < n$ individuals for variation. The selection operator determines from which individuals the search will be continued.

A *genetic operator* or *variation operator* $v : \mathcal{G}^\mu \to \mathcal{G}^\lambda$ creates λ offspring out of the μ selected parents from population $P(t)$. These λ new individuals become part of population $P(t+1)$. In other words, λ new search points are visited in genotype space. If $\mu < \lambda$ a parent produces more than one offspring. Usually recombination in GP creates two offspring from two parents, i.e., $\mu = \lambda = 2$, while mutation or reproduction produce $\mu = \lambda = 1$. All genetic operators must guarantee, first, that no syntactically incorrect programs are generated during evolution (*syntactic closure*). Second, the value and the type of each instruction argument must be drawn from defined ranges (*semantic protection*). The calculation of a new search point is much less expensive than the fitness evaluation in GP and may be neglected.

1.3   Linear Genetic Programming

In recent years different variants of genetic programming have emerged. All follow the basic idea of GP to automatically evolve computer programs. Three basic forms of representation may be distinguished for genetic programs. Besides the traditional *tree* representations, these are *linear* and *graph* representations [9].

The tree programs used in Koza-style genetic programming correspond to expressions (syntax trees) from a functional programming language. This classical approach is also referred to as *tree-based genetic programming* (TGP). Functions are located at inner nodes, while leaves of the tree hold input values or constants. In contrast, *linear genetic programming* (LGP) is a GP variant that evolves sequences of instructions from an imperative programming language or from a machine language. In this book instructions are restricted to *operations* – including conditional operations – that accept a *minimum* number of constants or memory variables, called *registers*, and assign the result to another register, e.g., $r_0 := r_1 + 1$.

The term *linear* refers to the structure of the (imperative) program representation. It does not stand for functional genetic programs that are restricted to a linear list of nodes only. Moreover, it does not mean that the method itself is linear, i.e., may solve linearly separable problems only. On the contrary, genetic programs normally represent highly non-linear solutions due to their inherent power of expression.

The use of linear bit sequences in GP again goes back to Cramer and his JB language [30]. A more general linear approach was introduced in [7]. Nordin's idea of subjecting machine code to evolution was the first GP approach [90] that operated directly on an imperative representation. It was subsequently expanded and developed into the AIMGP (*Automatic Induction of Machine code by Genetic Programming*) approach [93, 9]. In AIMGP individuals are manipulated as binary machine code in memory and are executed directly without passing an interpreter during the fitness calculation. This results in a significant speedup compared to interpreting systems. In [93] machine code GP and the application of this linear GP approach to different problem domains have been studied.

In this book we will concentrate on fundamental aspects of the linear program representation and examine its differences to a tree representation. Advanced LGP techniques are developed with the goal to be as independent as possible from any special type of imperative programming language. Transfer of results to machine code GP is nevertheless possible over wide areas. The methods we present here are not meant to be specific to a certain application area, but can be applied to a wide range of problems.

There are two basic differences between a linear program and a tree program:

(1) A linear genetic program can be seen as a data flow graph produced by multiple usage of register content. That is, on the functional level the evolved imperative structure represents a special *directed graph*. In traditional tree GP the data flow is more rigidly determined by the tree structure of the program.

The *higher variability* of linear program graphs allows the result of subprograms (subgraphs) to be reused multiple times during calculation. This permits linear solutions to be more compact in size than tree solutions and to express more complex calculations with less instructions. The step size of variations may also be easier to control in a program structure with higher degrees of freedom than in a tree structure. How much advantage evolution can take of these features will strongly depend on the design of appropriate variation operators.

(2) Special noneffective code segments coexist with effective code in linear genetic programs. They result from the imperative program structure – not from program execution – and can be detected efficiently and completely. Such *structurally noneffective* code manipulates registers not having an impact on the program output at the current position. It is thus not connected to the data flow generated by the effective code. In a tree program, by definition, all program components are connected to the root. As a result, the existence of noneffective code necessarily depends on program semantics.

Noneffective code in genetic programs is also referred to as *introns*. In general, it denotes instructions without any influence on the program behavior. Noneffective code is considered to be beneficial during evolution for two major reasons. First, it may act as a protection that reduces the effect of variation on the effective code. Second, noneffective code allows variations to remain neutral in terms of fitness change. In linear programs introns may be created easily at each position with almost the same probability.

According to the above notion, we distinguish between an *absolute program* and an *effective program* in linear GP. While the former includes all instructions, the latter contains only the structurally effective instructions. The (*effective*) *length* of a program is measured in the number of (effective) instructions it holds. Each program *position* or *line* is supposed to hold exactly one instruction. Even if the absolute length of a program has reached the maximum complexity it can still vary in the size of its effective code. In our approach the effective length of a program is particularly important since it reflects the number of executed instructions and, thus, the execution time.

A more detailed introduction to linear GP will be given in Chapter 2. For a detailed description of tree-based GP we refer the reader to Chapter 8.

1.4   Motivation

The traditional tree representation of programs is still dominating research in the area of GP, even though several different GP approaches and program representations exist. A general motivation for investigating different representations in evolutionary computation is that for each representation form, as is the case for different learning methods in general, *certain* problem domains may exist that are more suitable than others. This holds true even if the *No Free Lunch* (NFL) theorem [139] states that there is no search algorithm better on average than any other search algorithm over the set $F = \{f : \mathcal{S} \to W\}$ of *all* functions (problems) f for a finite search space $\mathcal{S}$.

A special concern of this book will be to convince the reader that there are some important advantages of a linear representation of programs compared to a tree representation. Linear GP is not only the evolution of imperative programs, but may be seen as the evolution of special program graphs. Mostly due to its weaker constraints the representation allows (1) smaller variation step sizes and (2) more compact (effective) solutions that may be executed more efficiently.

It can be observed that linear GP is often used in applications or for representation-independent GP techniques, but is less often considered for providing a basic understanding of GP or for the analysis of representation-specific questions. We aim to fill this gap with the present book. Basically, the research focus is on structural aspects of the linear representation rather than on problem-specific or semantic aspects, like the evolved programming language.

First, an exhaustive analysis of the program representation is performed regarding the imperative and functional structure. Analyzing program structure at runtime serves as a tool for better understanding the functionality of linear GP. Information about program structure is further exploited for various techniques, including the acceleration of runtime and the design of more efficient genetic operators among others.

The general objective will be the enhancement of linear GP on the methodical level in order to produce more precise prediction models, in the first place, and more efficient prediction models, in the second place. In particular, the control of variation step size on the symbolic level will turn out to be a key criterion for obtaining more successful solutions. Other important points of interest in this context, will be the control of neutral variations and the amount of noneffective code that emerges in programs.

The second major objective will be the analysis of general GP phenomena, such as intron code, neutral variations, and code growth, for the linear variant of GP.

PART I

FUNDAMENTAL ANALYSIS

Chapter 2

BASIC CONCEPTS OF LINEAR GENETIC PROGRAMMING

In this chapter linear genetic programming (LGP) will be explored in further detail. The basis of the specific linear GP variant we want to investigate in this book will be described, in particular the programming language used for evolution, the representation of individuals, and the specific evolutionary algorithm employed. This will form the core of our LGP system, while fundamental concepts of linear GP will also be discussed, including various forms of program execution.

Linear GP operates with imperative programs. All discussions and experiments in this book are conducted independently from a special type of programming language or processor architecture. Even though genetic programs are interpreted and partly noted in the high-level language C, the applied programming concepts exist principally in or may be translated into most modern imperative programming languages, down to the level of machine languages.

2.1 Representation of Programs

The imperative programming concept is closely related to the underlying machine language, in contrast to the functional programming paradigm. All modern CPUs are based on the principle of the von Neumann architecture, a computing machine composed of a set of registers and basic instructions that operate and manipulate their content. A program of such a register machine, accordingly, denotes a sequence of instructions whose order has to be respected during execution.

```
void gp(r)
  double r[8];
{  ...
    r[0] = r[5] + 71;
//  r[7] = r[0] - 59;
    if (r[1] > 0)
    if (r[5] > 2)
      r[4] = r[2] * r[1];
//  r[2] = r[5] + r[4];
    r[6] = r[4] * 13;
    r[1] = r[3] / 2;
//  if (r[0] > r[1])
//    r[3] = r[5] * r[5];
    r[7] = r[6] - 2;
//  r[5] = r[7] + 15;
    if (r[1] <= r[6])
      r[0] = sin(r[7]);
}
```

Example 2.1. LGP program in C notation. Commented instructions (marked with //) have no effect on program output stored in register r[0] (see Section 3.2.1).

Basically, an *imperative instruction* includes an operation on *operand* (or *source*) *registers* and an assignment of the result of that operation to a *destination register*. Instruction formats exist for zero,[1] one, two or three registers. Most modern machine languages are based on 2-register or 3-register instructions. Three-register instructions operate on two arbitrary registers (or constants) and assign the result to a third register, e.g., $r_i := r_j + r_k$. In 2-register instructions, instead, either the implemented operator requires only one operand, e.g., $r_i := sin(r_j)$, or the destination register acts as a second operand, e.g., $r_i := r_i + r_j$. Due to a higher degree of freedom, a program with 3-register instructions may be more compact in size than a program consisting of 2-register instructions. Here we will study 3-register instructions with a free choice of operands.

In general, at most one operation per instruction is permitted which usually has one or two operands. Note that a higher number of operators or operands in instructions would not necessarily increase expressiveness or variability of programs. Such instructions would assign the result of a more complex expression to a register and would make genetic operations more complicated.

In the LGP system described here and outlined in [21] a genetic program is interpreted as a variable-length sequence of simple C instructions. In order to apply a program solution directly to a problem domain without

---

[1]0-register instructions operate on a stack.

using a special interpreter, the internal representation is translated into C code.[2] An excerpt of a linear genetic program, as exported by the system, is given in Example 2.1. In the following, the term *genetic program* always refers to the internal LGP representation that we will discuss in more detail now.

2.1.1 Coding of Instructions

In our implementation all registers hold floating-point values. Internally, constants are stored in registers that are write-protected, i.e., may not become destination registers. As a consequence, the set of possible constants remains fixed. Constants are addressed by indices in the internal program representation just like variable registers and operators. Constant registers are only initialized once at the beginning of a run with values from a user-defined range. This has an advantage over encoding constants explicitly in program instructions because memory space is saved, especially insofar as real-valued constants or larger integer constants are concerned. A continuous variability of constants by the genetic operators is really not needed and should be sufficiently counterbalanced by interpolation in the genetic programs. Furthermore, a free manipulation of real-valued constants in programs could result in solutions that may not be exported accurately. Because floating-point values can be printed only to a certain precision, rounding errors might be reinforced during program execution.

Each of the maximum of four instruction components, the instruction identifier and a maximum of three register indices, can be encoded into one byte of memory if we accept that the maximum number of variable registers *and* constant registers is restricted to 256. For most problems LGP is run on this will be absolutely sufficient.

So for instance, an instruction $r_i := r_j + r_k$ reduces to a vector of indices $< id(+), i, j, k >$. Actually, an instruction is held as a single 32-bit integer value. Such a coding of instructions is similar to a representation as machine code [90, 9] but can be chosen independently from the type of processor to interpret the program. In particular, this coding allows an instruction component to be accessed efficiently by casting the integer value which corresponds to the instruction into an array of 4 bytes. A program is then represented by an array of integers. A compact representation

---

[2]For the program instructions applied throughout the book translation is straightforward. Representation and translation of more advanced programming concepts will be discussed briefly later in this chapter.

like this is not only memory-efficient but allows efficient manipulation of programs as well as efficient interpretation (see Section 2.2).

In the following we will refer to a *register* only as a variable register. A constant register is identified with its constant value.

In linear GP a user-defined number of variable registers, the *register set*, is made available to a genetic program. Besides the minimal number of *input registers* required to hold the program inputs before execution, additional registers can be provided in order to facilitate calculations. Normally these so-called *calculation registers* are initialized with a constant value (e.g., 1) each time a program is executed on a fitness case. Only for special applications like time series predictions with a defined order on the fitness cases it may be advantageous to change this. Should calculation registers be initialized only once before fitness evaluation, an exchange of information is enabled between successive executions of the same program for different fitness cases.

A sufficient number of registers is important for the performance of linear GP, especially if input dimension and number of input registers are low. In general, the number of registers determines the number of program paths (in the functional representation) that can be calculated in parallel. If an insufficient number is supplied there will be too many conflicts between registers and valuable information will be overwritten.

One or more input/calculation registers are defined as *output register(s)*. The standard output register is register r_0. The imperative program structure also facilitates the use of multiple program outputs, whereas tree GP can calculate only one output (see also Section 8.1).

2.1.2   Instruction Set

The *instruction set* defines the particular programming language that is evolved. The LGP system is based on two fundamental *instruction type* – operations[3] and conditional branches. Table 2.1 lists the general notation of all instructions used in experiments throughout the book.

Two-operand instructions may either possess two indexed variables (registers) r_i as operands or one indexed variable and a constant. One-operand instructions only use register operands. This way, assignments of constant values, e.g., $r_0 := 1+2$ or $r_0 := sin(1)$, are avoided automatically (see also Section 7.3). If there cannot be more than one constant per instruction, the percentage of instructions holding a constant is equal to the propor-

---

[3]Functions will be identified with operators in the following.

Table 2.1. LGP instruction types.

Instruction type	General notation	Input range
Arithmetic operations	$r_i := r_j + r_k$	$r_i, r_j, r_k \in \mathbb{R}$
	$r_i := r_j - r_k$	
	$r_i := r_j \times r_k$	
	$r_i := r_j \ / \ r_k$	
Exponential functions	$r_i := r_j^{(r_k)}$	$r_i, r_j, r_k \in \mathbb{R}$
	$r_i := e^{r_j}$	
	$r_i := ln(r_j)$	
	$r_i := r_j^2$	
	$r_i := \sqrt{r_j}$	
Trigonomic functions	$r_i := sin(r_j)$	$r_i, r_j, r_k \in \mathbb{R}$
	$r_i := cos(r_j)$	
Boolean operations	$r_i := r_j \wedge r_k$	$r_i, r_j, r_k \in \mathbb{B}$
	$r_i := r_j \vee r_k$	
	$r_i := \neg \, r_j$	
Conditional branches	$if \ (r_j > r_k)$	$r_j, r_k \in \mathbb{R}$
	$if \ (r_j \leq r_k)$	
	$if \ (r_j)$	$r_j \in \mathbb{B}$

tion of constants p_{const} in programs. This is also the selection probability of a constant operand during initialization of programs and during mutations. The influence of this parameter will be analyzed in Section 7.3. In most other experiments documented in this book $p_{const} = 0.5$ will be used.

In genetic programming it must be guaranteed somehow that only valid programs are created. The genetic operators – recombination and mutation – have to maintain the *syntactic correctness* of newly created programs. In linear GP, for instance, crossover points may not be selected inside an instruction and mutations may not exchange an instruction operator for a register. To assure *semantic correctness*, partially defined operators and functions may be protected by returning a high value for undefined input, e.g., $c_{undef} := 10^6$. Table 2.2 shows all instructions from Table 2.1 that have to be protected from certain input ranges and provides their respective definition. The return of high values will act as a penalty for programs that use these otherwise undefined operations. If low values would be returned, i.e., $c_{undef} := 1$, protected instructions may be exploited more easily by evolution for the creation of semantic introns (see Section 3.2.2).

In order to minimize the input range assigned to a semantically senseless function value, undefined negative inputs have been mapped to defined

Table 2.2.   Definitions of protected instructions.

Instruction	Protected definition			
$r_i := r_j \ / \ r_k$	$if \ (r_k \neq 0)$	$r_i := r_j \ / \ r_k$	$else$	$r_i := r_j + c_{undef}$
$r_i := r_j{}^{r_k}$	$if \ (\lvert r_k \rvert \leq 10)$	$r_i := \lvert r_j \rvert^{r_k}$	$else$	$r_i := r_j + r_k + c_{undef}$
$r_i := e^{r_j}$	$if \ (\lvert r_j \rvert \leq 32)$	$r_i := e^{r_j}$	$else$	$r_i := r_j + c_{undef}$
$r_i := ln(r_j)$	$if \ (r_j \neq 0)$	$r_i := ln(\lvert r_j \rvert)$	$else$	$r_i := r_j + c_{undef}$
$r_i := \sqrt{r_j}$	$r_i := \sqrt{\lvert r_j \rvert}$			

absolute inputs in Table 2.2. This permits evolution to integrate protected instructions into robust program semantics more easily. Keijzer [58] recommends the use of interval arithmetic and linear scaling instead of protecting mathematical operators for symbolic regression.

The ability of genetic programming to find a solution strongly depends on the expressiveness of the instruction set. A *complete* instruction set contains all elements that are necessary to build the optimal solution, provided that the number of variables registers and the range of constants are sufficient. On the other hand, the dimension of the search space, which contains all possible programs that can be built from these instructions, increases exponentially with the number of instructions and registers. If we take into account that the initial population usually represents a small fraction of the complete search space, the probability of finding the optimal solution or a good approximation decreases significantly with too many basic program elements that are useless. Moreover, the probability by which a certain instruction is selected as well as its frequency in the population influence the success rate of finding a solution. In order to exert better control over the selection probabilities of instruction types, the instruction set may contain *multiple instances* of an instruction.

We will not regard program functions with *side effects* to the problem environment, only those that return a single value in a strict mathematical sense. Side effects may be used for solving control problems. For instance, a linear program may represent a list of commands (plan) that direct a robot agent in an environment. Fitness information may then be derived from the agent's interactions with its environment by *reinforcement learning*. In such a case, genetic programs do not represent mathematical functions.

2.1.3   Branching Concepts

Conditional branches are an important and powerful concept in genetic programming. In general, programming concepts like branches or loops allow the control flow given by the structure of the representation to be altered. The control flow in linear genetic programs is linear while the data flow is organized as a directed graph (see Section 3.3). With conditional branches the control flow (and hence the data flow) may be different for different input situations, for instance, it may depend on program semantics.

Classification problems are solved more successfully or even exclusively if branches are provided. Branches, however, may increase the complexity of solutions by promoting specialization and by producing semantic introns (see Chapter 3). Both tendencies may lead to less robust and less general solutions.

If the condition of a branch instruction, as defined in Table 2.1, is false only *one* instruction is skipped (see also discussion in Section 3.3.2). Sequences of branches are interpreted as *nested branches* in our system (similar to interpretation in C). That is, the next non-branch instruction in the program is executed only if all conditions are true and is skipped otherwise. A combination of conditional branch(es) and operation is also referred to as a *conditional operation*:

```
if (<cond1>)
if (<cond2>)
<oper>;
```

Nested branches allow more complex conditions to be evolved and are equivalent to connecting single branch conditions by a logical AND. A disjunction (OR connection) of branch conditions, instead, may be represented by a sequence of conditional instructions whose operations are identical:

```
if (<cond1>)
<oper>;
if (<cond2>)
<oper>;
```

Alternatively, successive conditions may be interpreted as being connected either by AND or by OR. This can be achieved in the following way: A Boolean operator is encoded into each branch identifier. This requires the information of a binary flag only, which determines how the condition of a branch instruction is connected to a potentially preceeding or, alternatively, succeeding one in the program (AND or OR). The status of these flags may be changed during operator mutations. The transformation of this representation into a C program becomes slightly more complicated because each sequence of branches has to be substituted by a single branch with an equivalent condition of higher order.

2.1.4   Advanced Branching Concepts

A more general branching concept is to allow conditional forward jumps over a variable number of instructions. The number of instructions skipped may be either unlimited or it may be selected randomly from a certain range. In the latter case the actual length of a jump may be determined by a parameter that is encoded in the branch instruction itself, e.g., using the identifier section or the unused section of the destination register. It is also possible to do without this additional overhead by using constant block sizes. Because some instructions of a skipped code block are usually not effective, evolution may control the semantic effect of a jump over the number of noneffective instructions within jump blocks.

A transformation of such branches from the internal program representation into working C code requires constructions like:

```
if (<cond>) goto <label X>;
<...>
<label X>;
```

where *unique* X labels have to be inserted at the end of each jump block.

If one wants to avoid branching into blocks of other branches, jumps should not be longer than the position of the *next* branch in a program. In this way, the number of skipped instructions is limited implicitly and does not have to be administrated within the branches. Translation into C is then achieved simply by setting {...} brackets around the jump block.

An interesting variant of the above scheme is to allow jumps to *any* succeeding branch instruction in the program. This can be realized by using an additional pointer with each branch instruction to an arbitrary successor branch (*absolute jump*). *Relative jumps* to the kth *next* branch in program with $1 \leq k \leq k_{max}$ are also possible, even if such connections are separated more easily by insertions/deletions of a new branch instruction. A pointer to a branch that does not exist any more may be automatically replaced by a valid pointer after variation. The last branch in a program should always point to the end of the program ($k := 0$). Hence, control flow in a linear genetic program may be interpreted as a *directed acyclic branching graph* (see Figure 2.1). The nodes of such a *control flow graph* represent subsequences of (non-branch) instructions.

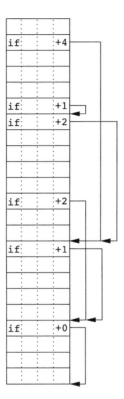

Figure 2.1. Branching graph: Each branch instruction points to a specified succeeding branch instruction.

In [57] a more general concept of a branching graph is proposed for the imperative representation. Each node contains an instruction block that ends with a single *if-else*-branch. These branches point to two alternative decision blocks which represent two independent successor nodes. Thus, instructions may not only be skipped within an otherwise linear control flow but real parallel subprograms may exist in programs. This form of representation is called a *linear graph* since it defines a graph-based control flow on linear genetic programs. Recall that the term *linear genetic program* derives from the linear flow of control that is given by the linear arrangement of instructions. In Section 3.3 we will see that the data flow is graph-based already in simple linear genetic programs.

In general, a complex non-linear control flow requires either more so-phisticated variation operators or repair mechanisms to be applied after variation. For branching graphs a special crossover operator may be constrained so that only complete nodes or subgraphs of nodes are exchanged between programs with a certain probability. That is, crossover points would fall upon branch instructions only. Unrestricted linear crossover (see Section 2.3.4) may be applied between graph nodes (instruction blocks) only.

A final branching concept whose capability is discussed here for linear GP uses an additional `endif` instruction in the instruction set. Nested constructions like:

```
if (<cond>)
<...>
endif
```

are interpreted such that an `endif` belongs to an `if` counterpart if *no* branch or *only closed* branching blocks lie in between. An instruction that cannot be assigned in this way may either be deleted from the internal representation or contribute to noneffective code. The strength of such a concept is to permit an (almost) unconstrained and complex nesting of branches while jumps into other branching blocks cannot occur. A transformation into C code is achieved simply by setting {...} brackets around valid branching blocks instead of `endif` and by not transforming invalid branch instructions at all. In a similar way `if-else-endif` constructions may be realized.

2.1.5   Iteration Concepts

Iteration of code by loops plays a rather unimportant role in genetic programming. Most GP applications that require loops involve control problems with the combination of primitive actions of an agent being the object of evolution. Data flow is usually not necessary in such programs. Instead, each instruction performs actions with side effects on the problem environment and fitness is derived from a reinforcement signal. For the problem classes we focus on here, supervised classification and approximation, iteration is of minor importance. That is not to say that a reuse of code by iterations could not result in more compact and elegant solutions.

In functional programming the concept of loops is unknown. The implicit iteration concept in functional programs denotes *recursions* which are, however, hard to control in tree-based genetic programming [142]. Otherwise, iterated evaluations of a subtree can have an effect only if functions produce side effects. In linear GP, assignments represent an implicit side effect on memory locations as part of the imperative representation. Nevertheless, the iteration of an instruction segment may only be effective if it includes at least one effective instruction *and* if at least one register acts as both destination register and source register in the same or a combination of (effective) instructions, e.g., $r_0 := r_0 + 1$.

In the following, possible iteration concepts for linear GP will be presented. These comprise *conditional loops* and loops with a *limited* number of iterations.

One form of iteration in linear programs is a conditional backward jump corresponding to a `while` loop in C. The problem with this concept is that infinite loops can be easily formed by conditions that are always fulfilled. In general, it is not possible to detect all infinite loops in programs, due to the *halting problem* [36]. A solution to remedy this situation is to terminate a genetic program after a maximal number of instructions. The result of the program would then, however, depend on the execution time allowed.

The more recommended option is a loop concept that limits the number of iterations in each loop. This requires an additional control flow parameter which may either be constant or be varied within loop instructions. Such a construct is usually expressed by a `for` loop in C. Because only overlapping loops (not nested loops) need to be avoided, an appropriate choice to limit the size of loop blocks may be the coevolution of `endfor` instructions. Analogous to the interpretation of branches in Section 2.1.4, a `for` instruction and a succeeding `endfor` define a loop block provided that *only closed loops* lie in between. All other loop instructions are not interpreted.

2.1.6 Modularization Concepts

For certain problems modularization may be advantageous in GP. By using subroutines repeatedly within programs, solutions may become more compact and the same limited program space can be used more efficiently. A problem may also be decomposed into simpler subproblems that can be solved more efficiently in local submodules. In this case, a combination of subsolutions may result in a simpler and better overall solution.

The most popular modularization concept in tree-based genetic programming is the so-called *automatically defined function* (ADF) [65]. Basically, a genetic program is split up into a main program and a certain number of subprograms (ADFs). The main program calculates its output by using the coevolved subprograms via function calls. Therefore, ADFs are treated as part of the main instruction set. Each module type may be composed of different sets of program components. It is furthermore possible to define a usage graph that defines which ADF type may call which other ADF type. Recursions are avoided by prohibiting cycles. The crossover operator has to be constrained in such a way that only modules of the same type can be recombined between individuals.

ADFs are an *explicit* modularization concept since the submodules are encapsulated with regard to the main program and may only be used locally in the same individual. Each module is represented by a separate tree expression [65] or a separate sequence of instructions [93]. To ensure encapsulation of modules in linear programs, disjoint sets of registers have to be used. Otherwise, unwanted state transitions between modules might occur.

ADFs denote subsolutions that are combined by being used in a main program. In Chapter 11 of this book another explicit form of modularization, the evolution of program *teams*, is investigated. A team comprises a fixed number of programs that are coevolved as one GP individual. In principle, all members of a team are supposed to solve the same problem by receiving the same input data. These members act as modules of an overall solution such that the member outputs are combined in a predefined way. A better performance may result from collective decision making and a specialization of relatively independent program modules.

A more *implicit* modularization concept that prepares code for reuse is *module acquisition* [5]. Here substructures up to a certain maximum size – not only including full subtrees – are chosen randomly from better programs. Such modules are replaced by respective function calls and moved into a global library from where they may be referenced by other individuals of the population. In linear GP code replacements are more complicated because subsequences of instructions are usually bound to a complex register usage in the imperative program context.

A similar method for automatic modularization is *subtree encapsulation* [115] where randomly selected subtrees are replaced by symbols that are added to the terminal set as primitive atoms.

Complex module dependencies may hardly emerge during evolution if modularization is not really needed for better solutions. In general, if a programming concept is redundant, the larger search space will negatively influence the ability to find a solution. Moreover, the efficiency of a programming concept or a program representation in GP always depends on the variation operators. Thus, even if the expressiveness or flexibility of a programming concept is high, it may be more difficult for evolution to take advantage of that strength.

2.2   Execution of Programs

The processing speed of a learning method may seriously constrain the complexity or time-dependence of an application. The most time-critical steps in evolutionary algorithms are the fitness evaluation of individuals and/or the calculation of new search points (individuals) by variation operators. In genetic programming, however, computation costs are dominated by the fitness evaluation because it requires multiple executions of a program, at least one execution per fitness case. Executing a genetic program means that the internal program representation is interpreted following the semantics of the programming language.

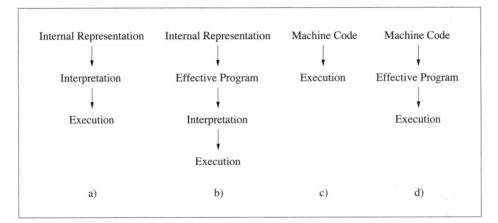

Figure 2.2. Different forms of program execution including (a) interpretation of programs in GP, (b) elimination of noneffective code in LGP, (c) direct execution of machine code in AIMGP, and (d) combination of b) and c).

For instance, interpretation in tree GP systems works by traversing the tree structure of programs in preorder or postorder. While doing so, operators are applied to operand values that result recursively from executing all subtrees of the operator node first.

In a special variant of linear GP, called *Automatic Induction of Machine code by Genetic Programming* (AIMGP) [90, 9], individuals are represented and manipulated as binary machine code. Because programs can be executed directly without passing an interpreter, machine code GP enjoys a significant speedup in execution compared to interpreting GP systems. Due to its dependence on specific processor architectures, however, machine code GP is restricted in portability. Moreover, a machine code system may be restricted in functionality due to, e.g., the number of hardware registers resident in the processor.

In this book we use a different method to accelerate execution (interpretation) of linear genetic programs. The special type of noneffective code which results from the imperative program structure can be detected efficiently in linear runtime (see [21] and Section 3.2.1). In LGP this noneffective code is removed from a program before fitness calculation, i.e., before the resulting effective program is executed over multiple fitness cases. By doing so, the evaluation time of programs is reduced significantly, especially if a larger number of fitness cases is to be processed (see below and Chapter 4). In the example program from Section 2.1 all commented instructions are noneffective under the assumption that program output is stored in register r[0].

Since AIMGP is a special variant of linear GP, both acceleration techniques may be combined such that a machine code representation is preprocessed by a routine extracting effective parts of code. This results in the four different ways of executing programs in genetic programming that are illustrated in Figure 2.2.

An elimination of introns – as noneffective code is frequently called – will be relevant only if a significant amount of this code is created by the variation operators. In particular, this is the case for linear crossover (see Section 2.3.4).

An additional acceleration of runtime in linear GP can be achieved if the fitness of an individual is recalculated only after effective code has undergone change (see Section 5.2). Instead of the evaluation *time*, this approach reduces the *number* of evaluations (and program executions) performed during a generation.

2.2.1   Runtime Comparison

The following experiment illustrates the difference in processing speed of the four ways of program execution depicted in Figure 2.2. In order to guarantee a fair comparison between machine code GP and interpreting GP, an interpreting routine has been added to an AIMGP system. This routine *interprets* the machine code programs in C so that they produce exactly the same results as without interpretation. Both interpreting and non-interpreting runs of the system are accelerated by a second routine that removes the noneffective code. Table 2.3 reports general settings of system parameters for a polynomial regression task.

Table 2.3. Parameter settings

Parameter	Setting
Problem type	polynomial regression
Number of examples	200
Number of generations	200
Population size	1,000
Maximum program length	256
Maximum initial length	25
Crossover rate	90%
Mutation rate	10%
Number of registers	6
Instruction set	$\{+,-,\times\}$
Constants	$\{0,..,99\}$

Table 2.4 compares the average *absolute* runtime[4] for the four different configurations with respect to interpretation and intron elimination. Without interpretation, programs are executed directly as machine code. Ten runs have been performed for each configuration while using the same set of 10 different random seeds. Runs behave exactly the same for all configurations apart from their processing speed. The average length of programs in the population exceeds 200 instructions by about generation 100. The intron rate converges to about 80% on average.

Table 2.4. Absolute runtime in seconds (rounded) averaged over 10 independent runs.

Runtime (sec.)	No Interpretation (I_0)	Interpretation (I_1)
No Intron Elimination (E_0)	500	6250
Intron Elimination (E_1)	250	1375

The resulting *relative* acceleration factors are listed in Table 2.5. If both the direct execution of machine code *and* the elimination of noneffective code are applied in combination, runs become about 25 times faster for the problem considered under the system configuration above. Note that the influence of intron elimination on the interpreting runs (factor 4.5) is more than two times stronger than on the non-interpreting runs (factor 2). This reduces the advantage of machine code GP over interpreting LGP from a factor of 12.5 to a factor of 5.5. Standard machine code GP without intron elimination, instead, seems to be around 3 times faster than linear GP including this extension.

---

[4] Absolute runtime is measured in seconds on a Sun SPARC Station 10.

Table 2.5.   Relative runtime for the four configurations of Table 2.4.

$E_0I_0 : E_0I_1$	1 : 12.5
$E_1I_0 : E_1I_1$	1 : 5.5
$E_0I_0 : E_1I_0$	1 : 2
$E_0I_1 : E_1I_1$	1 : 4.5
$E_0I_0 : E_1I_1$	1 : 2.75
$E_1I_0 : E_0I_1$	1 : 25

Clearly, the performance gain by intron elimination will depend on the proportion of (structurally) noneffective instructions in programs. In contrast to the size of effective code, this is less influenced by the problem definition than by variation operators and system configuration (see Chapters 5 and 7).

2.2.2   Translation

From an application point of view the best (generalizing) program solution is the only relevant result of a GP run. The internal representation (coding) of this program could be exported as is and an interpreter would be required to guarantee that the program will behave in an application environment exactly as it did in the GP system. In order to avoid this, LGP exports programs as equivalent C functions (see Example 2.1 and

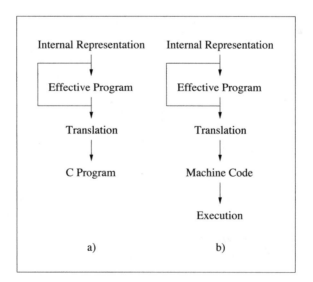

Figure 2.3.   Translation of internal representation into (a) C program and (b) machine code.

Figure 2.3). As has been explained in Section 2.1.2, single programming concepts are transformed into C by translating internal programs into an existing (imperative) programming language. This way, solutions may be integrated directly into an application context (software) without additional overhead.

Such a translation has the additional benefit to allow more freedom on the internal representation. The representation may be chosen (almost) freely, e.g., in favor of better evolvability and better variability in GP. Because normally just a few (best) individuals are exported during a run, even complex transformations may not be time-critical.

The same advantage – higher flexibility – together with a higher processing speed motivates a translation from the evolved LGP language into a binary machine language (*compilation*) just before the fitness of a program is evaluated (see Figure 2.3). This allows a more efficient evaluation of programs, especially if noneffective code is removed prior to translation. Note that the direct variation of machine code programs in AIMGP systems is less important for runtime. Instead, the speed advantage almost exclusively results from a direct execution of machine code. The disadvantage of this technique is the higher compiler overhead that needs to be taken into account.

2.3   Evolution of Programs

Algorithm 2.1 constitutes the kernel of our LGP system. In a *steady-state* evolutionary algorithm like this, generations are not fixed, in contrast to a *generational* EA. For the latter variant, the current generation is identified with a population of parent programs whose offspring migrate to a *separate* population pool. After the offspring pool is fully populated it replaces the parent population and the next generation begins. In the steady-state model there is no such centralized control of generations. Instead, offspring replace existing individuals in the *same* population. It is common practice to define *generation equivalents* in steady-state EAs as regular intervals of fitness evaluations. Only new individuals have to be evaluated if the fitness is saved with each individual in the population. A generation (equivalent) is complete if the number of new individuals equals the population size.

ALGORITHM 2.1 (*LGP algorithm*)

1. *Initialize* the population with random programs (see Section 2.3.1) and calculate their fitness values.

2. Randomly *select* $2 \times n_{ts}$ individuals from the population without replacement.

3. Perform two *fitness tournaments* of size n_{ts} (see Section 2.3.2).

4. Make *temporary copies* of the two tournament winners.

5. *Modify* the two winners by one or more variation operators with certain probabilities (see Section 2.3.4).

6. *Evaluate* the fitness of the two offspring.

7. If the current best-fit individual is replaced by one of the offspring *validate* the new best program using unknown data.

8. *Reproduce* the two tournament winners within the population with a certain probability or under a certain condition by replacing the two tournament losers with the temporary copies of the winners (see Section 2.3.3).

9. Repeat steps 2 to 8 until the maximum number of generations is reached.

10. *Test* the program with minimum validation error.

11. Both the best program during training and the best program during validation define the output of the algorithm.

Fitness of an individual program is computed by an *error function* on a set of input-output examples $(\vec{i_k}, o_k)$. These so-called *fitness cases* define the problem that should be solved or approximated by a program. A popular error function for approximation problems is the *sum of squared errors* (SSE), i.e., the squared difference between the predicted output $gp(\vec{i_k})$ and the desired output o_k summed over all n training examples. A squared error function penalizes larger errors more heavily than smaller errors. Equation 2.1 defines a related measure, the *mean square error* (MSE).

$$\text{MSE}(gp) = \frac{1}{n} \sum_{k=1}^{n} (gp(\vec{i_k}) - o_k)^2 \qquad (2.1)$$

For classification tasks the *classification error* (CE) calculates the number of examples wrongly classified. Function *class* in Equation 2.2 hides the classification method that maps the continuous program outputs to discrete class identifiers. While a better fitness means a smaller error the best fitness is 0 in both cases.

$$\mathrm{CE}(gp) = \sum_{k=1}^{n} \{1 \mid class(gp(\vec{i_k})) \neq o_k\} \tag{2.2}$$

The generalization ability of individual solutions is observed *during* training by calculating a *validation error* of the current best program. The training error function is applied to an unknown *validation data set* which is sampled differently from the training data, but from the same data space. Finally, among all the best individuals emerging over a run the one with minimum validation error (point of best generalization) is tested on an unknown *test data set*, once *after* training. Note that validation of the best solutions follows a fitness gradient. Validating all individuals during a GP run is not reasonable, since one is not interested in solutions that perform well on the validation data but have a comparatively bad fitness on the training data set.

Whether an individual is selected for variation or ruled out depends on relative fitness comparisons during selection. In order to not loose information, a copy of the individual with minimum validation error has to be kept outside of the population. The individual of minimum training error (best individual) does not need protection since it cannot be overwritten as long as the training data is fixed during evolution.

Training data may be resampled every mth generation or even each time before an individual is evaluated. On the one hand, resampling introduces noise into the fitness function (*dynamic fitness*). This is argued to improve the generalization performance compared to keeping the training examples constant over a run because it reduces *overtraining*, i.e., an overspecialization of solutions to the training data. On the other hand, resampling may be beneficial if the database that constitutes the problem to be solved is large. A relatively small subset size may be used for training purposes while all data points would be exposed to the genetic programs over time. As a result, not only the fitness evaluation of programs is accelerated but the evolutionary process may converge faster. This technique is called *stochastic sampling* [9].

2.3.1 Initialization

The initial population of a genetic programming run is normally generated randomly. In linear GP an upper bound for the initial program length has to be defined. The lower bound may be equal to the absolute minimum length of a program – one instruction. A program is created so that its length is chosen randomly from this predefined range with a uniform probability.

There is a trade-off to be addressed when choosing upper and lower bounds of program length: On the one hand, it is not recommended to initialize exceedingly long programs, as will be demonstrated in Section 7.6. This may reduce their variability significantly in the course of the evolutionary process. Besides, the smaller the initial programs are, the more thorough an exploration of the search space can be performed at the beginning of a run. On the other hand, the average initial length of programs should not be too small, because a sufficient diversity of the initial genetic material is necessary, especially in smaller populations or if crossover dominates variation.

2.3.2   Selection

Algorithm 2.1 applies *tournament selection*. With this selection method individuals are selected randomly from the population to participate in a tournament where they compete for the best fitness. Normally selection happens without replacement, i.e., all individuals of a tournament must be different. The *tournament size* n_{ts} determines the selection pressure that is imposed on the population individuals. If a tournament is held between *two* individuals (and if there is only one tournament used for selecting the winner) this corresponds to the minimum selection pressure. A lower pressure is possible with this selection scheme only by performing $m > 1$ tournaments and choosing the *worst* among the m winners.

In standard LGP *two* tournaments happen in parallel to provide two parent individuals for crossover. For comparison purposes, this is practiced here also in cases where only mutation is applied (see Chapter 6). Before the tournament winners undergo variation, a copy of each winner replaces the corresponding loser. This reproduction scheme constitutes a steady-state EA.

Tournament selection, together with a steady-state evolutionary algorithm, is well suited for parallelization by using isolated subpopulations of individuals, called *demes* (see also Section 4.3.2). Tournaments may be performed independently of each other and do not require global information about the population, like a global fitness ranking (*ranking selection*) or the average fitness (*fitness proportional selection*) [17] would do. Local selection schemes are arguably better to preserve diversity than global selection schemes. Moreover, individuals may take part in a tournament several times or not at all during one steady-state generation. This allows evolution to progress with different speeds in different regions of the population.

2.3.3   Reproduction

A full reproduction of winners guarantees that better solutions always survive in a steady-state population. However, during every replacement of individuals a certain amount of genetic material gets lost. When using tournament selection this situation can be influenced by the *reproduction rate* p_{rr}. By using $p_{rr} < 1$ the EA may *forget* better solutions to a certain degree. Both reproduction rate and selection pressure (tournament size) have a direct influence on the convergence speed of the evolutionary algorithm as well as on the loss of (structural and semantic) diversity.

The reproduction rate could also be allowed to exceed the standard setting 1 ($p_{rr} > 1$). An individual would then be reproduced *more than once* within the population. As a result, both the convergence speed and the loss of diversity will be accelerated. Obviously, too many replications of individuals lead to an unwanted premature convergence and subsequent stagnation of the evolutionary process. Note that more reproductions are performed than new individuals are created.

Instead of, or in addition to, an explicit reproduction probability, implicit conditions can be used to determine when reproduction shall take place (see Section 10.5).

2.3.4   Variation

Genetic operators change the contents and the size of genetic programs in a population. Figure 2.4 illustrates *two-point linear crossover* as it is used in linear GP for recombining two genetic programs [9]. A segment of random position and arbitrary length is selected in each of the two parents and exchanged. In our implementation (see also Section 5.7.1) crossover exchanges equally sized segments if one of the two children would exceed the maximum length otherwise [21].

Crossover is the standard *macro operator* applied to vary the length of linear genetic programs on the level of instructions. In other words, instructions are the smallest units to be changed. *Inside* instructions *micro mutations* randomly replace either the instruction identifier, a register or a constant (if existent) by equivalents from predefined sets or valid ranges. In Chapter 5 and Chapter 6 we will introduce more advanced genetic operators for the linear program representation.

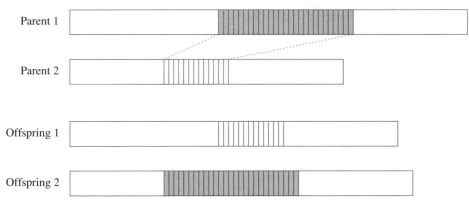

Figure 2.4. Crossover in linear GP. Continuous sequences of instructions are selected and exchanged between parents.

In general, there are three different ways in which variation operators may be selected and applied to a certain individual program before its fitness is calculated:

☐ Only *one* variation is performed per individual.

☐ *One* variation operator is applied *several* times.

☐ *More than one* variation operator is applied.

The advantage of using only one genetic operation per individual is a lower total variation strength. This allows artificial evolution to progress more specifically and in smaller steps. By applying several genetic operations concurrently, on the other hand, computation time is saved such that less evaluations are necessary. For example, micro mutations are often applied together with a macro operation.

Note that in all three cases, there is only one offspring created per parent individual, i.e., only one offspring gets into the population and is evaluated. However, similar to multiple reproduction of parents one may generate more than one offspring from a parent. Both options are, however, not realized by Algorithm 2.1.

Chapter 3

CHARACTERISTICS OF THE LINEAR REPRESENTATION

In the first instance linear genetic programming has been introduced for the benefit of shorter execution time. Genetic programs written as binary machine code do not have to pass through a time-consuming interpretation step (see Section 2.2). In this chapter we investigate other, more general features of the linear representation. One basic difference to a tree representation is the emergence of unused code parts in linear genetic programs that are independent of program semantics. Another fundamental difference is that the data flow in a linear genetic program has a directed graph structure that is more general than a tree.

3.1 Effective Code and Noneffective Code

Introns in nature are subsequences of DNA residing within the region of a gene and holding information that is not expressed in the phenotype of an organism or, more precisely, that is not translated into a protein sequence.[1] The existence of introns in eukaryotic genomes may be explained in different ways:

(1) Because the information for a gene is often located on different *exons*, i.e., gene parts that are expressed, introns may help to reduce the number of destructive recombinations between chromosomes by simply reducing the probability that recombination points will fall within an exon region

---

[1] The definition of introns is changing over time. In recent years, some non-intron sequences have been found to not be translated into proteins either, in the course of alternative splicing, a combinatorial mechanism to generate proteins. Even more recently, non-protein-coding but expressed DNA has been found to play a key role in gene regulation. Here we only refer to the early simple definition of introns.

[136]. Thus, functionally complete protein segments encoded by specific exons are more frequently mixed than interrupted during evolution.

(2) Perhaps even more important for understanding the evolution of higher organisms is the realization that new code can be developed "silently", without exposing each intermediate variation step to fitness selection.

In genetic programs there may be segments of code that are either essential or redundant for the program solution. Redundant code fragments are often called *introns*[2] like their natural counterpart. Actually, introns in GP may play a similar role as introns in nature. First, introns reduce the destructive influence of variations on the effective part of programs. In doing so, they may protect the information holding code from being separated and destroyed. Second, the existence of noneffective code allows code variations to be neutral in terms of a fitness change. This protects genetic manipulations from direct evolutionary pressure. In linear GP we distinguish effective instructions from noneffective instructions:[3]

DEFINITION 3.1 (*effective/noneffective instruction*)
An instruction of a linear genetic program is *effective* at its position iff it influences the output of the program for at least one possible input situation. A *noneffective* or *intron* instruction, respectively, is without any influence on the calculation of the output for all possible inputs.

One noneffective instruction is regarded as the smallest unit. A noneffective instruction may be removed from a program without affecting its semantics – either independently or only in combination with other noneffective instructions. In analogy to biology an *intron* in LGP may be defined as any instruction or combination of instructions where this is possible. A second, weaker intron definition postulates the program behavior to be unchanged only for the fitness cases [92]:

DEFINITION 3.2 (*noneffective instruction 2*)
An instruction of a linear genetic program is *noneffective* iff it does not influence the program output for the fitness cases.

The condition in Definition 3.2 does not necessarily hold for unknown data inputs. If the generalization performance of best individuals is checked during training and some of these introns would be removed before the

---

[2]Even if intron code is redundant in a program, it might have been important for finding that solution.

[3]Although the terms *intron* and *noneffective code* are used synonymously in the GP community, we prefer the latter.

validation error is calculated, the behavior of the program may not be the same any more.

DEFINITION 3.3 (*effective/noneffective register*)
A register is *effective* for a certain program position iff its manipulation can affect the behavior, i.e., an output, of the program. Otherwise, the register is *noneffective* at that position.

Effective instructions following Definition 3.1 necessarily manipulate effective registers (see Definition 3.3). But an operation can still be noneffective even if its result is assigned to an effective register.

When using single conditional instructions as introduced in Section 2.1.3 a branch instruction is effective only if it directly precedes an effective instruction. Otherwise it is noneffective. That is, a conditional instruction is effective as a whole if this is true for its operation.

3.2 Structural Introns and Semantic Introns

The above considerations suggest an additional classification of introns in linear GP. This is based on a special type of noneffective code that results from the imperative structure of programs – not from program semantics. Hence, two types of noneffective instructions may be discerned: structural introns and semantic introns [21].

DEFINITION 3.4 (*structural intron*)
Structural introns denote single noneffective instructions that emerge in a linear program from manipulating noneffective registers.

Actually, the term *structural intron* refers to the functional structure of linear genetic programs that constitutes a directed graph, as will be demonstrated in Section 3.3. Structural introns belong to a part of the graph that is not connected to the program output. That is, these instructions do not contribute to the *effective data flow*. Structural introns do not exist in tree-based GP, because in a tree structure, by definition, all program components are connected to the root. Thus, introns in tree programs can only result from program semantics.

In linear GP semantic introns may be defined as follows:

DEFINITION 3.5 (*semantic intron*)
A *semantic intron* is a noneffective instruction or a noneffective combination of instructions that manipulates effective register(s).

In other words, a semantic intron is structurally effective by this definition, otherwise it would be a structural intron. The state of effective registers manipulated by a semantic intron is the same before and after the intron has been executed – if we assume that operations do not induce side effects. For instance, instruction $r_0 := r_0 \times 1$ is a semantic intron if register r_0 is effective. While all structural introns are noneffective after Definition 3.1 and Definition 3.2, semantic introns may be noneffective after Definition 3.2 only. But note that not all semantic introns depend necessarily on fitness cases. More examples of semantic introns will be given in Section 3.2.2.

Following Definitions 3.4 and 3.5 we distinguish *structurally effective* code from *semantically effective* code. While the former may still contain semantic introns the latter code is supposed to be intron-free. However, even if all intron instructions can be removed from a program, it might not have minimum size (see Section 3.2.4).

Regarding Definition 3.1 only, structural introns may also be designated as *neutral noneffective* code and semantic introns as *neutral effective* code, respectively. Such naming would conform to the distinction of *neutral noneffective* variations and *neutral effective* variations, as will be defined in Section 5.1.1. It has to be noted, however, that neutral code does not only result from neutral variations (see Chapter 10). This produces confusion. The different intron definitions will become clearer in the following sections.

Whether a branch is a structural intron or a semantic intron depends again on the status of the operation that directly follows. Semantic introns include branch instructions, too, whose condition is always true, at least for all fitness cases. In this case, all other branches are skipped that follow directly in a sequence (nested branch, see Section 2.1.3). Likewise, an operation is not executed if the condition of a directly preceding (nested) branch is always false. All such *non-executed* instructions are special semantic introns (see also Section 3.2.2).

3.2.1   Detecting and Removing Structural Introns

In biology introns are removed from *messenger*RNA (mRNA) through RNA splicing and editing. mRNA is a copy of DNA code and functions as an intermediate information carrier on the way to protein biosynthesis [136]. A biological reason for the removal of introns could be that genes are more efficiently translated during protein biosynthesis in this way. Without being in conflict with ancient information held in introns, this might have an advantage, presumably through decoupling of DNA size from direct evolutionary pressure.

The imperative program structure in linear GP permits structurally non-effective instructions to be identified efficiently. This, in turn, allows the corresponding effective instructions to be extracted from a program during runtime and to be copied to a temporary program buffer once before the fitness of the program is calculated (see Figure 3.1). By only executing this effective program when testing fitness cases, evaluation can be accelerated significantly. Thereby, the representation of individuals in the population remains unchanged while valuable computation time for non-effective code is saved. No potentially relevant genetic material is lost and intron code may play its role during the evolutionary process. In analogy to the elimination of introns in nature, the linear genetic code is interpreted more efficiently. Because of this analogy the term *intron* might be more justified here than in tree-based GP where introns are necessarily semantic and, thus, cannot be detected and removed as easily.

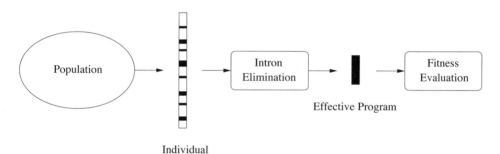

Figure 3.1. Intron elimination in LGP. Only effective code (black) is executed.

Algorithm 3.1 detects all structural introns in a linear genetic program which does not employ loops (backward jumps) or jumps over more than one instruction [21]. More generally, such an *elimination of dead code* represents a form of code optimization that is applied, for instance, during compilation [1]. The algorithm includes a simple *dependence analysis* which identifies all instructions influencing the final program output. All depending effective instructions are marked in a program by using one bit of the instruction coding (see Section 2.1.1) as an *effectiveness flag*. Copying all marked instructions into a buffer results in the corresponding *effective program*. In the sample program from Section 2.1 all instructions marked with // are structural introns provided that the program output is stored in register r[0] at the end of execution.

ALGORITHM 3.1 (*detection of structural introns*)

1. Let set R_{eff} always contain all registers that are effective at the current program position. $R_{eff} := \{\ r \mid r \text{ is output register } \}$.
   Start at the last program instruction and move backwards.

2. Mark the next preceding operation in program with destination register $r_{dest} \in R_{eff}$. If such an instruction is not found then $\rightarrow$ 5.

3. If the operation directly follows a branch or a sequence of branches then mark these instructions too. Otherwise remove r_{dest} from R_{eff}.

4. Insert each source (operand) register r_{op} of newly marked instructions in R_{eff} if not already contained. $\rightarrow$ 2.

5. Stop. All unmarked instructions are introns.

For a program of length n instructions the algorithm needs linear calculation time $O(n)$. Indeed, detecting and removing the structurally noneffective code from a program only requires about the same time as calculating one fitness case. The more fitness cases are processed by the resulting effective program the more computational overhead will be saved. A good estimate of the overall acceleration factor in runtime is

$$\alpha_{acc} = \frac{1}{1 - p_{intron}} \tag{3.1}$$

where p_{intron} is the average percentage of intron code in a genetic program and $1 - p_{intron}$ the respective percentage of effective code.

By omitting the execution of noneffective instructions during program interpretation a large amount of computation can be saved. The removal of structural introns may, however, be relevant only if a sufficient proportion of this noneffective code occurs with the applied variation operators (see Chapter 5). System parameters like the maximum program length influence this proportion because effective length may grow even after absolute length has reached a maximum. Moreover, the creation of structural introns is facilitated if a higher number of registers is provided. Should only one register be available, this type of code would not occur at all. We will demonstrate in Section 7.1 that prediction performance suffers if the number of registers is chosen either too small or too large.

3.2.2   Avoiding Semantic Introns

After structural introns have been identified and removed completely by Algorithm 3.1, semantic introns may still be present in the remaining program code. In general, a detection of semantic introns is much more difficult and may be done only incompletely (see Section 3.2.4). As an inherent part of the program structure, the structurally noneffective code does not directly depend on the applied set of instructions. This type of noneffective code may be implemented easily by linear genetic programming, even in great quantities. Structural introns reduce much of the pressure that would otherwise lie on genetic programs to develop semantic introns. This would mostly happen to reduce the variation step size in semantically effective code (see Section 5.9.1 and Chapter 10). Structural introns thus allow effective solutions to be more compact in size.

The proportion of semantic introns may be further reduced by controlling the formation of this code explicitly. Although these introns cannot be completely avoided in genetic programming some rules can be formulated that help to avoid at least simple instances of semantic introns, without significantly restricting the freedom of variation or the expressiveness of the function set. The harder it becomes for the system to develop non-effective code that depends on program semantics, the more this code should be ruled out by structural introns.

The potential of linear GP to develop semantic introns strongly depends on the set of instruction operators provided and the set of constants. To restrict the rate of semantic introns and to keep the (structurally) effective size of programs small, both sets should be chosen with a minimum tendency for creating semantic introns. Below different *types of semantic introns* possible with instruction set $\{+, -, \times, /, x^y, if >, if \leq\}$ (see Table 2.1) are given by example, together with some rules for how each type may be avoided. The classification into categories is not meant to be totally disjoint. Some examples may be borderline cases and fit in more than one class.

All semantic introns denote noneffective code for *all* possible input situations (following intron Definition 3.1). We do not regard instructions as introns that are noneffective for certain input ranges or fitness cases only (see Definition 3.2). In the following, register r_0 is supposed to be effective (otherwise introns would be structural).

Examples of semantic introns of type 1 are:

1. (a) $r_0 := r_0 + 0$
   (b) $r_0 := r_0 \times 1$
   (c) $r_0 := r_0{}^1$

(d) $r_2 := r_0 + r_0$
     $r_1 := r_2 - r_0$
     $r_0 := r_1 + 0$

Such introns become less likely if the particular constants 0 and 1 are not explicitly provided to act as neutral elements in operations. It is especially easy and effective to do without constant 0, since it is not really useful for calculation but has a high potential for creating semantic introns.

Semantic introns of type 2 are instructions preceding the following instructions and influencing only the content of effective register r_i:

2. (a) $r_0 := r_i \times 0$

   (b) $r_0 := r_i{}^0$

   (c) $r_1 := r_0 - r_0$
        $r_0 := r_i \times r_1$

This intron type can include many noneffective instructions. Note that even if value 0 is excluded from the set of constants it may still be calculated and assigned to a variable register, independent from the register contents (see context example 2c). However, the more complex such intron constructs become the more context-dependent they are and the more likely they will be destroyed during variation.

Introns of type 3 result from registers like r_0 whose contents become constant by calculation, i.e., do no longer depend on other register variables:

3. (a) $r_0 := r_i - r_i$

   (b) $r_0 := r_i / r_i$

   (c) $r_1 := r_i + c$
        $r_0 := r_1 - r_i$

Again, all preceding instructions are semantic introns that manipulate register r_i exclusively. The reader may recall that instructions with only constant operands are not possible (see Section 2.1.1). One operand is always variable. To make the emergence of type 3 introns more difficult subtraction and division of identical registers might be forbidden explicitly. An example of a type 4 intron is shown next:

4. $r_1 := r_0 + 1$
    $r_0 := r_1 - 1$

It includes all *combinations* of instructions that may be symbolically simplified without requiring any (semantically equivalent) *replacement* through other instructions (see Section 3.2.4). The same is true for type 1 introns that comprise a single instruction only. Such introns are difficult to avoid in general, especially if many redundant calculations are involved. It may be questioned, however, if complex context-dependent introns occur frequently and survive during program evolution.

By closer inspection one can see that register r_1 has to be noneffective at the position of intron example 4 in a program. Otherwise, these instructions might not be removed without changing the (effective) program. In general, all registers that are manipulated in semantic introns must be either (structurally) noneffective or their original contents before the intron is restored after the last instruction of the intron has been executed.

Typically, the undefined range of a protected operator is exploited for the induction of type 5 introns:

5. (a) $r_0 := r_i/0$
   (b) $r_1 := r_0 - r_0$
   $r_0 := r_i/r_1$

This variant can be avoided by penalty as described in Section 2.1.2. Type 6 is a special case of semantic intron:

6. (a) $if\ (r_i > r_i)$
   $r_0 := r_j + c$
   (b) $r_2 := r_i + r_i$
   $r_1 := r_2 - r_i$
   $if\ (r_1 > r_i)$
   $r_0 := r_j + c$
   (c) $r_0 := r_i + 2$
   $r_1 := r_0 - r_i$
   $if\ (r_1 \leq 1)$
   $r_0 := r_j + r_k$
   (d) $if\ (r_i > 2)$
   $if\ (r_i \leq 1)$
   $r_0 := r_j + r_k$

The operation is not executed at all because the branching condition cannot be met. As a result, all preceding instructions, whose effectiveness depends only on the skipped instruction become noneffective, too. Example 6a cannot occur if identical registers cannot be compared. More context-dependent conditions (6b) are not affected by such a restriction, but are created with less likelihood. Conditions like in example 6c that are unsatisfiable for all possible register values emerge from comparison of constant values even if a direct comparison of two constant values is avoided. A conjunction of contradicting conditions (6d) emerges less likely if only one type of comparison ($>$ or $<$) is allowed to the system. This will not significantly restrict the expressiveness of the programming language. Alternatively, sequences of branches might be explicitly forbidden.

Type 7 represents the opposite case to type 6. That is, a conditional operation is always executed because the condition is always true:

7. (a) $if \ (r_i \leq r_i)$
         $r_0 := r_j + c$

   (b) $r_1 := r_i + 2$
       $r_0 := r_1 - r_i$
       $if \ (r_0 > 1)$
       $r_0 := r_j + r_k$

Here the branch instruction itself is a sematic intron as well as all preceding instructions that are effective only in the false case.

8. $if \ (r_1 > 1)$
   $if \ (r_1 > 1)$
   $r_0 := r_j + r_k$

Finally, redundant branch instructions that may occur in nested branches constitute introns of type 8.

3.2.3   Detecting Semantic Introns

The specific measures proposed in the previous section reduce the probability that semantically noneffective code occurs in linear genetic programs. It is generally not necessary and not cost effective to apply expensive algorithms that detect and remove semantic introns during runtime. Usually the evolutionary process is already accelerated significantly by eliminating the larger number of structural introns (see Algorithm 3.1).

Nevertheless, a removal of semantic introns makes sense for a better understanding and interpretation of a certain program solution and, thus, to gain information about the application domain. Another motivation to further reduce the (structurally) effective size *after* evolution may be a higher efficiency in time-critical application domains.

Algorithms that detect certain types of (structural or semantic) noneffective code as specified by Definition 3.1 should be deterministic. Probabilistic algorithms that require the execution of a program necessarily depend on a representative set of input-output examples. Such algorithms may identify instructions whose intron status depends on certain input situations (see Definition 3.2). Since normally not all possible inputs can be verified for a problem, such intron instructions may become effective when being confronted with unknown data.

The following probabilistic algorithm (similar to the one documented in [9]) detects semantic introns. All structural introns, instead, are detected as a side effect even if much more inefficiently than by Algorithm 3.1. Hence, computation time may be saved if the program is already free from structural introns.

ALGORITHM 3.2 (*elimination of semantic introns*)

1. Calculate the fitness $\mathcal{F}_{ref}$ of the program on a set of m data examples (fitness cases) as a reference value. Start at the first program instruction at position $i := 1$.

2. Delete the instruction at the current program position i.

3. Evaluate the program again.

4. If its fitness $\mathcal{F} = \mathcal{F}_{ref}$ then the deleted instruction is an intron. Otherwise, reinsert the instruction at position i.

5. Move to the next instruction at position $i := i + 1$.

6. Stop, if the end of program has been reached. Otherwise $\rightarrow$ 2.

Algorithm 3.2 needs calculation time $O(m \cdot n^2)$ because of n fitness evaluations, $m + 1$ program executions per fitness evaluation, and n (effective) program instructions at maximum. This is too inefficient for removing introns during runtime. The higher computational costs would hardly be paid by the savings obtained during the fitness evaluation.

Unfortunately, Algorithm 3.2 will not recognize semantic introns that are more complex than one instruction (see Section 3.2.2). One possibility to find all semantic introns in a linear genetic program for a certain set of fitness cases (following Definition 3.2) is to repeat the algorithm for all k-party combinations of arbitrary program instructions with $k = 1, 2, .., n$.

3.2.4   Symbolic Simplification

Introns have been defined in Section 3.1 as single instructions or combinations of instructions that may be removed without replacement *and*
without affecting program semantics. But even if a linear genetic program is completely free from semantic and structural introns, the size
of the remaining (semantically) effective code is not necessarily minimal.
The following example (type 9) is not an intron, but may be referred to
as a *mathematically* or *semantically equivalent extension*. It represents
all formulations of a subprogram that are more complicated than necessary. Such combinations of instructions cannot be removed, but may
be replaced by less complex, semantically equivalent code (*semantically
equivalent replacement*).

9. $r_0 := r_0 + 1$
   $r_0 := r_0 + 1$
   $\Leftrightarrow$
   $r_0 := r_0 + 2$

A (structurally effective) program can be transformed into a functional
tree expression by a successive replacement of variables (see Section 3.3.4)
provided that program operators do not induce side effects. During such
a transformation process the expression can be simplified successively by
applying rules of *symbolic calculation*. In doing so, semantic intron instructions by Definition 3.1 are removed deterministically. The probabilistic Algorithm 3.2, instead, removes noneffective code by Definition
3.2 only and does not resolve mathematically equivalent extensions.

In general, detecting absolutely *all* noneffective code and semantically
equivalent extensions is an unsolvable problem. Reducing a program to
an equivalent of minimum size corresponds to the more general problem
of whether two programs are equivalent or not. This *program equivalence
problem* is in general undecidable because it may be reduced to the undecidable *halting problem* [36, 1]. However, in GP we normally regard
finite programs. If no loops or only loops with a finite number of iterations are permitted (see Section 2.1.5), genetic programs will always
terminate. Then we may assume that at least theoretically all (semantic)
introns can be detected. Unfortunately, the reduction of an expression
to an equivalent expression of minimum size (unique except for isomorphism) is already NP-complete [1]. This is true because the NP-complete
satisfiability problem may be reduced to this *simplification problem*. A
general Boolean expression will be unsatisfiable if and only if it simplifies
to false.

In the following let the terms *intron* or *noneffective* instruction always denote a structural intron unless stated otherwise. Accordingly, *effective* programs still include semantic introns. As we will see below, the modification of an instruction may change the effectiveness status of other preceding instructions in a linear program – comprising both deactivations and reactivations. Therefore, the terms *active* and *inactive* code will be used as synonyms for effective and noneffective code, respectively.

3.3 Graph Interpretation

The imperative representation of a linear program can be transformed into an equivalent functional representation as a graph by means of Algorithm 3.3. In [11] we showed a simpler version of the algorithm applicable to *effective* programs. The directed structure of the resulting graph better reflects functional dependencies and *data flow* in linear genetic programs than the simple succession of instructions. The graph is acyclic if loops do not occur in the imperative program. Special cases of programming concepts like loops and branches shall be excluded from the following considerations for simplicity. Instead, we concentrate on the transformation of linear genetic programs consisting of sequences of simple operations into *directed acyclic graphs* (DAGs). Again, it has to be assumed that program operators/functions do not induce side effects in the problem environment. Otherwise, the linear execution order of instructions would be less flexible than is required here.

ALGORITHM 3.3 (*transformation of an LGP program into a DAG*)

1. Start with the last instruction in program at position $i := n$ ($n =$ program length). Let set $S := \emptyset$ always contain all variable sinks of the current graph.

2. If destination register $r_{dest} \notin S$ then create a new start node (a new contiguous graph component) with label r_{dest} and $S := S \cup \{r_{dest}\}$.

3. Go to the (variable) sink node in the graph with label r_{dest}.

4. Assign the operator of instruction i to this node.

5. Repeat steps 6 to 8 for each operand register r_{op} of instruction i.

6. If there is no (variable or constant) sink node with label r_{op} then create a new node with that label.

7. Connect nodes r_{dest} and r_{op} by a directed edge.
   (r_{dest} becomes inner node and r_{op} becomes sink node.)

8. If not all operations are commutative then label this edge with k if r_{op} is the kth operand.

9. Replace r_{dest} in S by all non-constant operand registers r_{op} of instruction i if not already contained.

10. If $i > 1$ then go to instruction $i := i - 1$ in program and $\rightarrow$ 2.

11. Stop. Delete all register labels from inner nodes.

The number of imperative instructions corresponds exactly to the number of inner nodes in the program graph resulting from Algorithm 3.3. Each inner node represents an operator and has as many outgoing edges as there are operands in the corresponding imperative instruction, i.e., one or two (see Section 2.1). Thus, each program instruction is interpreted as a small subtree of depth one.

Sink nodes, i.e., nodes without any outgoing edges, are labeled with register identifiers or constants. The number of these *terminals* is restricted by the total number of (different) registers and constants in the terminal set. This is different in a tree representation where a terminal may occur multiple times because each node is referenced only once, by definition.

Only sink nodes that represent a (variable) register are replaced regularly by operator nodes in the course of the algorithm. These are the only points at which the graph may grow. Since loops are not considered, the only successors of such sink nodes may become other existing sink nodes or new nodes. At the end of the transformation process these sinks represent the input variables of the program. Note that the data flow in such functional programs runs in the opposite direction in which the edges point.

Sink nodes that represent a constant value are only created once during the transformation process and may be pointed to from every program position. The same is true for constant inputs.

A DAG that results from applying Algorithm 3.3 may be composed of several *contiguous components*. Each of these subgraphs has only one start node from where all its other nodes are reached by at least one (directed) path. *Start* nodes have indegree 0. There may be as many start nodes (contiguous components) in the DAG as there are instructions in the imperative program. The last instruction in the program that manipulates an output register corresponds to a start node that initiates an *effective component*. If there is only one output register defined, exactly one graph component is effective. The rest of the graph is *noneffective*, i.e., corresponds to noneffective instructions (structural introns).

The different contiguous components of a DAG may either be disconnected or may overlap in parts by forming a *weakly contiguous component*. We state that in the latter case all operator nodes are connected (disregarding the direction of edges) but that they may not be reached from the same start node (on a directed path).

Note that noneffective components are not necessarily disconnected from an effective component. Graph edges may point from a noneffective (operator) node to an effective (operator) node, but not the other way around. Thus, noneffective components cannot influence the program output because the data flow in the effective component (*effective data flow*) is directed from sinks to the (effective) start node. Also note that all components (including disconnected ones) still share the same set of sinks in this graph representation.

In the following we assume that the linear program is fully effective in terms of Definition 3.4 and that only one output register is defined. Such a program is translated into a DAG that constitutes only a single contiguous component. The start node may also be denoted as the *root* of the DAG.

After each iteration of Algorithm 3.3 all non-constant sink nodes correspond exactly to the effective registers at the current program position. In particular, set S is equal to set R_{eff} in Algorithm 3.1. Because the number of effective registers is bound by the total number of registers, the number of variable sink nodes is bound as well. This number determines the width of program graph. For problem configurations with a moderate number of inputs and registers the program graph is supposed to grow in depth rather than in width. The depth is restricted by the length of the imperative program because each imperative instruction corresponds to exactly one inner node in the graph. A narrow but deep graph structure may be referred to as "linear", just like its imperative equivalent.

The actual width of a program graph indicates the number of parallel calculation paths in a linear genetic program. It can be approximated by the maximum or the average number of registers that are effective at a program position (see also Section 3.4). Recall that the performance of linear GP strongly depends on a sufficient number of registers. The less registers available, the more conflicts may occur by overwriting of information during calculations. The more registers are provided, instead, the more local sets of registers may be used for calculating independent program paths.

It follows from the above discussion that the runtime of Algorithm 3.3 is $O(k \cdot n)$ where n is the number of effective instructions and k is the number of registers. If the total number of (input) registers is small, runtime is approximately linear in n.

The linear program in Example 3.1 corresponds exactly to the DAG in Figure 3.2 after applying Algorithm 3.3.

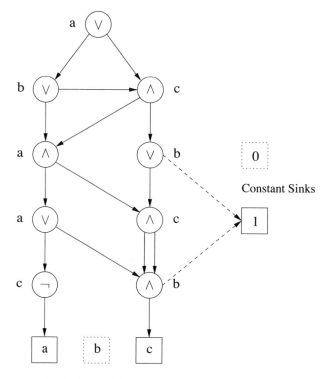

Variable Sinks

Figure 3.2. Functional equivalent to the effective imperative program in Example 3.1. Operator nodes are labeled with the destination registers of the corresponding instructions (see Algorithm 3.3). Output register **a** marks the start node. (Outgoing edges are not labeled because the order of operands is arbitrary here.)

Both the imperative representation and the functional representation consist of structurally effective code here that is free from unused instructions or unvisited graph components, respectively. This argument holds if we assume that the output of the imperative program is stored in register **a** at the end of execution. In Example 3.1 only two of the three possible inputs are used. At the beginning of program execution these inputs are held in registers **a** and **c**. *Used* program inputs designate all register operands that are directly read before being overwritten. In the corresponding graph representation used inputs denote sink nodes (terminals).

b := **c** ∧ 1
c := ¬ **a**
a := c ∨ b
c := b ∧ b
b := c ∨ 1   (x)
a := a ∧ c   (x)
c := a ∧ b
b := a ∨ c
a := b ∨ c

Example 3.1. Effective imperative program using Boolean operator set {∧, ∨, ¬}. Output and (used) input registers of the program are printed in bold.

3.3.1   Variation Effects

In linear GP already small mutations of the imperative representation resulting in the exchange of a register may have a large effect on the functional program structure and on data flow. Even if the absolute program structure is altered only slightly the effective program may change dramatically. Many instructions preceding the mutated instruction may be deactivated or reactivated. These *minimum mutations* are possible due to weaker constraints of the functional structure and due to the existence of non-contiguous graph components in linear programs. In tree GP, mutations cannot redirect single edges without loosing the underlying subtree. The number of child nodes (operands) is usually not variable.

b := c ∧ 1
c := ¬ a   (i)
a := c ∨ b   (i)
c := b ∧ b
b := c ∨ 1
a := **b** ∧ c
c := a ∧ b
b := a ∨ c
a := b ∨ c

Example 3.2. Linear program from Example 3.1 after register mutation. Operand register **a** has been exchanged by register **b** in the 6th line. Instructions marked with (i) are structural introns.

Example 3.2 demonstrates the effect of a register mutation on the program from Example 3.1. In particular, the first operand register **a** has been exchanged by register **b** in instruction 6. Subsequently two former

effective instructions – marked with (i) – are deactivated, i.e., are identified as structural introns now by Algorithm 3.1. Applying Algorithm 3.3
to this program results in the modified graph of Figure 3.3 which shows
a noneffective (and weakly connected) component.

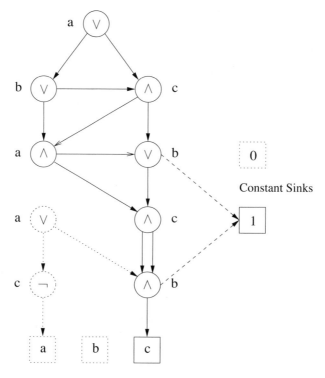

Figure 3.3. Graph interpretation of example program 3.2. Graph is effective except
for the dotted component.

In general, by changing an *operand* register on the imperative program
level a single edge is redirected in the corresponding graph. The exchange
of a *destination* register, on the other hand, may result in more redirections
of edges.

3.3.2   Interpretation of Branches

Throughout this book we restrict ourselves to the simple branching concept of Section 2.1.3 which only considers single conditional operations.
These have a minimal effect on the imperative control flow but may significantly change the data flow in a genetic program. Conditional instructions
have a high expressive power because leaving out or executing a single in-

struction can deactivate much of the preceding effective code or reactivate preceding noneffective instructions in turn. The more registers are available the more likely instructions operate on different sets of registers and the less likely the different data flows will intersect.

A single branch instruction is interpreted as an *if-else* node in a functional representation with a maximum of four successor nodes: one or two successors for the condition plus one successor each for its true or false outcome. In the true case the conditioned operation is executed and overwrites a certain register contents. In the false case the previous content of this register remains the current one and the corresponding calculation is connected to the following data flow.

a := c ∧ 1
b := c ∨ 0
if (b)
a := b ∨ c

Example 3.3. Conditional branch.

All instructions in Example 3.3 constitute one branching node plus context nodes as depicted in Figure 3.4. We assume that register **a** and, thus, all instructions are effective. If condition **b** = 1 is fulfilled in program line 3, the value of register **a** is calculated in the subsequent line. Otherwise, the value of **a** is not changed from the first line.

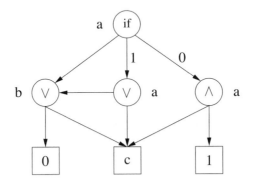

Figure 3.4. Functional equivalent to the conditional branch in Example 3.3. Edge followed in true (false) case is labeled with 1 (0).

Conditional jumps over single instructions in linear GP are at least as powerful for the modification of data flow as branch nodes in tree-based GP. In both instances only *one* point in data flow is affected. A conditional jump over more than one instruction, by comparison, would be interpreted as multiple branching nodes with identical condition. Accordingly, *several* branching points (program paths) are affected simultaneously on the functional level.

Conditional segments seem to be more powerful than conditional instructions, but they suffer from serious drawbacks. First, changing multiple branching nodes simultaneously will be more difficult to handle by evolution. Especially if jumps over branches into other conditional segments are allowed in the programs, the control flow in linear programs becomes somewhat chaotic. Second, larger jumps will induce larger variation steps in case the branching condition is modified or if the branch instruction is removed altogether. Whole branching blocks may suddenly be executed for most inputs. This makes both a stepwise improvement of solutions and a reduction of variation step size more difficult as will be discussed in Chapter 5. Third, conditional jumps over more than one instruction have a high potential for creating semantic introns and tend to produce larger structurally effective programs. On the strength of these arguments we may assume that the use of single conditional instructions provides enough freedom of expression for GP solutions.

3.3.3   Evaluation Order

The calculation proceeds in imperative programs by a sequence of transitions between different states of registers. While assignments to memory variables are an implicit part of imperative programs, in a pure functional program only values exist. Nevertheless, assignments – to a temporary stack – are needed during the interpretation of programs.

If a functional genetic program is executed the *evaluation order* of nodes depends on the way the graph is traversed. This path is not unique because the successor nodes of an inner node may be visited in arbitrary order – if we again exclude functions with side effects. The evaluation of nodes in a (contiguous) DAG may be performed as in trees in postfix order or prefix order. If the subgraphs of all outgoing edges have been processed, i.e., if all operand values are calculated, the result of a node can be computed. Because subprograms may be used more than once in a graph – in contrast to a tree – the result of evaluation should be saved in each node in order to not evaluate subgraphs twice. The final program result is stored at the root, the only node without incoming edges.

In an imperative genetic program the *evaluation order* is determined by the linear sequence of instructions. By using advanced programming concepts like loops or conditional branches, the execution order of instructions (*control flow*) may differ from the linear structural order. The instruction order of a program may be varied partly without leading to different behavior. This can happen for both effective and noneffective instructions. For instance, the order of the two effective instructions marked with (x) in Example 3.1 may be inverted, without altering the data flow or the output of the program. In fact, a functional transformation of the modified program will result in exactly the same graph, shown in Figure 3.2. Any reordering of instructions that preserves the dependencies in a program and, therefore, does not change the execution order of depending instructions is equivalent.

While the imperative structure arranges all instructions in a certain order, such an order is not defined in a functional representation which renders the latter less variable. As a result, only the transformation of a linear program into a graph is unique (except for isomorphism), but not the reverse transformation.

The imperative structure of programs is more variable based on a second reason: Internal register identifiers, used temporarily during calculation, may be replaced by other identifiers without changing program behavior.

Only the structural order of operands and the number of operands have to be respected in the imperative representation which is the same as in the functional representation.

3.3.4 Tree Interpretation

An effective linear program can be transformed into a functional expression by a successive replacement of register variables starting with the last effective instruction. The result of this instruction is always assigned to an output register. If there is more than one program output defined, a tree expression will need to be created for each output register.

In order to transform the noneffective imperative code the whole process has to be restarted from the last non-processed instruction in the program until all instructions have been processed. Except for the last instruction, instructions may have to be processed more than once. Because each component of the resulting functional program appears as a separate tree (expression), the whole linear genetic program is represented as a *forest*.

These tree programs normally contain many identical subtrees. The deeper a tree node is located the more frequently its corresponding subtree occurs.

The size of a tree grows exponentially with the program length n: Let there be only 1 register and only operations with 2 register operands in the imperative program.[4] Then the corresponding tree representation is perfectly balanced and contains $2^n - 1$ operator nodes and 2^n (identical) terminal nodes. The corresponding effective graph, by comparison, has only as many nodes as there are effective instructions (n) plus 1 terminal node.

On the one hand, this calculation example demonstrates the high expressive power of linear genetic programs. On the other hand, graph solutions are more compact in size than tree solutions because subgraphs can be reused several times. The reuse of register content is also the reason why ADFs are less important in linear GP than in tree-based GP [94].

However, we cannot conclude automatically that linear GP is more powerful than tree-based GP only because the constraints of the graph structure are weaker. The design of appropriate genetic operators is a very important aspect to be added to the expressiveness of a representation (see Chapters 5 and 6).

3.4 Analysis of Program Structure

In this section algorithms are described that extract information about the specific structure of a linear genetic program. All algorithms operate directly on the imperative representation which also is a representation for special program graphs, as demonstrated in the previous section. Three different features are analyzed that all refer to the effective part of a program.

$b := c \wedge 1$
$c := \neg a$
$a := c \vee \mathbf{b}$
$c := \mathbf{b} \wedge \mathbf{b}$
$b := c \vee 1$
$a := a \wedge c$
$c := a \wedge \mathbf{b}$
if ($\mathbf{b}$)
$b := a \vee c$
$a := \mathbf{b} \vee c$

Example 3.4. Linear program from Example 3.1 with branch. All dependencies of register **b** are bold printed. The dependence degree is 3 for the 1st and the 5th instruction from the top and 1 for the second last instruction.

---

[4]Then all instructions are necessarily effective.

First, there is the actual *number of effective registers* at an effective or absolute program position. This information is provided by means of Algorithm 3.1. If set $R_{eff}(i)$ holds all registers that are effective at a position i then $\frac{1}{n+1} \sum_{i=0}^{n} R_{eff}(i)$ denotes the average number of effective registers in a program of n instructions (and $n+1$ intermediate positions). This value corresponds approximately to the average width of the (effective) graph equivalent to the instruction sequence.

In a tree program each node is reached via a unique path from the root, i.e., each node has indegree 1 except for the root (indegree 0). In a graph-structured program, instead, many program paths may lead to the same node. In principle, the indegree of a node is restricted only by the total number of nodes n times the maximum outdegree m of a node. The narrower a graph develops the more program paths lead through a particular operator node.

DEFINITION 3.6 (*degree of effectiveness/dependence*)
The *degree of effectiveness* or *dependence* of an effective operation denotes the number of operand registers in (succeeding) instructions that directly use its result. Let the dependence degree of a branch instruction be identically equal to the dependence degree of its conditioned operation.

Algorithm 3.4 calculates the *degree of effectiveness* in a (structurally) effective program (see Definition 3.6). Each of the $d_{eff}(i)$ operands guarantees that operation i is (structurally) effective. In other words, an operand register guarantees the effectiveness of the next preceding assignment to this register that is not conditional *and* of all conditional assignments to this register that lie in between (see Example 3.4). On the functional level the effectiveness degree corresponds to the number of edges that go into an instruction node, i.e., the *connectivity degree* or, more precisely, the *indegree* of the node.

ALGORITHM 3.4 (*degree of effectiveness/dependence*)

1. Assume that all n instructions of a program are effective after Definition 3.4. Start at the last instruction in program at position $i := n$ and move backwards. Let $d_{eff}(i)$ denote the *degree of effectiveness* of an instruction at position i. $d_{eff}(i) := 0$ for $i = 1, .., n$.

2. If instruction i is a branch then $d_{eff}(i) := d_{eff}(i + 1)$ and $\rightarrow 7$.

3. $j := i$.

4. If $j < n$ then go to instruction $j := j + 1$. Otherwise $\rightarrow 7$.

5. If destination register $r_{dest}(i)$ of instruction i equals m operand registers $r_{op}(j)$ in instruction j then $d_{eff}(i) := d_{eff}(i) + m$.

6. If neither instruction j nor $j - 1$ are branches and $r_{dest}(i) = r_{dest}(j)$ then $\rightarrow$ 7. Otherwise $\rightarrow$ 4.

7. If $i > 1$ then go to instruction $i := i - 1$ and $\rightarrow$ 2.

8. Stop. The average effectiveness degree of program instructions is defined as $D_{eff} := \frac{1}{n} \sum_{i=1}^{n} d_{eff}(i)$.

The runtime of Algorithm 3.4 is bound by $O(n^2)$ with n being the effective program length. In the worst case scenario no instruction depends on any other. On average, however, runtime can be expected to be much shorter since usually a register will be used several times (temporarily) as a destination register or operand register, especially if only a few registers are available. In the best case each instruction only depends on the instruction that directly follows while computational costs are linear in n. This happens, for instance, if only one program register is available. If Algorithm 3.4 is applied to determine the effectiveness degree of a single instruction, it requires computation time $O(n)$.

Finally, Algorithm 3.5 calculates the average *effective dependence distance* in a program (see Definition 3.7). On the one hand, this quantity gives information about the relative position of effective instructions depending on each other. Since loops are not considered, an instruction necessarily follows the instructions in a program whose result it uses.

DEFINITION 3.7 (*effective dependence distance*)
The *effective dependence distance* denotes the relative distance (in effective instructions) of an effective instruction to the first succeeding instruction that depends on it.

On the other hand, this measure indicates how similar the position of an instruction in an imperative program is to the position of its corresponding node in the functional graph. Two instruction nodes depending on each other are always directly connected in the functional graph. The closer these instructions are in the imperative code, on average, the more similar are the relative positions of instructions and nodes. It follows from Algorithm 3.3 that the last instruction of an effective linear program forms the root of its equivalent directed graph. Theoretically, however, it is possible that single instructions are located high up in the effective program while their corresponding node is close to the graph root.

ALGORITHM 3.5 (*effective dependence distance*)

1. Assume that all n instructions of a program are effective after Definition 3.4. Start at the first non-branch instruction at a position i. Let $\delta_{eff}(i)$ denote the effective dependence distance between instruction i and the next instructions depending on it. $\delta_{eff}(i) := 0$ for $i = 1, .., n$.

2. $j := i$.

3. $\delta_{eff}(i) := \delta_{eff}(i) + 1$.

4. If $j < n$ then go to instruction $j := j + 1$. Otherwise $\rightarrow 6$.

5. If the destination register of instruction i equals an operand register in instruction j then $\rightarrow 6$. Otherwise $\rightarrow 3$.

6. Go to the next succeeding instruction $i := i + k$ $(k \geq 1)$ that is not a branch.
   If this does not exist then $\rightarrow 7$. Otherwise $\rightarrow 2$.

7. Stop. The average distance of two depending instructions is $\Delta_{eff} :=$
$$\frac{1}{n} \sum_{i=1}^{n} \delta_{eff}(i).$$

Algorithm 3.5 resembles Algorithm 3.4 in its basic structure and in runtime.

The effective dependence distance is not only influenced by the instruction order but also by the number and the usage of registers. The minimum distance of two depending instructions is one which will always be the case if only one register is used. In this case, the functional graph equivalent is reduced to a linear list of operator nodes, each connected by one or two edges. The more registers provided the more registers that may be effective and the wider the functional graph that may develop. Wider and longer graphs require a longer imperative representation. But only for wider graphs the average dependence distance increases because it is less likely that two depending instructions will occur one after the other in the imperative program. On the other hand, the more complex the register dependencies are, i.e., the higher their dependence degree is, the less variable the order of effective instruction becomes. This may decrease the effective dependence distance.

3.5   Graph Evolution

Because the imperative representation can be interpreted as a special graph representation, linear GP is reducible to the evolution of program graphs. What may be asked in this context is whether a direct evolution of a (less constrained) DAG representation may be more advantageous than evolution on the linear structure. In the imperative representation the (register) dependence of two instructions is influenced by both their position in the program and the dependencies of the instructions that lie in between.

We have seen above that the mutation of a single operand register may reactivate or deactivate other preceding instructions. Former effective (active) instructions become noneffective (inactive) if no other dependence to an effective instruction exists than the one that has been canceled. These deactivated instructions form a single contiguous graph component of the DAG that is disconnected from the effective component because the only existing connection has been removed.

If variations would happen directly on program graphs the degree of freedom would be higher for connecting nodes. If single edges may be redirected without restrictions on a functional level, the corresponding changes on the imperative code level may comprise much more complex transformations than exchanging a single register identifier.

The imperative representation defines a linear evaluation order on the effective and the noneffective instructions. This order does not exist in the functional representation where the evaluation order is less constrained and only determined by the connections of nodes. The imperative order determines and restricts the possible functional connections. A connection to the destination register of *any* preceding instruction is not possible, at least not by exchanging just a single register operand. Because registers are used multiple times in a program, only the next preceding assignment to a certain register may be reached in this way. The more registers that are provided, however, the less a restriction of variability this constitutes. In principle, all transformations are possible in an imperative representation, but it might require more or larger variation steps to achieve the same result.

The higher variability of a graph representation, however, does not automatically guarantee better access to solutions. Too many degrees of freedom tend to be disadvantageous. By coevolving an order of instruction nodes in linear GP not only the number of possible connections is restricted but promising connections are better preserved. So the probability is increased that functionally disconnected nodes can be reconnected in the evolutionary process. A limitation of connections further supports the emergence of structurally noneffective code, i.e., non-contiguous components.

Also recombination is less complicated between linear sequences of instructions than between graphs. If an instruction segment (subgraph) is exchanged, the new parts are automatically reconnected on the functional level in a defined manner. If not to an operator node, edges point to one of the graph sinks, i.e., a program input (see Section 3.3).

The most important property, however, is that a linear order of operations implicitly avoids cycles of register dependencies by allowing instructions to use only the result of *previous* instructions in a program. If graph programs are evolved without avoiding the formation of cycles, they may not terminate by themselves but the execution has to be stopped after a maximum number of nodes has been visited. Moreover, during variations special attention has to be paid to all operator nodes receiving the correct number of inputs. Depending on whether edges point in data flow direction or usage direction, either the correct number of incoming or outgoing edges has to be checked.

Otherwise the evaluation order of nodes becomes indefinite and a stack (or another state memory) is needed to determine both the exchange of data between nodes (data flow) and the decision of which path is visited next (control flow) [135, 20]. That is, the evaluation order has to be explicitly coevolved with the graphs.

If an evolved graph structure is supposed to be acyclic without restricting the freedom of node connections or the number of node evaluations, this had to be verified explicitly after each variation. The detection of all cycles in a graph is, however, computationally expensive. In linear GP such constraints do not have to be observed during variation but result implicitly from the linear sequence of instructions.

3.6 Summary and Conclusion

The properties of the special LGP representation that is analyzed in this book may be summarized as follows:

☐ On the imperative level a linear genetic program represents a sequence of instructions that comprise single operations or conditional operations with a minimum number of operands. This implies that the control flow is always forward-directed.

☐ On the functional level a linear genetic program describes a directed acyclic graph (DAG) with a minimum outdegree per operator node. The indegree of nodes is unrestricted in principle. It follows that the data flow in linear genetic programs is graph-based.

☐ Linear GP allows structurally noneffective code to coexist in programs that results from manipulating unused registers. In the corresponding graph structure this code may be composed of several disconnected or only weakly connected subgraphs. The effective code forms a connected graph component, instead, if the genetic programs return one output only.

☐ All operators used in linear genetic programs are mathematical functions without side effects. That is, a genetic program itself always represents a function.

A linear program defined like this may still be transformed into a tree expression. Since each tree is a special DAG this is achieved by copying all subgraphs successively whose start node has more than one incoming edge (starting with the root).

We showed different algorithms to extract features from linear genetic programs about their functional or imperative structure. This includes the detection of structural introns which is possible in runtime $O(n)$ when n is the number of instructions. Moreover, an algorithm was presented that transforms a linear program into a DAG. Other more specific features comprise the:

☐ Number of effective registers

☐ Degree of dependence (effectiveness)

☐ Effective dependence distance

The number of effective registers at a certain program position may serve as an approximation for the width of the effective graph component. The width of a graph component is limited by the maximum number of available registers. The effectiveness degree of an instruction equals the indegree of its corresponding graph node. The distance of an effective instruction to the first succeeding instruction (in the effective program) that depends on it, instead, has no equivalent on the functional level.

Chapter 4

A COMPARISON WITH NEURAL NETWORKS

The ability of a learning model to generalize, i.e., to predict the outcome of unknown input situations, is an important criterion when comparing the performance of different machine learning methods. This is all the more true for real-world applications in data mining. This chapter compares the generalization performance of LGP on several medical classification problems with results obtained by neural networks using RPROP learning.

Both the time that is necessary for learning a prediction model and the time needed for its execution are critical when operating with large data sets as they occur in medical applications. Two methods are therefore applied for the acceleration of LGP: (1) The absolute runtime is reduced by using Algorithm 3.1 for the elimination of noneffective code; (2) The effective training time is reduced on a generational basis by means of a deme approach and an elitist migration strategy.

4.1 Medical Data Mining

Genetic programming and artificial neural networks (ANNs) can be seen as alternative and perhaps competing techniques to solve classification and approximation problems. In the analysis of medical data neural networks have become an alternative to classical statistical methods. Ripley [112, 113] and Lisboa [78] have reviewed several NN techniques in medicine including methods for diagnostic and prognostic tasks, especially survival analysis. Most applications of NNs in medicine refer to classification tasks. Comprehensive lists of medical applications of neural networks can be found in [14, 114].

Gray *et al.* [42] report from an early application of GP to cancer diagnosis with results better than those of a neural network. GP and other evolutionary techniques have recently become more widespread in medical diagnosis and prognosis [102, 131]. Again, most of these tasks are from the realm of classification and approximation [18, 86, 106, 15, 32, 35, 145]. Various refinements of the classical GP approach are used [89, 19, 51, 132], as are hybridization techniques [123, 13, 69].

In this chapter genetic programming is applied to medical data widely tested in the machine learning community. More specifically, LGP is tested on six diagnostic problems that have been taken from the PROBEN1 benchmark set of real-world problems [109]. The main objective is to show that for these problems (L)GP is able to achieve classification rates and generalization performance competitive with neural networks. The application further demonstrates the ability of genetic programming in *data mining*, where general descriptions of information are to be found in large real-world databases.

4.2 Benchmark Data sets

Table 4.1 gives a brief description of six diagnostic problems and the diseases that are to be predicted. For a more detailed description the reader may consult [109]. Medical diagnosis mostly describes classification tasks which are much more frequent in medicine than approximation problems.

Table 4.1. Medical diagnostic tasks of PROBEN1 benchmark data sets.

Problem	Diagnosis
cancer	benign or malignant breast tumor
diabetes	diabetes positive or negative
gene	intron-exon, exon-intron or no boundary in DNA sequence
heart	diameter of a heart vessel is reduced by more than 50% or not
horse	horse with a colic will die, survive or must be killed
thyroid	thyroid hyperfunction, hypofunction or normal function

The data sets have been taken unchanged from an existing collection of real-world benchmark problems, PROBEN1 [109], that has been established originally for neural networks. The results obtained with one of the fastest learning algorithms for feed-forward neural networks (RPROP) accompany the PROBEN1 benchmark set to serve as a direct comparison with other methods. Comparability and reproducibility of the results are facilitated by careful documentation of the experiments. Following the benchmarking idea the results for neural networks have been adopted from [109] and verified. Our main objective was to realize a fair comparison between GP and NNs in medical classification and diagnosis. We will show that for all problems discussed the performance of GP in generalization comes very close to or is even better than the results documented for NNs.

All PROBEN1 data sets originate from the *UCI Machine Learning Repository* [88]. They are organized as a sequence of independent sample vectors divided into input and output values. For a better processing by neural networks the representation of the original (raw) data sets has been preprocessed in [109]. Values have been normalized, recoded, and completed. All inputs are restricted to the continuous range [0,1] except for the **gene** data set which holds values −1 or +1 only. For the outputs a binary *1-of-m encoding* is used where each bit represents one of the m possible output classes of the problem definition. Only the correct output class carries a "1" while all others carry "0". It is characteristic for medical data that they suffer from unknown attributes. In PROBEN1 most of the UCI data sets with missing inputs have been completed by 0 (30% in the case of the **horse** data set).

Table 4.2. Problem complexity of PROBEN1 medical data sets.

Problem	#Attributes	#Inputs		#Classes	#Samples
		continuous	*discrete*		
cancer	9	9	0	2	699
diabetes	8	8	0	2	690
gene	60	0	120	3	3175
heart	13	6	29	2	303
horse	20	14	44	3	364
thyroid	21	6	15	3	7200

Table 4.2 gives an overview of the specific complexity of each problem expressed in the number of attributes, divided into continuous and discrete inputs, plus output classes and number of samples. Note that some attributes have been encoded into more than one input value.

4.3 Experimental Setup

4.3.1 Genetic Programming

We employ the LGP approach that has been outlined in Chapter 2. For each data set an experiment with 30 runs has been performed with LGP. Runs differ only in their choice of a random seed. Table 4.3 lists the choice of parameters used for all problems here.

Table 4.3.   Parameter settings used for LGP.

Parameter	Setting
Number of generations	250
Population size	5,000
Number of demes	10
Migration rate (of best)	5%
Classification error weight	1
Maximum program length	256
Maximum initial length	25
Crossover rate	90%
Mutation rate	90%
Instruction set	$\{+, -, \times, /, sin, e^x, if >, if \leq\}$
Constants	$\{0, .., 255\}$

For benchmarking, the partitioning of the data sets has been adopted from PROBEN1. The *training set* always includes the first 50% of all samples, the next 25% is defined as the *validation set* and the last 25% of each data set is the *test set*. In PROBEN1 three different compositions of each data set were prepared, each with a different order of samples. This increases the confidence that results are independent of the particular distribution into training, validation and test set.

The fitness of an individual program is always computed using the complete training set. According to the LGP algorithm described in Section 2.3 generalization performance of the best-so-far individual is checked during training by calculating its error using the validation set. The test set is used only for the individual with minimum validation error after training.

The applied fitness function $\mathcal{F}$ has two parts, a continuous component and a discrete component (see Equation 4.1). The continuous *mean square error* (MSE) calculates the difference between the predicted output (vector) $gp(\vec{i_k})$ of an individual program gp and the desired output (vector) $\vec{o_k}$ for all n input-output samples $(\vec{i_k}, \vec{o_k})$ and $m = |\vec{o_k}|$ outputs. The discrete *mean classification error* (MCE) is computed as the average number of incorrectly classified examples.

$$
\begin{aligned}
\mathcal{F}(gp) &= \text{MSE} + w \cdot \text{MCE} \\
&= \frac{1}{n \cdot m} \sum_{k=1}^{n} (gp(\vec{i_k}) - \vec{o_k})^2 + \frac{w}{n} \cdot \text{CE}
\end{aligned}
\tag{4.1}
$$

The MCE is weighted by a parameter w. In this way, the classification performance of a program determines selection more directly while the MSE component still allows continuous fitness improvements. For fair comparison, the *winner-takes-all* classification method has been adopted from [109]. Each output class corresponds to exactly one program output. The class with the highest output value designates the response according to the 1-of-m output representation introduced in Section 4.2.

The generation in which the individual with the minimum validation error appeared defines the *effective training time*. The classification error of this individual on the test set characterizes the generalization performance that is of main interest here.

4.3.2 Population Structure

In evolutionary algorithms the population of individual solutions may be subdivided into multiple subpopulations. Migration of individuals among the subpopulations causes evolution to occur in the population as a whole. Wright [140] first described this mechanism as the *island model* in biology and reasoned that in semi-isolated subpopulations, called *demes*, evolution progresses faster than in a single population of equal size. This inherent acceleration of evolution by demes could be confirmed for EAs [133] and for GP in particular [130, 4]. One reason for this acceleration may be that genetic diversity is better preserved in multiple demes with a restricted migration of individuals. Diversity, in turn, influences the probability that the evolutionary search hits a local minimum. A local minimum in one deme might be overcome by other demes with a better search direction. A nearly linear acceleration can be achieved in evolutionary algorithms if demes are run in parallel on multi-processor architectures [4].

A special form of the island model, the *stepping stone model* [60], assumes that migration of individuals is only possible between certain adjacent demes which are organized as graphs with fixed connecting links. Individuals can reach remote populations only after passing through these neighbors. In this way, the possibility that there will be an exchange of individuals between two demes depends on their distance in the graph topology. Common topologies are ring or matrix structures.

In our experiments, the population is subdivided into 10 demes each holding 500 individuals. This partitioning has been found to be sufficient for investigating the effect of multiple demes. The demes are connected by a directed ring of migration links by which every deme has exactly one successor (see Figure 4.1). After each generation a certain percentage of *best* individuals, which is determined by the *migration rate*, emigrates from each deme into the successor deme thereby replacing the worst individuals. Primarily, demes are used here to allow locally best solutions a higher reproduction by migration. By copying the best solutions of a deme into several others learning may accelerate because these individuals might further develop simultaneously in different subpopulations. In general, a more frequent reproduction of better individuals in the population increases the probability that these solutions are selected and improved. However, it may cause a premature loss of diversity, too. This negative influence is partly counteracted by the use of demes. Additionally, the migration of best is not free between demes, but restricted to only certain migration paths that are organized as a directed ring. Together with a modest migration rate this has been found to be a good compromise between faster fitness progress and preservation of diversity.

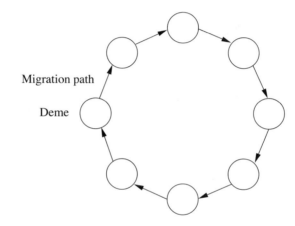

Figure 4.1.   Stepping stone model of directed migration on a ring of demes.

4.3.3   Neural Networks

Experimental results in [109] have been achieved using standard multi-layer perceptrons (MLPs) with fully connected layers. Different numbers of hidden units and hidden layers (one or two) have been tried before arriving at the best network architecture for each problem. The training method was RPROP [111], a fast and robust backpropagation variant. For further information on the RPROP parameters and the special network architectures the reader may consult [109].

The generalization performance on the test set is computed for the state of the network with minimum validation error. *Effective training time* of the neural network is measured in number of epochs until this state is reached. One *epoch* has passed once all training samples have been presented to the network.

4.4   Experiments and Comparison

4.4.1   Generalization Performance

Table 4.4 shows the classification error rates obtained with genetic programming and neural networks, respectively, for the medical data sets discussed in Section 4.2. Best and average CE of all GP runs are documented on the validation set and test set for each medical data set, together with the standard deviation. A comparison with the test classification error of neural networks (reprinted from [109]) is the most interesting here. For that purpose the difference Δ between the average test errors of NN and GP is printed in percent of the largest value. A positive Δ indicates improved GP results over NN. A negative Δ indicates better NN results, respectively. Unfortunately, the classification results on the validation set and the results of best runs are not specified in [109] for NNs.

Table 4.4. Classification error rates of GP and NN for PROBEN1 medical data sets. Difference Δ in percent. Positive Δ indicates improved GP results over NN.

	GP						NN		
Problem	Validation CE (%)			Test CE (%)			Test CE (%)		Δ (%)
	best	*mean*	*std.dev.*	*best*	***mean***	*std.dev.*	***mean***	*std.dev.*	
cancer1	1.7	2.5	0.3	0.6	2.2	0.6	1.4	0.5	−36.7
cancer2	0.6	1.4	0.4	4.0	5.7	0.7	4.8	0.9	−16.6
cancer3	1.7	2.6	0.4	3.5	4.9	0.6	3.7	0.5	−24.9
diabetes1	20.3	22.2	1.1	21.4	24.0	1.4	24.1	1.9	+0.6
diabetes2	21.4	23.2	1.3	25.0	27.9	1.5	26.4	2.3	−5.1
diabetes3	25.5	26.7	0.7	19.3	23.1	1.3	22.6	2.2	−2.2
gene1	7.8	11.2	2.3	9.2	13.0	2.2	16.7	3.8	+22.2
gene2	9.1	12.9	2.3	8.5	12.0	2.2	18.4	6.9	+35.1
gene3	7.2	10.8	2.1	10.1	13.8	2.1	21.8	7.5	+36.6
heart1	7.9	10.5	2.4	18.7	21.1	2.0	20.8	1.5	−1.4
heart2	14.5	18.6	2.4	1.3	7.3	3.3	5.1	1.6	−29.8
heart3	15.8	18.8	1.5	10.7	14.0	2.0	15.4	3.2	+9.2
horse1	28.6	32.4	2.2	23.1	30.6	2.2	29.2	2.6	−4.5
horse2	29.7	34.3	2.7	31.9	36.1	2.0	35.9	2.5	−0.7
horse3	27.5	32.7	1.9	31.9	35.4	1.8	34.2	2.3	−3.6
thyroid1	0.8	1.3	0.3	1.3	1.9	0.4	2.4	0.4	+19.8
thyroid2	1.1	1.6	0.3	1.4	2.3	0.4	1.9	0.2	−17.3
thyroid3	0.9	1.5	0.2	0.9	1.9	0.4	2.3	0.3	+17.2

Our results demonstrate that LGP is able to reach a generalization performance similar to multi-layer perceptrons using the RPROP learning rule. The rather small number of runs performed for each data set may, however, give an order of magnitude comparison only. In addition, the results for GP are not expected to rank among the best, since parameter settings have not been adjusted to each benchmark problem. This has deliberately not been carried out in order to show that even a common choice of the GP parameters can produce reasonable results. In contrast, at least the NN architecture has been adapted specifically for each data set in [109]. Finally, the PROBEN1 data sets are prepared for being advantageous to NNs but not necessarily to GP, particularly in regard to the coding of input attributes and outputs whose dimensions are larger than in the original UCI data sets (see Section 4.2). For instance, even if multiple program outputs required for a winner-takes-all classification are easy to handle in linear GP by using multiple output registers, they do not necessarily produce better results.

Notably, for the gene problem the test classification error (average and standard deviation) has been found to be much better with GP. This is another indication that GP is able to handle a very high number of inputs efficiently (see Table 4.2). On the other hand, cancer turned out to be considerably more difficult for GP than for NN judged by the percentage difference in average test error.

Looking closer, classification results for the three different data sets of each problem show that the difficulty of a problem may change significantly with the distribution of data into training, validation and test set. Especially the test error differs with the three different distributions. For instance, the test error is much smaller for data set heart2 than for heart1. For some data sets the training, validation and test sets cover the problem data space differently, i.e., are less strongly correlated. As a result a strong difference between validation and test error might occur, as in the case of cancer and heart.

Not for all problems, especially diabetes, heart, and horse, the best classification results have been produced with conditional branches. This might be due to the fact that if branches are not necessary for a good solution they promote rather specialized solutions. Another reason may be the rather poor correlation of training data and generalization data here [109]. Other problems, particularly gene, have worked better with branches. Branches have been found to have a much smaller influence on the generalization performance than on the training performance (not documented). The similarity of the gain in performance strongly depends on the correlation of training data and generalization data.

4.4.2 Effective Training Time

The effective training time specifies the number of *effective* generations or epochs, respectively, until the minimum validation error occurred. We can deduce from Tables 4.2 and 4.5 that more complex problems cause more difficulty for GP and NN and, thus, a longer effective training time. A comparison between generations and epochs is, admittedly, difficult, but it is interesting to observe that effective training time for GP shows lower variation than for NN.

Table 4.5. Effective training time of GP and NN (rounded).

Problem	GP		NN	
	#Eff. Generations		#Eff. Epochs	
	mean	*std.dev.*	*mean*	*std.dev.*
cancer1	26	24	95	115
cancer2	26	25	44	28
cancer3	17	11	41	17
diabetes1	23	14	117	83
diabetes2	28	25	70	26
diabetes3	21	15	164	85
gene1	77	21	101	53
gene2	90	20	250	255
gene3	86	14	199	163
heart1	17	14	30	9
heart2	20	14	18	9
heart3	21	18	11	5
horse1	18	16	13	3
horse2	19	16	18	6
horse3	15	14	14	5
thyroid1	55	18	341	280
thyroid2	64	15	388	246
thyroid3	51	14	298	223

4.4.3 Acceleration of Absolute Runtime

Table 4.6 shows the percentage of noneffective instructions (and effective instructions) averaged over all programs of a run and over multiple runs (30 here) as identified by Algorithm 3.1 for the medical problems under consideration. The potential acceleration of runtime, that is obtained when removing these introns before a program is evaluated, directly results from the intron rates (using Equation 3.1). Very often, intron rates of 80% have been observed which corresponds to an average decrease in runtime by the intron elimination of about a factor of 5. This performance improvement is of practical significance especially when operating with large data sets as they occur in medicine. A further benefit of the reduced execution time is that the effective linear genetic programs may operate more efficiently in time-critical applications. The reader may recall that the elimination of introns cannot have any influence on the fitness or classification performance (see Section 3.2.1).

Table 4.6. Percentage of introns and effective code per run in percent of the absolute program length. Factors show speedup if only the effective code is executed. Notable differences exist between problems.

Problem	Introns (%)		Eff. Code (%)		Speedup
	mean	*std.dev.*	*mean*	*std.dev.*	
cancer	65.5	2.8	34.6	2.8	2.9
diabetes	74.5	0.6	25.5	0.6	3.9
gene	90.5	1.1	9.5	1.1	10.5
heart	88.2	0.9	11.8	0.9	8.5
horse	90.8	0.4	9.2	0.4	10.9
thyroid	72.2	1.8	27.8	1.8	3.6

From Table 4.6 it may also be concluded that the average percentages of effective program size strongly vary with the problem. The standard deviation of program size has proven to be amazingly small between single runs of the same problem. The differences between the three data sets tested for each problem are found even smaller and are, therefore, not specified here.

Different instruction types may cause different computational costs, of course. Compared to most operations, branch instructions are rather cheap in execution time, for instance. Additional computation is saved with branches because not all (conditional) operations of a program are executed for each training sample. In general, the calculation of the relative speedup factors relies on the assumption that the different components of the instruction set are approximately uniformly distributed in the population – over the effective code as well as over the noneffective code.

4.4.4   Acceleration of Effective Training Time

Another important result of our GP experiments is that effective training time can be reduced considerably by using semi-isolated subpopulations together with an elitist migration strategy (as described in Section 4.3.2). Moreover, this is possible without leading to a notable decrease in generalization performance. A comparable series of runs without demes but with the same population size (5,000) has been performed for the first data set of each problem. The average classification rates documented in Table 4.7 differ only slightly from the results obtained with a demetic population (see Table 4.4).

Table 4.7. Classification error rates of GP without demes. Average results similar to results with demes (see Table 4.4).

Problem	GP without Demes					
	Validation CE (%)			Test CE (%)		
	best	*mean*	*std.dev.*	*best*	*mean*	*std.dev.*
cancer1	1.1	2.1	0.5	1.2	2.9	1.2
diabetes1	19.3	21.4	0.7	20.3	24.4	1.7
gene1	7.7	11.0	3.0	9.0	12.6	3.1
heart1	7.9	11.0	3.0	18.7	22.3	2.9
horse1	26.4	32.4	1.9	22.0	30.7	3.5
thyroid1	0.7	1.3	0.4	1.2	2.0	0.5

Table 4.8 compares the effective training time using a panmictic (non-demetic) population with the respective results from Table 4.5 after the same maximum number of 250 generations. On average, the number of effective generations is reduced by a factor of about 3. Thus, a significantly faster convergence of runs is achieved by using a demetic approach that allows only better individuals to migrate without compromising quality of the results.

Table 4.8. Effective training time of GP with and without demes. Significant acceleration with demes and an elitist migration strategy.

Problem	GP with Demes		GP without Demes		
	#Eff. Generations		#Eff. Generations		Speedup
	mean	*std.dev.*	*mean*	*std.dev.*	
cancer1	26	24	62	67	2.4
diabetes1	23	14	62	53	2.7
gene1	77	21	207	42	2.7
heart1	17	14	68	75	4.0
horse1	18	16	59	63	3.3
thyroid1	55	18	200	36	3.6

Not surprisingly, programs grow less within a smaller number of effective generations (not shown). In this way, a demetic population controls program size, at least of the best generalizing solutions.

4.4.5   Further Comparison

Note that reducing the (relative) training time on a generational basis affects the absolute training time, too, because runs may be stopped earlier. Comparing the absolute runtime of genetic programming and feed-forward neural networks, the fast NN learning algorithm has been found to be superior. One should keep in mind, however, that large populations have been used with the GP runs to guarantee a sufficient diversity and a sufficient number of (not too small) subpopulations. Because we concentrate on a comparison in classification performance the parameters of the LGP system have not been optimized for runtime. Nevertheless, the proposed speedup techniques for (L)GP help to reduce the difference in runtime to NN, especially if smaller populations of genetic programs are used.

In contrast to neural networks, GP is not only capable of predicting outcomes but may also provide insight into and a better understanding of the medical diagnosis by an analysis of the learned models (genetic programs) [89]. Knowledge extraction from genetic programs is more feasible with programs that are compact in size and free from redundant information. Thus, the elimination of noneffective code in our LGP system may serve another purpose in generating more intelligible results than do NNs.

4.5   Summary and Conclusion

We reported on LGP applied to a number of medical classification tasks. It was demonstrated that, on average, genetic programming performs competitive to RPROP neural networks with respect to the generalization performance.

The runtime performance of genetic programming becomes especially important for time-critical applications or when operating with large data sets from real-world domains like medicine. Two techniques were presented that reduced the computational costs significantly.

First, the elimination of noneffective code from linear genetic programs resulted in an average decrease in runtime of about a factor of 5 here. Second, by using a demetic population in combination with an elitist migration strategy the number of effective generations was reduced by a factor of about 3, without decreasing the performance of the evolutionary algorithm.

PART II

METHOD DESIGN

Chapter 5

LINEAR GENETIC OPERATORS I – SEGMENT VARIATIONS

Crossover has been the traditional operator in tree-based GP for varying the content and size of programs. In this chapter we systematically introduce crossover and mutation operators for the linear program representation and compare their influence on prediction performance and the complexity of evolved solutions.

We can distinguish between two different levels of variation done by these operators. *Macro variations* operate on the instruction level (or *macro level*). In this perspective, an instruction represents the smallest unit. *Micro variations* operate on the level of instruction components (*micro level*) and manipulate registers, operators, and constants. Only macro variations influence program growth. Macro variations may be further divided into *segment variations* and *instruction variations*, depending on whether a contiguous subsequence of instructions or only one instruction is subjected to change. Only segment variations will form the subject of this chapter. Other variations will be treated in a subsequent chapter.

We will see that the performance of a variation operator strongly depends on its maximum (and average) step size on the symbolic program structure, on its influence on code growth, and on the proportion of effective and neutral variations. Among other things, macro mutations with minimum step size will turn out to be most effective provided that a change of the structurally effective code can be guaranteed. We will also investigate how linear genetic programs can be manipulated more efficiently through respecting their functional structure.

5.1   Variation Effects

Basically, two different effects of a variation operator can be distinguished in evolutionary computation. These are its effects on the genotype and its effects on the phenotype. In GP the genotype is represented by the program structure while the phenotype is determined by the semantics (execution behavior) of the program.

5.1.1   Semantic Variation Effects

The phenotype quality is measured by a fitness function $\mathcal{F} : \mathcal{P} \rightarrow \mathbb{R}_0^+$. Fitness distributions have been proposed as a means for understanding (semantic) variation effects in evolutionary computation. In [43] the *fitness distribution* (FD) of a variation operator v is described as the probability distribution of the offspring fitness $\mathcal{F}_o$ depending on the fitness of parent(s) $\mathcal{F}_{\{p\}}$:

$$\mathrm{FD}_v(\mathcal{F}_{\{p\}}) := \mathrm{Prob}(\mathcal{F}_o | \mathcal{F}_{\{p\}}). \tag{5.1}$$

A fitness distribution is quite complex and, in general, rather difficult to compute. In practice it is usually sufficient to focus on important features of the fitness distribution [91, 53] which can serve as an approximation to the actual distribution. If we assume that a better fitness always means a *smaller* value of $\mathcal{F}$ ($\mathcal{F}$ being an error function), the following definitions are valid.

DEFINITION 5.1 (*constructive/destructive/neutral variation*)
A variation is defined as *constructive* iff the difference between the fitness $\mathcal{F}_p$ of a parent individual and the fitness $\mathcal{F}_o$ of its offspring is positive, i.e., $\mathcal{F}_p - \mathcal{F}_o > 0$. In the case of a negative difference, i.e., $\mathcal{F}_p - \mathcal{F}_o < 0$, we refer this as a *destructive* variation. Finally, a genetic operation is *neutral* if it does not change the fitness, i.e., $\mathcal{F}_p = \mathcal{F}_o$.[1]

In the LGP algorithm of Section 2.3 two offspring are created from two parents in each iteration. Either recombination is applied once between both parents and produces two offspring or mutation is applied on each parent separately. In both cases we compare the parent and the offspring with the same index, i.e., p_1 with o_1 and p_2 with o_2. That is, the state of a program at a certain position in memory is compared before and after it has been varied.

---

[1]We stick here to exact neutrality, but realize that other definitions are possible, too. Sometimes the fitness cannot be calculated exactly, and sometimes, the definition might consider fitness values as equal within a certain tolerance interval. For a recent review of near-neutrality in Biology, see [96].

We are interested in the *proportion* of constructive, destructive, and neutral operations per generation. Such measurements are sensitive to the *direction* of semantic variation effects, but neglect other features of a fitness distribution, like the *amount* of a fitness change (see Section 5.3).

5.1.2 Structural Variation Effects

The program structure or genotype can also be subjected to measurements. The quantity of interest is the proportion of effective and noneffective variations as defined by:

DEFINITION 5.2 (*effective/noneffective variation*)
A genetic operation applied to a linear genetic program is called *effective* iff it affects the *structurally* effective code according to Definition 3.4. Otherwise, a variation is called *noneffective*.

Note that even if effective code is altered the program output for the set of fitness cases considered might be the same. An effective variation is merely meant to bring about a structural change of the effective program. There is no change of program semantics (fitness) guaranteed, mostly due to the existence of semantic introns. From the above definitions it follows that all structurally noneffective variations are semantically neutral but not the other way around.

Measuring the *amount* of structural change between parent and offspring requires the definition of a structural distance metric between genetic programs (see below and Chapter 10).

5.2 Effective Variation and Evaluation

In principle, there are two different ways to identify effective variations. Either the effectiveness is implicitly guaranteed by the genetic operator itself (see Section 6.2.3) or the effective code of an individual is compared explicitly before and after the variation (see Section 5.7.4). The latter method will be necessary with recombination.

By using Algorithm 3.1 the effective code of parent and offspring can be identified and extracted in linear computation time $O(n)$ where n denotes the maximum program length. In doing so, the two effective programs may be compared in worst case by $O(n)$ comparisons of instructions which is reduced to comparisons of integers in our implementation (see Section 2.1.1). An effective variation has been detected after the comparison failed for one instruction position.

In order to avoid another application of Algorithm 3.1 before fitness evaluation, the effective code of each program should be saved separately. A less memory-intensive alternative we apply here marks all effective instructions within the program representation (see Section 3.2.1). An update flag for each program decides whether the effective code has already been calculated or not.

If a variation has been identified as *noneffective* the effective code is unchanged. In this case, a new fitness evaluation of the offspring is unnecessary and can be skipped since its behavior clearly cannot be different from the parent. This produces a difference between comparing variation operators on the basis of *generations* (number of varied individuals) and *evaluations* (number of effective variations) because it is no longer guaranteed that each new (varied) individual will be evaluated. Evaluating individuals only after effective variations will be referred to as *effective evaluation* in the following.

Besides the removal of noneffective code before fitness evaluation, this method is a further technique to accelerate runtime of linear GP. Depending on the rate of noneffective operations induced by a variation operator, a high amount of fitness evaluations might be saved. The overall acceleration in runtime can be expressed by the factor

$$\alpha_{acc} = \frac{n_{var}}{n_{(eff)var}} \tag{5.2}$$

where $n_{(eff)var}$ is the number of (effective) variations.

In general, fitness evaluation is by far the most time-consuming step in a GP algorithm. Computational costs for variation may be neglected if the time for calculating a new search point is linear in program size. This holds for both techniques, the detection of effective variations, as well as the detection of effective code.

5.3   Variation Step Size

We now return to the amount of structural program change. Let *variation step size* denote the distance between a parent individual gp_p and its offspring gp_o that results from the application of one or more variation operators.

The *phenotype distance* or *semantic step size* is calculated by a semantic distance metric $d_\mathcal{P} : \mathcal{P} \times \mathcal{P} \rightarrow \mathbb{R}_0^+$. The absolute difference in fitness $d_\mathcal{P}(gp_p, gp_o) := |\mathcal{F}(gp_p) - \mathcal{F}(gp_o)|$ identifies a phenotype with its fitness value. This is a gross simplification because the fitness function $\mathcal{F}$ cannot expected to be bijective in general (see Section 1.2). Usually many more genetic operations are destructive than constructive in GP, while fitness deteriorations will, on average, be larger than improvements. As a result, the average fitness distance $\mathcal{E}(|\mathcal{F}(gp_p) - \mathcal{F}(gp_o)|)$ is often dominated by large negative terms. In order to avoid this dominance, positive and negative fitness changes should be computed separately.

Measuring the *genotype distance* or *structural step size* $d_\mathcal{G}(gp_p, gp_o)$ requires an appropriate distance metric $d_\mathcal{G} : \mathcal{G} \times \mathcal{G} \to \mathbb{N}_0^+$ to be defined on the program structure. We measure all structural step sizes absolutely in instructions, not relative to the program length. Relative step sizes are more difficult to control and to minimize during a run since programs grow. Moreover, the corresponding semantic step size may be only partly proportional to the length of the linear genetic program.

DEFINITION 5.3 (*structural step size*)
For macro operators in linear GP let the (absolute) *structural step size* be defined as the number of instructions that are added to a linear program *plus* the number of instructions that are removed during one variation step from parent to offspring program.

Definition 5.3 is more precise than simply calculating the distance in program length if code is both inserted and deleted in one step, e.g., during crossover. It is also more precise than using the (average) segment length only since an exchange of code may be more destructive than a deletion or an insertion. This definition only disregards the possibility that the actual step size may be smaller due to an exchange of similar code segments at similar positions.

Accordingly, the *effective step size* may be defined intuitively as the number of inserted and/or deleted effective instructions. When using unrestricted segment variations the effective step size is sufficiently approximated in this way. Nonetheless, such a definition is imprecise since additional instructions may become effective or noneffective upstream from the varied program position (*variation point*). In particular if the absolute variation step size is minimal, i.e., one instruction, these side effects within the linear program structure become relevant. Thus, the following definition is more suitable:

DEFINITION 5.4 (*effective step size*)
The *effective step size* is defined as the number of instructions that are added to or removed from the *effective* program including instructions that change their effectiveness status, i.e., that are deactivated or reactivated, as a consequence of the variation of parent to offspring.

We note in passing that micro mutations affect, by definition, a single instruction component only. That is, their absolute step size is always constant and minimum. Nonetheless, their effective step size may be much larger. This is the case, for instance, if an effective instruction register is replaced on which the effectiveness of many other instructions depends.

On the functional level the absolute step size measures the total number of deleted or inserted graph nodes. The effective step size, instead, counts all instruction nodes that are connected to or disconnected from the effective graph (see Section 3.3). Thus, effective step size can better observe the functional structure of a linear program. The distance between the effective code of parent and offspring is more precise because it is more closely related to fitness distance. That is, a smaller effective step size may be assumed to lead to a smaller change in fitness. In Chapter 9 we will present distance metrics that calculate effective distance between linear genetic programs. This information is used to explicitly control the variation step size on *effective* code. In the present chapter, however, the absolute variation step size is controlled on the *full* program structure.

The proportion of noneffective code within a linear genetic program and the absolute program size influence the effective step size that is induced by segment variations, both for recombination and mutation. A higher intron rate will lead to less effective instructions being deleted and/or inserted during variation. So despite the fact that introns do not directly contribute to the fitness of a program, they increase average fitness and survivability of its offspring. More generally, an explicit or implicit reduction of effective step size increases the *effective fitness* [91] or the *evolvability* [3] of the population of programs. The notion of effective step size allows the evolvability of linear genetic programs to be measured and explicitly controlled. In doing so, the effective step size considers not only structural aspects of a genetic program, like the intron rate, but also the influence of the absolute step size of the variation operator. We will demonstrate in this chapter (and in Chapter 9) that a minimization of effective step sizes, i.e., a maximization of the effective fitness, yields the best performance.

5.4 Causality

In the following, unless otherwise stated, the term *step size* will refer to the absolute *structural* variation distance. In evolutionary computation the term originates from the idea of a *fitness landscape* [83, 54] where all possible solutions of the (genotype) search space are organized in a structural neighborhood – by using a structural distance metric – and their fitness values constitute a relatively smooth surface. In GP the surface of the fitness landscape depends not only on the problem definition (fitness function) but also on the system configuration, in particular the set of program instructions. The application of a variation operator corresponds to performing one step on the fitness landscape. Both the roughness of the surface and the step size of the variation operator determine the success of the evolutionary search process.

On the one hand, the variation operator has to allow progress in steps that are small enough to approach a global optimum solution or at least a good local optimum. That means, it should *exploit* the fitness information of adjacent search points by a *gradient descent*. It can be considered a strength of evolutionary algorithms that the exact gradient is not followed, but rather a *gradient diffusion* process takes place [110]. Due to new search points being selected randomly without a constant direction, an evolutionary search will less likely get stuck in local minima (suboptima) of the fitness landscape. Usually there is more than one global optimum in the genotype space since programs with optimum fitness are not unique in their structure, what is known as code redundancy.

On the other hand, the average variation step size must not be too small. Otherwise the global evolutionary progress may be too restricted. A sufficient proportion of larger steps may be required to avoid the evolutionary process getting bogged down early in a local suboptimum. That is, sufficient *exploration* of the fitness landscape has to be maintained. This may depend, however, on other factors like population size and diversity of the population material. Moreover, exploration requires a sufficient proportion of neutral variations, which will allow *random walks* (*neutral walks*) over the fitness landscape.

This chapter will show that linear genetic programming benefits strongly from a reduction of variation step size. Even minimum step sizes on the program structure seem to be still large enough to escape from local minima.[2] This might be interpreted in such a way that an *exploration-exploitation trade-off* does not exist. But keep in mind that the fitness landscape is not perfectly smooth, especially when operating on a symbolic representation. Even small changes of the program structure may still result in large changes of program semantics.

Strong causality requires a completely "smooth" fitness landscape [110], i.e., small changes of position (individual) in the high-dimensional landscape always imply small changes in height (fitness). Therefore, this fea-

---

[2]The fitness function always minimizes a prediction error here.

ture postulates Equation 5.3 to be valid for any three search points:

$$\forall p_1, p_2, p_3 \in \mathcal{G} : d_{\mathcal{G}}(p_1, p_2) \leq d_{\mathcal{G}}(p_1, p_3) \Leftrightarrow d_{\mathcal{P}}(p_1, p_2) \leq d_{\mathcal{P}}(p_1, p_3) \quad (5.3)$$

Strong causality is, however, not a necessary condition for the proper working of evolutionary algorithms in general. Indeed, this condition is not strictly fulfilled by most evolutionary algorithms. Already from observations in nature we may not assume a strong causality between genotype and phenotype. In biological evolution the DNA may be subject to large modifications without affecting the organism significantly. Sometimes large modifications of the phenotype may result from only little genotype changes. Nevertheless, the vast majority of natural variations on genotype level is rather small and is expressed (if ever) in small variations of the phenotype. Among other things, this is due to the redundancy of the genetic code.

A fitness landscape should be smooth at least in local regions (*locally strong causality*) [110, 121]. Otherwise, evolutionary search may not be more powerful than random search. In an extremely rugged surface a search point (individual) would contain only little or no information about the expected fitness of its direct neighbors. Ruggedness of the fitness landscape is one aspect, but flatness of the fitness landscape is another. Flat regions make a problem hard for an evolutionary algorithm, because on such *fitness plateaus* no gradient information is available.

Neutral variations are important for problems with wide fitness plateaus occurring frequently with discrete fitness functions. In flat regions of the fitness landscape neutral variations maintain evolutionary progress by a random exploration in the genotype space. That is, the population spreads wider over a fitness plateau by neutral drift which increases the probability to find a better solution. If a *fitness gradient* is discovered the population will quickly concentrate on the neighborhood of this local optimum again, since individuals in that region will spread faster in the population.

Changing a small program component in genetic programming may lead to almost arbitrary changes in program behavior. On average, however, we may assume that the less instructions are modified the smaller the fitness change will be. With a high probability smaller variations in genotype space, i.e., smaller variation step sizes, result in smaller variations in phenotype space, i.e., smaller fitness distances. Such a *stochastic causality* or *weak causality* is a necessary precondition of a program representation and its genetic operators. In Section 9.7.1 a positive correlation between structural and semantic step sizes will be shown empirically for different variation operators and problems.

5.4.1   Self-Adaptation

Automatic optimization of variation parameters by self-adaptation has been applied successfully in different disciplines of evolutionary algorithms. In evolution strategies (ES) [110, 119] mutation step sizes are coevolved as part of the individual representation in the form of standard deviation parameters. In the most simple case there is only one mutation step size for all objective variables. Rather than using a deterministic control rule for the adaptation of such parameters, the parameters themselves are subject to evolution. Self-adaptation differs from a global adaptive parameter control because the parameters are adapted locally during evolution. The modification of parameters is under the control of the user by a fixed mutation step size, called *learning rate*. Selection is performed on the basis of an individual's fitness. The propagation or extinction of variation parameters in the population is therefore coupled with the fitness of the carrier individual. Consequently, the success of a certain parameter configuration directly depends on how the variation operator performs on an individual with these settings. It is generally recommended to mutate the variation parameters of an individual first before the new settings are applied for the variation of the individual. The reverse mechanism might suffer from a propagation of (good) individuals with rather bad parameters because those have not been used for finding the current position of the individual on the fitness landscape.

Good results may also be obtained by using a lower mutation rate for the parameters than for the actual individuals. Otherwise good individuals with bad parameter settings might spread too quickly in the population at the beginning of a run. This again may lead to an early loss of diversity while the search process gets caught in a local minimum. Note that the fitness of an individual does not depend directly on the quality of its variation parameters, but parameters will influence the average survival probability and potential fitness of its offspring.

The general motivation for self-adaptation and variable parameters is twofold: (1) It may outperform an optimal parameter *setting* that remains constant during a run and find the optimal *solution*, i.e., genetic program, faster; (2) it may be the only efficient way to find the (or a nearly) optimal setting. Especially if the dimension of the parameter vector is high, an optimal parameter configuration may hardly be detected just by choosing random fixed settings.

In Section 6.4.5 we will analyze a self-adaptation approach to optimize mutation step size in terms of the number of mutation points on the (symbolic) program representation.

5.5   Selection of Variation Points

Due to the hierarchy of nodes in tree programs a variation point (node) can be expected to be more influential the closer it lies to the root of the tree. If nodes are selected independent of their position, deeper nodes are automatically chosen more frequently because most nodes are closer to a leaf. In a completely balanced binary tree of n nodes exactly $\lfloor \frac{n}{2} \rfloor$ nodes are inner nodes and $\lceil \frac{n}{2} \rceil$ nodes are leaves. Thus, half of the variation points would fall upon constants or variables. This implicit bias of tree crossover results in a lower variation probability and, thus, in a loss of diversity in tree regions closer to the root. In order to compensate this tendency Koza [64] imposes an explicit counter bias on the crossover operator by selecting inner (function) nodes with a high probability (90 percent). An alternative solution is to select depth prior to selecting the actual node among all nodes of that depth with the same probability [46].

In a linear program the situation is different. One may assume that each program position has a similar influence on program semantics, at least if a rather moderate number of registers is provided. Recall that the internal structure of an LGP program, as defined in Chapter 3, represents a directed acyclic graph (DAG) that is restricted in width through the number of registers provided (see Section 3.3). In a tree each node can be reached via a unique path from the root, i.e., each node is connected to only one incoming edge. In a DAG more than one program path may lead to the same node, i.e., a node may be connected to several incoming edges. Therefore, it may be justified to select each instruction for variation with the same probability.

However, even if the *maximum* width of the graph representation is restricted and the number of incoming edges is free there is not enough information about the specific functional structure of a particular linear program. The algorithms that have been presented in Section 3.4 extract special features about the functional or imperative program structure. Among other things, this information can be used to bias the choice of variation points.

In Section 6.4.6 mutation points will be selected with different probability distributions depending on their effective position in the imperative representation. The relative position of an effective instruction in a program is of minor importance as long as all instructions are selected with the same probability. Only if selection of variation points is non-uniform, e.g., biased towards the end or the beginning of the imperative program, it becomes important that the relative position of an instruction is similar to the position of its corresponding node in the functional program. A small average effective dependence distance, for instance, indicates that the order of instructions is high, i.e., functionally dependent instructions lie close to each other in the imperative code.

5.6 Characteristics of Variation Operators

Together with the selection operator, the variation operators determine the efficiency of an EA and its representation of individuals. Before we discuss and compare various genetic operators for the linear program representation, we summarize some general features of variation operators and program representation that we believe are important for genetic programming. The following general rules are meant to be independent from a special type of program representation. Some of the design rules are also valid for evolutionary algorithms in general [33].

(1) Genetic programming is working with a variable-length representation that is supposed to grow during the course of a run. First, evolutionary search is, in general, more successful when starting with relatively small initial programs. Second, fitter solutions require a certain minimum complexity, i.e., they are located in more complex regions of the search space. Therefore, the variation operator(s) should allow *sufficient code growth* within a reasonable number of generations, acted upon by a selection operator that favors longer programs if they show better performance.

(2) *Local search* is an important property in every search algorithm. It means that a variation operator or a combination of variation operators should explore the region around the parent search point(s) more thoroughly than more distant regions of the search space. This implies that the structural similarity between parent and offspring should be higher, on average, than between arbitrary individuals. If we assume the fitness landscape to be smooth locally, good search points are at least partly adjacent to other good search points.

(3) We recommend the use of *minimal variation steps* on program size by the insertion or deletion of a single instruction. Usually even these small variations of program complexity induce sufficiently large semantic steps.

(4) The design of efficient genetic operators strongly depends on the representation of individuals. The phenotype function and its fitness should be efficiently computable from the genotype representation (*efficient interpretation*) to keep the time of fitness evaluation as short as possible. Moreover, the genotype representation should allow *efficient variation*. Ideally, computation time should be linear in program size.

(5) The program representation should offer sufficient freedom of variation (*high variability*) to allow small structural variations at each program position throughout the entire run. This will have the advantage that noneffective code may emerge at every position with about the same probability.

(6) In order to guarantee that all effects on a program are reversible, each genetic operator should be employed together with its inverse operator (*reversibility*). It may even be required that these two genetic operators be applied with the same probability (*symmetry*), i.e., without any bias towards a certain search direction.

(7) In general, variation operators are better *bias-free*, i.e., they should not let programs grow *without* fitness selection. Code growth should not occur just because certain genetic operators are applied.[3]

(8) Programs produced by a variation operator in GP must be valid in the underlying programming language, they must satisfy the constraints of a program structure in that language (*syntactic closure*). The feasibility of a program solution should either be guaranteed by the variation operators or, if this is not efficient, through a post-processing step with special repair mechanisms.

(9) In most program representations used in GP, redundant pieces of code can be identified. Unnecessary program growth in genetic programming has become known as the *bloat effect* (see also Chapter 10). In order to avoid large solutions that are inflexible during the evolutionary process and may increase evaluation time, variation operators should keep the rate of redundant code growth as small as possible (*minimum code redundancy*).

(10) By increasing the *effectiveness* of genetic operations, i.e., the probability that effective code is modified, less variations remain neutral in terms of a fitness change.[4] As a result, evolution may progress faster over the same number of generations. Provided that redundant code elements can be identified efficiently for a program representation, the effectiveness of variations may be increased, e.g., by an explicit removal of redundant code from programs in the population. Other possibilities will be introduced in this and the following chapter.

---

[3]Chapter 6 will show special operators, however, which may benefit from an *explicit growth bias*.

[4]The same effect is achieved by increasing variation step size.

5.7 Segment Variation Operators

We now explain in more detail the inner working of *segment variations*, operators that delete and/or insert an instruction segment whose length is normally restricted only by the program length. Different recombination and mutation operators are discussed for the linear program representation. Let us start with the standard variant of LGP which applies linear crossover.

5.7.1 Linear Crossover

Standard linear crossover always produces two offspring by exchanging two arbitrarily long, contiguous subsequences (*segments*) of instructions between two parent individuals. The principle has been illustrated in Figure 2.4. By definition, linear crossover guarantees a minimum segment length of one instruction (= minimum program length l_{min}). The implementation of linear crossover used in the following experiments is given by Algorithm 5.1. The identifier cross will be used to refer to this operator. The maximum length of segments ls_{max} is unrestricted, i.e., it equals the program length. The whole program code may thus be replaced in one genetic operation. Let the term *crossover point* denote the *first* instruction of a segment. The end of a segment is uniquely identified by the segment length. The position of the first instruction in a program is always 0 (see also Figure 5.1).

ALGORITHM 5.1 (*linear crossover*)
Parameters: two linear programs gp_1 and gp_2; minimum and maximum program length l_{min} and l_{max}; maximum segment length ls_{max}; maximum distance of crossover points dc_{max}; maximum difference in segment length ds_{max}.

1. Randomly select an instruction position i_k (crossover point) in program gp_k ($k \in \{1, 2\}$) with length $l(gp_1) \leq l(gp_2)$ and distance $|i_1 - i_2| \leq min(l(gp_1) - 1, dc_{max})$.

2. Select an instruction segment s_k starting at position i_k with length $1 \leq l(s_k) \leq min(l(gp_k) - i_k, ls_{max})$.

3. While difference in segment length $|l(s_1) - l(s_2)| > ds_{max}$ reselect segment length $l(s_2)$.

4. Assure $l(s_1) \leq l(s_2)$.

5. If $l(gp_2) - (l(s_2) - l(s_1)) < l_{min}$ or $l(gp_1) + (l(s_2) - l(s_1)) > l_{max}$ then

   (a) Select $l(s_2) := l(s_1)$ or $l(s_1) := l(s_2)$ with equal probabilities.

   (b) If $i_1 + l(s_1) > l(gp_1)$ then $l(s_1) := l(s_2) := l(gp_1) - i_1$.

6. Exchange segment s_1 in program gp_1 by segment s_2 from program gp_2 and vice versa.

If the crossover operation cannot be executed because one offspring would exceed the maximum program length, equally long segments are exchanged. In order to avoid a bias towards smaller segments, Algorithm 5.1 selects randomly one of the two segment lengths. The algorithm is still slightly biased in terms of selecting shorter segments more frequently, due to the fact that crossover points are selected *before* the segment length is determined. The selection of crossover points, however, is unbiased, i.e., their distribution is uniform over the program positions. Experimental results will show below that a restriction of the segment length is less critical than restricting the free choice of crossover points.

It is important to note that linear crossover is not explicitly biased towards creating larger individuals. Because, by definition, it only *moves existing* code within the population by mutual exchange between individuals and because individuals are selected randomly, the average program length is not growing without fitness selection.

One way to reduce the structural step size of linear crossover explicitly is to put a maximum limit on the *absolute* segment length. This way the amount of program change is decoupled from the program length. A *relative* upper bound for the segment length in percent of the current program length is not a feasible alternative. First, the segment length would still depend on the absolute program length. Because programs grow during a run such relative step sizes would increase, too. Second, the influence exerted by a segment of code is partially independent of the overall length of program this segment is inserted into (see also Section 10.7.6).

Another crossover parameter is the *maximum distance of crossover points* dc_{max} (in instructions) between both parents. A restriction of this distance reduces the probability that a piece of code may migrate to a far distant program position which implies a reduction of variation freedom.

A third parameter that influences the performance of crossover is the *maximum difference in segment length* ds_{max} between parents. Together with the absolute segment length, this parameter controls the step size of linear crossover. If $ds_{max} := 0$ program growth is impossible. By choosing a moderate value for ds_{max} a simple *size fair crossover* is realized in linear

GP. Such an operator is more complicated to realize with subtree crossover [72].

Figure 5.1 illustrates all three control parameters. The performance of linear crossover can also be influenced by the probability distribution of crossover points, segment length, or length differences. For instance, segment lengths may either be uniformly distributed over a maximum range (standard case) or normally distributed such that either smaller or larger segments are exchanged more frequently.

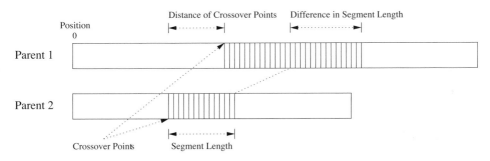

Figure 5.1. Basic parameters of linear crossover.

Obviously, there is an analogy between crossover of instruction sequences in linear GP and crossover of DNA strings in nature. In fact, this analogy to biological crossover was the original inspiration for the use of crossover in evolutionary algorithms. But there are some basic differences. The vast majority of crossover operations in nature is homologous and based on the chromosomal organization of DNA [136]. Biology causes homology through a strict base pairing of equally long DNA sequences while similarity of structure is closely related to similarity of function.

In [94] we propose the use of *homologous crossover* in linear GP. The basic idea is that similar sequences of instructions are exchanged during the course of evolution. This may be regarded as an indirect reduction of crossover step size. Homologous linear crossover also implies a restriction of both the average distance of crossover points and the average difference in segment length. Platel *et al.* [105] compute the optimal alignment with gaps between two program sequences – by minimizing a string edit distance [44] – before applying one-point linear crossover.

Other variants of linear crossover include *block crossover* [94] used with machine code and *page-based crossover* [49]. Both subdivide the programs into fixed-length instruction blocks and allow crossover point to fall only between blocks. In the latter case the number of blocks and, thus, the program length are fixed because crossover only swaps single pages between individuals. *Dynamic* page-based crossover [49] allows variable block lengths up to a predefined maximum, instead.

5.7.2   One-Point Crossover

Standard linear crossover may also be considered a *two-point crossover* operator because both the beginning and the end of the instruction segments exchanged are subject to variation. Segments may be located in the midst of a program. With *one-point crossover* (abbr. onepoint), programs are swapped at one point only. That is, the end of the code segment swapped is always identical to the end of program (see Algorithm 5.2). If a new individual would exceed the maximum program length, the two crossover points are chosen at equal positions in both parents, instead. Compared to two-point crossover, one-point crossover necessarily leads to larger absolute step sizes since larger segments of instructions are exchanged. Furthermore, the absolute step size may not be restricted that easily by a control parameter, at least not without restricting the free choice of crossover points.

ALGORITHM 5.2 (*one-point crossover*)
Parameters: two linear programs gp_1 and gp_2; minimum and maximum program length l_{min} and l_{max}; maximum distance of crossover points dc_{max}.

1. Randomly select an instruction position i_k (crossover point) in program gp_k ($k \in \{1,2\}$) with length $l(gp_1) \leq l(gp_2)$ and distance $|i_1 - i_2| \leq min(l(gp_1) - 1, dc_{max})$.

2. $l(s_1) := l(gp_1) - i_1$,
   $l(s_2) := l(gp_2) - i_2$.

3. Assure $l(s_1) \leq l(s_2)$.

4. If $l(gp_2) - (l(s_2) - l(s_1)) < l_{min}$ or $l(gp_1) + (l(s_2) - l(s_1)) > l_{max}$ then

   (a) If $l(gp_1) \geq l(gp_2)$ then $i_1 := i_2$ else $i_2 := i_1$.
   (b) Go to → 2.

5. Exchange segment s_1 in program gp_1 by segment s_2 from program gp_2 and vice versa.

5.7.3   One-Segment Recombination

Crossover requires, by definition, that information is *exchanged* between individual programs. However, an exchange always includes two operations on an individual, the *deletion* and the *insertion* of a subprogram. The imperative program representation allows instructions to be deleted without replacement since instruction operands, e.g., register pointers, are always defined. Instructions may also be inserted at any position without a preceding deletion, at least if the maximum program length is not exceeded. But if we want linear crossover to be less disruptive it may be a good idea to execute only one operation per individual.

These considerations motivate a *one-segment* or *one-way recombination* (abbr. oneseg) of linear genetic programs as described by Algorithm 5.3. Standard linear crossover may also be referred to as *two-segment recombination*, in these terms.

ALGORITHM 5.3 (*one-segment recombination*)
Parameters: two linear programs gp_1 and gp_2; insertion rate p_{ins}; deletion rate p_{del}; minimum program length l_{min}; maximum program length l_{max}; maximum segment length ls_{max}.

1. Randomly select recombination type *insertion* | *deletion* for probability p_{ins} | p_{del} and with $p_{ins} + p_{del} = 1$.

2. If $l(gp_1) < l_{max}$ and (*insertion* or $l(gp_1) = l_{min}$) then:

   (a) Randomly select an instruction position i in program gp_1.

   (b) Randomly select an instruction segment s from program gp_2 with length $1 \leq l(s) \leq min(l(gp_2), ls_{max})$.

   (c) If $l(gp_1) + l(s) > l_{max}$ then reselect segment s with length $l(s) := l_{max} - l(gp_1)$

   (d) Insert a copy of segment s in program gp_1 at position i.

3. If $l(gp_1) > l_{min}$ and (*deletion* or $l(gp_1) = l_{max}$) then:

   (a) Randomly select an instruction segment s from program gp_1 with length $1 \leq l(s) \leq min(l(gp_2), ls_{max})$.

   (b) If $l(gp_1) - l(s) < l_{min}$ then reselect segment s with length $l(s) := l(gp_1) - l_{min}$

   (c) Delete segment s from program gp_1.

4. Repeat steps 1 to 3 with exchanged program identifiers gp_1 and gp_2.

In traditional tree-based GP an exchange of subtrees during crossover is necessary because the constraints of the tree structure require removed code to be replaced. Nevertheless, pure deletions or insertions of subtrees can be implemented in the following manner: A deleted subtree is substituted by one of its subtrees. Likewise, a subtree is inserted at a random position such that the old subtree becomes a leaf of the new one.

Whether a segment is deleted from an individual or whether a segment is inserted from another individual depends on a *deletion rate* p_{del} and an *insertion rate* p_{ins}. These allow a *growth bias* or a *shrink bias* to be adjusted for one-segment recombination, depending on whether $p_{ins} > p_{del}$ or $p_{ins} < p_{del}$. Such an *explicit bias* allows programs to grow without fitness information. Note that an explicit bias may not be realized with crossover because it does not alter the average program length in the population. Only two-segment mutations (see Section 5.7.5) allow a more frequent exchange of smaller segments by larger ones (or vice versa). Since program growth is controlled more precisely over the maximum segment length, however, we apply one-segment recombination without an explicit bias, i.e., $p_{ins} = p_{del}$, in the following.

5.7.4   Effective Recombination

In principle, there are two possibilities to increase the number of effective variations and, thus, to reduce the probability that a variation stays neutral in terms of a fitness change. Either the noneffective code in programs is reduced actively or genetic operations concentrate on the effective part of the code.

To examine whether noneffective code influences recombination of effective code, we may remove all noneffective instructions immediately *after* each variation from the new individuals in the population[5] using Algorithm 3.1. In contrast to removing structural introns before the fitness calculation, the population comprises only *effective programs* and each variation automatically becomes effective. Due to the absence of noneffective instructions, effective step sizes will be larger and variations may be more destructive on the effective code. We name this variant *effective recombination* or *effective crossover* (abbr. effcross) [23].

Some researchers [124] propose to remove redundant code parts before tree crossover to reduce code growth. Other researchers [16] reduce the rate of neutral crossover operations by avoiding a crossover point falling upon an intron subtree. However, intron detection in tree-based GP is difficult, since only semantic introns exist. Detection can only be accomplished incompletely and strongly depends on the problem and the set of functions

---

[5]It has to be explicitly guaranteed that the absolute program length does not fall below the minimum (one instruction).

and terminals provided. In [124] unfulfilled if-statements are partially identified in tree programs and removed.

An alternative variant of effective recombination is realized by an explicit control of effectiveness. That means a variation is repeated until effective code has been altered. The effective code of two programs can be compared efficiently (see also Section 5.2). Prior to that comparison, however, Algorithm 3.1 has to be executed on the new programs to determine their effective code. This approach does not affect the effective variation step size but only the rate of effective variations.

The effectiveness of crossover operations may already be guaranteed by selecting segments that hold *at least one* effective instruction. This crossover variant is called *effective deletion* (abbr. effdel). An exchange of identical effective pieces of code is not prohibited by this operator, but it will be less likely if the average length of exchanged segments is large.

5.7.5 Segment Mutations

The implementation of crossover/recombination operators we apply in this book always produces two offspring. To be able to compare the effects of crossover and mutation two individuals are always selected in our LGP Algorithm 2.1 for producing offspring, even with mutation.

One-segment recombination, as described by Algorithm 5.3, can be modified to serve as two variants of macro mutation operators. *One-segment mutation* is done by the insertion of a *randomly created* subsequence s of $l(s)$ instructions in Step 2(d) of Algorithm 5.3. In doing so, the maximum *length* of an inserted or deleted segment is still limited by the length of the other parent. This guarantees that the mutation operator is free from an explicit length bias, i.e., the average inflow of code into the population is not larger than the outflow.

Effective segment mutation is done by inserting a fully effective segment, i.e., by inserting $l(s)$ effective instructions at a position i as will be described in Section 6.2.3. Deleted segments must not be completely effective and may still contain noneffective instructions. As a result, the proportion of noneffective code will be reduced. Note that, on a functional level, an effective segment does not necessarily form a single contiguous component for itself even if all segment instructions are connected to the effective graph component.

Another approach to effective (two-)segment mutation may be based on linear crossover. In this variant random segments *replace* existing segments. In the following the resulting four different variants of segment mutation will be referred to as onesegmut, effonesegmut, segmut and eff-segmut.

5.7.6   Explicit Introns

The ratio of noneffective instructions to the total amount of code controls the influence of segment variations on the effective part of code. Because there is usually a maximum limit to program length this implicit control of effective step size may not prove sufficient. Inactive instructions can be easily reactivated if transferred from one individual into another. The effectiveness of inserted instructions depends strongly on their position and the context in which they are in the new program. It is very likely that this will be totally different from the original program and the protection effect of noneffective code can therefore be considered as rather weak.

One solution to this problem is to provide for special program elements that already represent intron code for themselves. In [92] we have introduced the idea of *explicitly defined introns* (EDIs) into linear GP. This stand-alone intron code does not depend on a special semantic or structural program context. Explicit introns are supposed to suppress the emergence of implicit introns in the course of a run. At the same time, they reduce the absolute program size which shall include only the operational (non-EDI) instructions here. In the presence of explicit introns there is less need for inducing implicit intron code. Explicit introns are not only more easily implemented in program code by evolution but are less brittle during manipulation by the genetic operators, too.

The higher proportion of noneffective code that occurs particularly with crossover, indirectly increases the size of effective code. Obviously, the more code that is inactive, the higher the probability for reactivation during a genetic operation. Thus, the more programs grow, the more difficult it becomes to maintain a small effective code size. If sufficient implicit introns are replaced by context-independent explicit introns, however, we may hope that a smaller (proportion of) effective code is possible.

In [92] an explicitly defined intron has been implemented by a separator that is held between all coding instructions in a linear program. The non-coding separators just include a mutable integer value n which represents a "virtual" sequence of n wildcards or *empty* instructions. During crossover the EDI value between two working instructions determines the probability that the crossover point falls between them. Crossover behaves just as if EDIs were real empty instructions. After crossover has been performed the EDI values at crossover points are updated accordingly in the offspring programs.

A different realization of explicit introns is demonstrated in [122] by including a special EDI function into the function set. Such functions ignore all its arguments except one which is returned unaltered – similar to branches that hold a condition which is always wrong. In tree-based GP this is necessary because the program structure requires that every node returns a value. All subtrees that are ignored represent inactive code, but may be reactivated after a crossover operation or if the EDI function is replaced by an effective node.

We investigate explicit introns here for linear GP in a simpler form than that in [92]. In our approach an EDI comprises a single empty instruction only and is "physically" evolved within imperative programs. *Empty instructions* neither perform an operation on register values, nor manipulate the content of registers. By definition, an empty instruction is not allowed to be changed. Neither can it be reactivated nor can a working instruction be transformed into an empty one. This would require a mutation operator that is restricted to coding instructions only. During initialization a certain percentage of empty instructions are seeded into a population of coding instructions. In this way, it is guaranteed that only crossover determines how the proportion of EDIs develops in the population during a run. Such "imperative" EDIs are defined on the imperative level only and have no equivalent on the functional level.

5.7.7 Building Block or Macro Mutation?

One of the questions frequently asked when comparing the effects of mutation with those of recombination, is whether recombination does indeed help as much as it was originally thought it would. Recombination clearly depends strongly on the composition of the population. But do building blocks in programs really exist?

Intuitively, GP individuals are composed of building blocks [50, 41, 64]. A *building block* may be any coherent fraction of program code, i.e., an arbitrary subtree in tree-based GP or a subsequence of instructions in linear GP. The *building block hypothesis* for general evolutionary algorithms has been adopted from genetic algorithms into genetic programming [107, 108]. It states that smaller substructures of individuals with a high positive effect on fitness will be combined via crossover to produce offspring with higher fitness, and that, thus, the frequency of these substructures increases in the population.

One problem with the building block hypothesis is the assumption that GP is able to decompose a problem into subproblems and to develop global solutions by composing partial solutions. Subprograms are to be relatively independent from each other and are to have an additive influence on the fitness, i.e., the fitness function ought to be *separable* to a certain degree.

What are we to do with the fact that in GP the fitness advantage or disadvantage of a certain piece of code strongly depends on its position within the program? The usually complex interaction of registers in linear GP reduces the possibility that a subprogram may behave similarly in another program context. Depending on the number of available registers, as well as the length of the subsequence this would require many nodes to be reconnected appropriately in the functional graph equivalent. However in actuality, de- or re-activation of instructions may easily destroy the functionality of building blocks.

If the building block hypothesis would not be valid, recombination would act as simply another macro mutation, restricted however, to inserting genetic material already present in the population. In that case, one might expect an open macro mutation to do better. However, even if the building block hypothesis were true for a certain recombination-based GP approach, nothing precludes a pure mutation-based approach to exist that performs equally as well or better. A qualified answer to whether recombination or mutation is more powerful might be given depending on criteria like the (average) variation step size and the degree of innovation that is induced by a genetic operator, to name just two parameters.

Traditional tree-based genetic programming [64] started by using crossover for the majority of variations. The role of mutation was initially considered of minor importance and mutation frequency was adjusted to a low probability. Later on, however, researchers realized that mutation operators perform quite well on trees. For instance, Angeline [6] compared normal crossover with a "crossover" operator where one parent individual is created randomly. These *subtree mutations* work mechanically similar to crossover which allowed a fair comparison. From the competitive performance of subtree mutations Angeline concluded that subtree crossover was to be more accurately described as a macro mutation. Other comparisons of subtree crossover and mutations in tree-based GP [46, 29, 81] report on similar results. However, to this day the jury is still out. GP algorithms seem to be remarkably robust to parameter changes, and only react with strong signals once extreme choices are taken (for example 0% mutation or crossover).

From what has been observed in the literature, it may be concluded that mutation-based variation and crossover-based variation in tree GP have been found competitive with each other. Sometimes one approach was slightly more successful than the other, depending on details. Section 5.9.2 will compare recombination and segment mutations in linear GP.

5.8 Experimental Setup

5.8.1 Benchmark Problems

We have now seen an impressive set of different choices available to the system designer. These different variation operators will be discussed in this section and compared on the basis of benchmark problems. For experiments we have chosen (symbolic) regression and classification tasks throughout most of the book, because many real-world applications may be reduced to one of these problem classes.

The first problem requires a surface reconstruction from a set of data points. The surface is given by the two-dimensional *mexican hat* function of Equation 5.4.

$$f_{mexicanhat}(x, y) = \left(1 - \frac{x^2}{4} - \frac{y^2}{4}\right) \times e^{\left(-\frac{x^2}{8} - \frac{y^2}{8}\right)} \qquad (5.4)$$

Figure 5.2 shows a three-dimensional plot of the function visualizing the surface that has to be approximated.

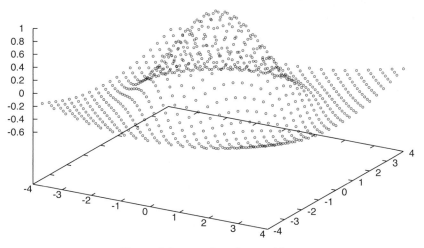

Figure 5.2. mexican hat problem.

The second problem is the popular *spiral* classification task [64]. In this problem, two interlaced spirals have to be distinguished in two-dimensional data space. All data points of a spiral belong to the same class as visualized in Figure 5.3.

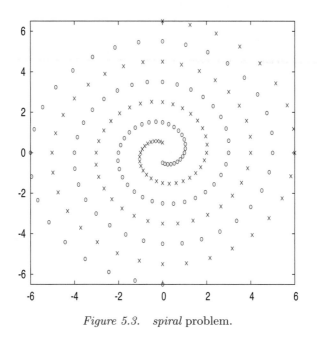

Figure 5.3.   *spiral* problem.

5.8.2   Parameter Settings

Table 5.1 summarizes attributes of the data sets that have been created for each problem. These include input dimension, output dimension, ranges of input and output values as well as number of training examples or fitness cases. Furthermore, problem-specific configurations of the LGP system are given comprising the fitness function, the composition of the function set, and the number of registers and constants.

It is important for the performance of linear GP to provide enough registers for calculation, especially if the input dimension is low. Therefore, the number of (calculation) registers – in addition to the minimum number of registers that is required for the input data – is an important parameter (see also Section 7.1). Recall that the number of registers determines the number of program paths that can be calculated in parallel. If that number is not sufficiently large there may be too many conflicts between instructions, e.g., by overwriting register content.

For classification tasks the fitness function is discrete and equals the *classification error* (CE), i.e., the number of incorrectly classified inputs. For approximation problems the fitness is the continuous *sum of square output errors* (SSE, see Section 2.3).

Table 5.1. Problem-specific parameter settings.

Problem	*mexican hat*	*spiral*
Problem type	regression	classification
Input range	$[-4.0, 4.0]$	$[-2\pi, 2\pi]$
Output range	$[-1, 1]$	$\{0, 1\}$
Number of inputs	2	2
Number of outputs	1	1
Number of output classes	—	2
Number of examples	400	194
Number of registers	$2 + 4$	$2 + 4$
Fitness function	SSE	CE
Instruction set	$\{+, -, \times, /, x^y\}$	$\{+, -, \times, /, sin, cos, if >\}$
Constants	$\{1, .., 9\}$	$\{1, .., 9\}$

The *spiral* problem at hand uses an *interval classification* method, i.e., if the output is smaller than 0.5 the answer of the program is interpreted as class 0, if it is equal or larger it is interpreted as class 1.

The instruction set used for the classification problem includes branches. The instruction set for the *mexican hat* problem is intentionally chosen to be incomplete, i.e., insufficiently powerful to build the optimum solution. In particular, the exponential function e^x was not included. Because the constant e is an irrational number it may only be approximated by a finite number of program instructions.

The general configuration of our linear GP system is given in Table 5.2. If not otherwise specified, this configuration is used in all experiments. As mentioned before, two tournament winners are either recombined or undergo mutation in Algorithm 2.1. Tournament selection is applied with a minimum of two participants per tournament and winning parents always replace losers.

Table 5.2. General parameter settings.

Parameter	Setting
Number of generations	1,000
Population size	1,000
Tournament size	2
Maximum program length	200
Initial program length	5–15
Macro variation rate	75%
Micro mutation rate	25%
Reproduction rate	100%

In most experiments in this chapter, macro operators are applied with a probability of 75 percent. This guarantees that the operators of interest for the comparison dominate the variation process. On the other hand, variation inside instructions is not reduced to zero but is maintained at 25 percent micro mutation probability.

For all problems we use a maximum number of 200 instructions. This has proven to be a sufficiently large size to represent the optimal solution provided that the function set is complete. This choice allows all operators tested to reach similar effective program sizes during 1,000 generations – including segment operators and instruction operators (see next chapter).

5.9   Experiments

All variation operators discussed so far involve single contiguous instruction *segments*. We will now take a look at experiments that have been conducted with such segment operators, both for recombination and segment mutation.

5.9.1   Comparison of Recombination Operators

In Tables 5.3 and 5.4 the different approaches to recombination operators are compared in terms of their influence on prediction performance, code growth and the probability distribution of variation effects. The mean prediction error is calculated over 100 independent runs, together with the statistical standard error. The number of hits is not given here because the optimal solution (fitness 0) has almost never been found by any crossover operator within a period of 1,000 generations. Both benchmark problems, *spiral* and *mexican hat*, show similar behavior in this regard. In order to reduce noise introduced through unequal initial populations, each test series is performed with the same set of 100 different random seeds.

Program length is averaged over all programs created during a run *and* in all 100 trials. Thus, the average effective program length gives more precise information about the average calculation time necessary for executing a program. Recall that the effective length corresponds to the number of instructions executed in our system (see Chapter 3.2.1). The proportion of effective code p_{eff} is given in percent with $p_{noneff} = 100 - p_{eff}$ being the percentage of structural introns.

Absolute length l_{abs} includes all instructions while effective length l_{eff} counts only instructions that are effective. As indicated in Section 5.7 the ratio of effective length and absolute length $\frac{l_{eff}}{l_{abs}}$ is an important parameter when using linear crossover. It determines the average number of effective

Table 5.3. *mexican hat*: Comparison of different recombination operators and configurations. Average results over 100 runs after 1,000 generations.

Operator	Config.	SSE		Length			Variations (%)		
		mean	*std.*	*abs.*	*eff.*	*%*	*constr.*	*neutral*	*noneff.*
cross		15.4	1.5	180	67	37	4.9	26	22
	effinit	13.3	1.4	178	65	37	5.0	26	22
	effdel	14.3	1.4	171	68	34	5.9	22	18
onepoint		21.9	1.3	188	66	35	2.8	78	69
oneseg		12.1	1.3	158	57	36	4.5	27	24
effcross		26.9	2.5	51	51	100	6.6	32	9
	effinit	6.1	0.8	111	111	100	9.4	12	1.8

Table 5.4. *spiral*: Comparison of different recombination operators and configurations. Average results over 100 runs after 1,000 generations.

Operator	Config.	CE		Length			Variations (%)		
		mean	*std.*	*abs.*	*eff.*	*%*	*constr.*	*neutral*	*noneff.*
cross		26.1	0.7	185	102	55	3.6	23	14
	effinit	24.3	0.7	183	104	57	3.5	24	14
	effdel	25.2	0.7	184	95	51	4.5	20	12
onepoint		32.0	0.9	190	89	47	0.9	81	32
oneseg		24.0	0.8	164	85	52	2.5	26	18
effcross		26.0	0.7	162	162	100	4.0	22	2.4
	effinit	18.8	0.7	164	164	100	3.9	20	0.6

instructions that may be deleted or selected from a parent program. This, in turn, influences the average effective step size as defined in Section 5.3.

Additionally, Tables 5.3 and 5.4 show the average proportion of *measured* constructive, neutral and noneffective variation (see Definition 5.1) effects among all variations during a run. The rates of destructive and effective variations, respectively, are obvious then.

Two-point crossover (cross) performs better than one-point crossover (onepoint). Interestingly, even if the average (absolute) step size is larger with only one crossover point per individual, a much higher proportion of operations is neutral. In the case of the *mexican hat* problem most of these variations are noneffective, i.e., do not alter the effective solution. Since the end points of segments are always the same, an exchange of (effectively) identical segments becomes much more likely.

Only slightly better results are obtained with one-segment recombination (oneseg) compared to standard crossover. We argued in Section 5.7.3 that those may reduce the variation step size. However, since the program size grows similarly large on average and because segment length is unrestricted with both variants, this effect may be less relevant here.

The effective crossover variant effcross is implemented in such a way that the (structural) noneffective code is removed completely after each variation (see Section 5.7.4). In doing so, only effective code finds its way into the population while deletions of instruction segments as well as all micro mutations automatically become effective.

One explanation why noneffective code grows with crossover may be found in a reaction of the system to protect the effective code from larger destructions (see also Chapter 10). A lack of structural introns in the population may be counteracted by a larger effective code only if the problem definition allows a sufficient amount of semantic introns (to be part of the effective code). Otherwise, a protection of the (semantically) effective code will be insufficient and the resulting larger effective crossover step size renders a continuous improvement of solutions more difficult.

As already noted, the ability to create semantic introns strongly depends on the configuration of the instruction set. On the other hand, a sufficient replacement depends on how far the search process profits from a growth of effective code. In contrast to the *mexican hat* problem, the discrete *spiral* problem allows good solutions to incorporate a relatively large amount of effective code. This is facilitated by using branching instructions that offer additional potential for creating semantic intron code (see Section 3.2.2).

Figures 5.4 and 5.5 compare the development of average length and average effective length in the population for both test problems. We just note here that the length of best solutions – if averaged over multiple runs – develops almost identically to the average length.

The standard deviation of effective length in the population is smaller than 10 instructions on average (not specified in Tables 5.3 and 5.4). One reason for the small standard deviation is the early restriction of (absolute) code growth for this genetic operator by the maximum size limit. As one can see, program growth is significantly reduced for *mexican hat* in effcross runs. Actually, absolute programs do not even become as long here as the effective code in cross runs. For the *spiral* classification, instead, the permanent loss of (noneffective) code is much better compensated by semantic intron code. The average program size nearly reaches the maximum length just like in runs with normal crossover.

The *mexican hat* results demonstrate that the existence of structurally noneffective code in linear GP offers an advantage over semantic introns because the former may be created more easily by evolution and be inde-

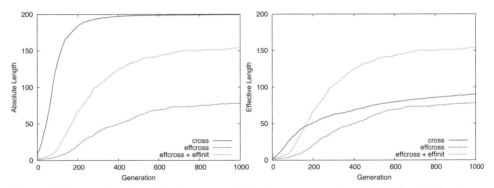

Figure 5.4. *mexican hat*: Development of absolute program length (left) and effective program length (right) for different crossover operators. Code growth significantly reduced by removing the noneffective code. Average figures over 100 runs.

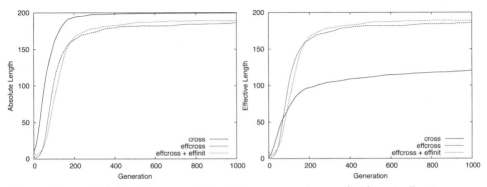

Figure 5.5. *spiral*: Development of absolute program length (left) and effective program length (right) for different crossover operators. Removal of structural introns compensated by more semantic introns. Note that absolute length and effective length are the same with effcross. Average figures over 100 runs.

pendent from the function set. In other words, the emergence of semantic intron code is suppressed in the presence of structural introns. The structurally noneffective code *reduces* the size of effective programs (*implicit parsimony pressure*, see also Section 8.4.1).

Furthermore, Figure 5.4 reveals that the removal of noneffective code is especially destructive at the beginning (first 50 generations) of an effcross run where effective solutions are most brittle since they have not developed a sufficient (effective) size for compensation yet. Programs become so small after the first generation that many are structurally identical – and even more programs are semantically identical. That is, the initial loss of code is accompanied by a high loss of diversity in the population. Hence, it is not surprising that the effective crossover variant profits much more from an effective initialization (effinit, see also Section 7.6) in terms of the prediction quality than is found with normal crossover. Effective initialization means that the initial programs are created such that they are completely effective while the absolute amount of genetic material stays the same. Due to this special form of initialization the program size probably doubles in Figure 5.4 because semantic introns are created in sufficient numbers. With the *spiral* problem, by comparison, the initial phase of code loss is much shorter (see Figure 5.4).

There is a small proportion of noneffective operations left that occurs with the effcross variant in Tables 5.3 and 5.4. This may result from the exchange of segments which are (effectively) identical. Such a situation becomes particularly likely if programs and segments comprise only a few instructions or if many programs are identical at the beginning of a run.

If it is just ensured that crossover operations are effective, i.e., delete *at least one* effective instruction (effdel), only slightly better results have been found compared to the standard approach. Because of the large absolute step size of crossover, we may assume that most crossover variations are effective anyway.

In general, the different crossover operators and configurations performed more similarly than what might have been expected. One reason is the maximum segment length (and thus the maximum step size) that is restricted by the program size only. Programs, however, grow similarly large for most recombination operators even without this growth control (see Chapter 10).

5.9.2 Comparison with Segment Mutations

Tables 5.5 and 5.6 summarize the results obtained with segment mutations. Recall that variant segmut replaces an instruction segment by a random segment of arbitrary length while the onesegmut variant deletes segments and inserts random ones in separate genetic operations. From a technical point of view, the first variant operates similar to standard crossover (cross) while the latter variant corresponds to one-segment recombination (oneseg).

All segment operators compared in this chapter are *unbiased* in terms of the program length, i.e., do not promote code growth. That means without fitness pressure (flat fitness landscape) there would be no relevant increase of program length. Therefore, and for the purpose of a fair comparison with recombination, segment mutations have been implemented in Section 5.7.5 such that the maximum segment length of both insertions and deletions depends on the length of programs in the population. This,

Table 5.5. *mexican hat*: Comparison of different segment mutation operators. Average results over 100 runs after 1,000 generations.

Operator	SSE		Length			Variations (%)		
	mean	*std.*	*abs.*	*eff.*	*%*	*constr.*	*neutral*	*noneff.*
segmut	12.6	1.3	72	28	39	5.1	26	18
effsegmut	4.1	0.3	31	23	76	7.6	19	6
onesegmut	4.2	0.5	92	38	42	4.6	26	21
effonesegmut	2.0	0.1	43	32	74	7.3	19	8

Table 5.6. *spiral*: Comparison of different segment mutation operators. Average results over 100 runs after 1,000 generations.

Operator	CE		Length			Variations (%)		
	mean	*std.*	*abs.*	*eff.*	*%*	*constr.*	*neutral*	*noneff.*
segmut	27.3	0.7	121	61	50	3.3	25	15
effsegmut	28.1	0.7	35	29	82	5.3	18	4
onesegmut	21.2	0.6	126	65	51	2.4	27	19
effonesegmut	19.1	0.5	67	54	81	4.1	18	4

however, guarantees similar segment lengths and step sizes as recombination only if programs grow similarly large.

It is an important result that recombination does not perform better than segment mutations here. Recall from the discussion in Section 5.7.7 that this may be taken as an argument against the building block hypothesis. Interestingly, with two-segment mutations (segmut) the prediction performance is hardly different from crossover. One-segment mutation (onesegmut) shows even improvements over one-segment recombination, especially for the *mexican hat* problem. As noted above, *mexican hat* is better solved with a reduced growth of programs, in contrast to the *spiral* problem.

The better performance of one-segment mutation compared to two-segment mutations may result from the absolute step size of two-segment variations (twice as large according to Definition 5.3). One-segment and two-segment mutations have a more pronounced difference in prediction error than the two corresponding recombination operators of Section 5.9.1. Note again that the average step size of segment mutations is smaller already because of a significantly smaller size of solutions. Moreover, results may be only slightly different beyond a certain average step size.

It is an interesting question why smaller effective programs occur with segment mutations than with recombination although in both cases the segment size is limited by the program size only. Possible reasons for this will be discussed in Section 10.8.1. We only note here that the difference in program size will increase if a maximum program length larger than 200 instructions is used since recombination is much more influenced by this choice.

A slightly better performance but definitely smaller solutions are obtained if it is explicitly guaranteed that each instruction of an *inserted* segment is created effective (**effonesegmut**). On the one hand, this reduces the rate of noneffective (and neutral) variations. Noneffective variations still occur with a small probability because of the 25 percent free micro mutations that are applied, together with each macro operator. Only some noneffective operations may result from segment deletions, since it is not explicitly guaranteed that deletions are effective.

On the other hand, the proportion of noneffective instructions is significantly smaller compared to a standard segment mutation. Hence, the effective step size may hardly be reduced by a higher rate of structural introns in programs. First, noneffective instructions are not directly created here, but may occur only indirectly by deactivations of depending instructions. Second, deleted segments may still contain noneffective instructions while inserted segments are fully effective. This corresponds to an explicit shrink bias in terms of the noneffective code.

When using effective two-segment mutations (**effsegmut**) code growth is even more reduced than with effective one-segment mutations (**effoneseg-mut**). The former operator allows noneffective code to be *replaced* by effective code but not vice versa. Performance is again improved significantly for *mexican hat*. As for the *spiral* problem, code growth may be restricted too much to let more efficient solutions emerge.

But why is the program length not increased by semantic introns here, as this has been observed with effective crossover (**effcross**) above? Apparently, the creation of both semantic and structural introns is much more limited when using (effective) segment mutations (see also Section 10.8.1).

5.9.3   Crossover Rate

In Section 5.8 we have decided to use a configuration of variation rates that assigns 75 percent to macro variations and 25 percent to micro mutations. Our motivation was that the variation should be dominated by the macro operators under comparison while still allowing enough modifications to happen inside instructions (micro mutations).

Tables 5.7 and 5.8 compare results for different crossover rates p_{cross} in percent while the percentage of micro mutations is $p_{micromut} = 100 - p_{cross}$, respectively. Only one variation is applied at a time, i.e., between two fitness evaluations. The more micro mutations there are, the smaller the average step size becomes, but the more variations remain noneffective and neutral. The advantage of smaller step sizes seems to outweigh the disadvantage of less effective variations, though. In both problem cases, the best performance has been achieved with the smallest crossover rates (10 percent). Although only a few macro variations are responsible for code growth, program size is still almost the same. This is basically a result of the large unlimited step size of crossover.

Table 5.7. mexican hat: Comparison of different crossover rates (in percent). Average results over 100 runs after 1,000 generations.

Crossover (%)	SSE		Length			Variations (%)		
	mean	*std.*	*abs.*	*eff.*	*%*	*constr.*	*neutral*	*noneff.*
10	**9.0**	1.2	121	54	45	1.5	46	44
25	12.7	1.5	150	64	43	1.8	42	40
50	13.8	1.4	170	64	38	2.7	36	33
75	15.4	1.5	180	67	37	4.9	26	22
100	23.5	1.4	182	48	26	6.1	27	22

Table 5.8. spiral: Comparison of different crossover rates (in percent). Average results over 100 runs after 1,000 generations.

Crossover (%)	CE		Length			Variations (%)		
	mean	*std.*	*abs.*	*eff.*	*%*	*constr.*	*neutral*	*noneff.*
10	**14.9**	0.7	142	88	62	0.6	42	30
25	17.6	0.7	164	99	60	0.9	39	27
50	23.0	0.7	178	99	56	1.9	31	22
75	26.1	0.7	185	102	55	3.6	23	14
100	34.5	0.6	187	98	53	5.8	17	8

The reader may note that there is a particularly large decrease in performance if crossover is applied exclusively compared to using micro mutations with their usual rate of 25 percent. Crossover can only recombine program components (instructions) that already exist in the previous generation but does not introduce new instructions. By the influence of selection and reproduction, however, the concentration of certain instructions may be reduced significantly which can be avoided already by applying mutations with a small percentage.

5.9.4   Analysis of Crossover Parameters

Linear crossover has been defined as the mutual exchange of a contiguous sequence of instructions between two individual programs in Section 5.7.1. In the following we analyze the influence of three crossover parameters

☐ Maximum length of segment

☐ Maximum difference in segment length

☐ Maximum distance of crossover points

on prediction performance, program growth and variation effects. Let the term *crossover point* always refer to the first absolute position of a segment. All actual length and distance quantities are measured in instructions and are uniformly distributed from the respective maximum range.

Tables 5.9 and 5.10 show the results of different maximum thresholds for the segment length, ranging from two[6] instructions to all instructions of a program, i.e., from maximum to no restrictions.

For both problems, *mexican hat* and *spiral*, the best fitness has been found if at most 5 instructions are allowed to be exchanged. Especially in the case of the *spiral* problem the growth of programs seems to be too restricted with segment length 2 to develop competitive solutions.

Basically, the relative influence on the fitness decreases with larger maximum segment length because of the following reasons. First, the average segment length is relatively small even for unrestricted two-point crossover – about 25 percent of the program length on average. Second, because of a virtually linear data flow, the influence of the segment length may be proportional to the program length only to a certain degree (see also Section 10.7.6). Finally, code growth is reduced significantly only when using relatively small upper bounds for the segment length. Due to restrictions by the maximum program length there is no significant difference in the program length beyond a certain maximum segment length any more. As noted before, a reduction of program length indirectly influences the average segment length again since a segment may not be larger than the program from which it originates.

The rate of effective code decreases with the maximum segment length, i.e., the rate of noneffective code increases. Since smaller segments mean

---

[6]Code growth would not be possible with maximum segment length 1 since crossover exchanges, by definition, include at least one instruction.

Table 5.9. *mexican hat*: Effect of maximum segment length using crossover (cross). Average results over 100 runs after 1,000 generations.

Maximum	SSE		Length			Variations (%)		
Segment Length	*mean*	*std.*	*abs.*	*eff.*	%	*constr.*	*neutral*	*noneff.*
2	4.3	0.6	50	31	63	3.8	29	26
5	**3.5**	0.5	107	50	47	3.5	31	28
10	8.5	1.2	146	58	40	3.6	31	28
20	10.9	1.3	169	65	38	3.9	30	26
50	13.3	1.3	177	65	37	4.5	27	24
–	15.4	1.5	180	67	37	4.9	26	22

Table 5.10. *spiral*: Effect of maximum segment length using crossover (cross). Average results over 100 runs after 1,000 generations.

Maximum	CE		Length			Variations (%)		
Segment Length	*mean*	*std.*	*abs.*	*eff.*	%	*constr.*	*neutral*	*noneff.*
2	17.4	0.6	54	38	70	1.6	29	21
5	**12.8**	0.6	125	77	61	1.7	33	20
10	18.8	0.6	166	99	60	2.0	29	18
20	22.0	0.7	180	102	56	2.7	26	17
50	24.8	0.7	185	103	56	3.2	24	15
—	26.1	0.7	185	102	55	3.6	23	14

smaller absolute step sizes there is less need to reduce the effective step size of crossover by developing more intron code (see also Chapter 10). In other words, less noneffective instructions need to be inserted together with the same number of effective instructions. It is interesting to note that the rates of noneffective and neutral variations are less affected in Tables 5.9 and 5.10 by comparison.

These results imply that the average variation step size of unrestricted standard crossover is too large. A strong restriction of the segment length, on the other hand, may not be regarded as real crossover any more. At least, the idea of combining advantageous building blocks from different programs may be questioned if the building blocks only comprise a few effective instructions.

For the following considerations we assume that segment length is unrestricted again. Instead, we limit the maximum *difference* in length between the two crossover segments exchanged. To this end, we select one segment freely in one of the parents. The position of the second segment is selected without restrictions from the other parent. Only for the length of this segment it is guaranteed that a maximum distance from the length

Table 5.11. mexican hat: Effect of maximum difference in segment length using crossover (cross). Average results over 100 runs after 1,000 generations.

Max. Segment	SSE		Length			Variations (%)		
ΔLength	*mean*	*std.*	*abs.*	*eff.*	*%*	*constr.*	*neutral*	*noneff.*
1	**3.6**	0.5	48	29	60	5.4	24	21
2	4.4	0.7	77	41	54	5.2	25	22
5	7.7	1.1	124	56	45	5.2	24	21
10	10.1	1.2	159	61	39	5.0	25	22
20	13.7	1.4	175	65	37	4.9	25	22
50	15.4	1.4	183	66	36	4.9	26	23
–	15.4	1.5	180	67	37	4.9	26	22

Table 5.12. spiral: Effect of maximum difference in segment length using crossover (cross). Average results over 100 runs after 1,000 generations.

Max. Segment	CE		Length			Variations (%)		
ΔLength	*mean*	*std.*	*abs.*	*eff.*	*%*	*constr.*	*neutral*	*noneff.*
1	20.8	0.6	56	41	73	3.6	22	14
2	**18.5**	0.7	91	63	69	3.6	23	13
5	20.6	0.7	151	91	60	3.4	25	15
10	23.3	0.7	173	97	56	3.6	24	15
20	24.6	0.6	182	100	55	3.5	24	15
50	25.5	0.6	186	101	55	3.6	23	15
—	26.1	0.7	185	102	55	3.6	23	14

of the first segment is not exceeded. In this way, a form of *size fair linear crossover* is implemented in linear GP (see also Section 5.7.1).

Tables 5.11 and 5.12 may be interpreted in such a way that a smaller maximum difference in segment length reduces the crossover step size in a similar way, as this resulted from using a smaller maximum segment length above. Apparently, the more similar the length of exchanged segments is the less programs can increase in length during a crossover operation.

In conclusion, the potential speed of code growth depends on both the size and the difference in size of the exchanged code fragments. However, while an exchange of very small segments may hardly be regarded as crossover, a size fair implementation can be. Size fair crossover is even more closely related to crossover in nature where recombined DNA strings are not only of a similar length but happen at similar positions (crossover points), too. Langdon [72] found that both, size fair and homologous crossover reduce bloat in tree genetic programming. Platel *et al.* [104] confirmed for linear genetic programming that homologous crossover gives size control.

Table 5.13. *mexican hat*: Effect of maximum distance of crossover points (cross). Average results over 100 runs after 1,000 generations.

Maximum	SSE		Length			Variations (%)		
Point Distance	*mean*	*std.*	*abs.*	*eff.*	*%*	*constr.*	*neutral*	*noneff.*
0	25.1	1.3	184	60	33	1.5	82	75
2	21.3	1.4	182	79	43	3.3	50	45
5	20.2	1.4	181	77	43	3.8	41	37
10	19.4	1.5	181	80	44	4.5	33	30
20	18.5	1.5	180	75	42	4.4	31	29
50	17.1	1.4	180	71	40	4.4	29	27
–	**15.4**	1.5	180	67	37	4.9	26	22

Table 5.14. *spiral*: Effect of maximum distance of crossover points (cross). Average results over 100 runs after 1,000 generations.

Maximum	CE		Length			Variations (%)		
Point Distance	*mean*	*std.*	*abs.*	*eff.*	*%*	*constr.*	*neutral*	*noneff.*
0	26.7	0.7	186	90	49	0.5	82	47
2	22.6	0.8	183	87	47	1.6	52	30
5	21.5	0.6	182	98	54	2.0	41	24
10	**20.3**	0.6	182	98	54	2.2	36	22
20	22.5	0.7	181	100	55	2.6	32	20
50	25.7	0.6	185	103	55	2.9	28	18
–	26.1	0.7	185	102	55	3.6	23	14

The distance of crossover points is investigated in the next experiment (see Tables 5.13 and 5.14).

Different maximum distances of crossover points in the two parent individuals have been tested. In contrast to other crossover parameters, results are more different here for the two test problems. While *mexican hat* is clearly better solved without such a restriction of variation freedom, the *spiral* problem seems to profit slightly from more similar positions of crossover points. If crossover points are selected below a certain optimum distance, however, the prediction error increases again. Apparently, if the emphasis is on equal positions, evolution will be significantly restricted in its ability to move code fragments from one program region to another. This may lead to a loss of code diversity among the population individuals. We may conclude that a free choice of crossover points in *both* parents is important

Compared to the two other parameters, the maximum distance of crossover points has a lower impact on the (effective) program size. Instead, the rate of noneffective (and thus neutral) variations increases significantly if the crossover points are chosen more similarly or even equal with distance 0. This is a direct consequence of the fact that the diversity of effective code is negatively affected because effectively identical segments are exchanged with high probability. Similar observations have been made with one-point crossover in Section 5.9.1 where the end points of segments – in contrast to the starting points – were always identical.

Consequently, only if both smaller differences in segment length and smaller distances of crossover points have a positive influence on the performance, homologous crossover – which combines both attributes – may be beneficial. Otherwise, these two criteria may antagonize each other.

5.9.5   Explicit Introns

Many implicit introns in linear genetic programs reduce the number of effective instructions that can be exchanged by crossover. However, this positive influence on the effective crossover step size is limited by reactivations of intron instructions. The higher the intron rate the more probable it is that such side effects occur. We test whether explicitly defined introns (EDIs, see Section 5.7.6) can provide a more reliable reduction of effective step sizes.

As mentioned earlier, explicit introns constitute a method for controlling the number of coding (non-EDI) instructions, i.e, the actual program complexity. Since both implicit structural introns and explicit introns can be removed efficiently before the fitness calculation in linear GP (see Section 3.2.1) an acceleration of runtime can only result from a smaller effective size.

We have seen above that the growth of effective code is accelerated significantly with crossover if all noneffective instructions are removed immediately after each operation. We concluded that without structural introns there is more need for expanding the effective code by semantic introns. While such effective variations necessarily increase the effective step size, explicit introns have been introduced for exactly the opposite reason. We may assume that the creation of semantic introns is more suppressed in the presence of explicit introns than this is true in the presence of structural introns.

In both Tables 5.15 and 5.16 a maximum initialization of individuals with explicit introns[7] reduces the average size of effective code by almost half

---

[7]Programs are filled with EDI instructions up to the maximum length.

and produces the best prediction results. Implicit introns emerge less frequently, depending on the amount of empty instructions that is provided in the initial population. Note that in all configurations the same amount of non-empty initial instructions is provided (10 instructions on average).

Even though the proportion of effective instructions decreases almost by half if the initial population has been filled up with explicit introns, intron segments are not exchanged more frequently. In the first place, this effect may be credited again to the large unrestricted step size of crossover. As a result, the rate of noneffective and neutral operations stays practically the same in Tables 5.15 and 5.16.

Table 5.15. mexican hat: Effect of empty instructions (EDIs) on crossover (cross). Number of empty instructions in an initial program equals n times the number of non-empty instructions (10 on average). Average results over 100 runs after 1,000 generations.

Initial EDIs	SSE		Length			EDIs		Variations (%)		
$n \times 10$	*mean*	*std.*	*abs.*	*eff.*	*%*	*#*	*%*	*constr.*	*neutral*	*noneff.*
0×	15.4	1.4	180	67	37	—	—	4.9	26	22
1×	11.4	1.3	186	50	27	73	39	4.9	26	22
2×	8.5	1.1	190	42	22	102	54	4.8	26	23
4×	7.5	1.1	194	37	19	123	63	4.8	26	23
max	**5.6**	0.7	200	30	15	147	74	4.5	28	25

Table 5.16. spiral: Effect of empty instructions (EDIs) on crossover (cross). Number of empty instructions in an initial program equals n times the number of non-empty instructions (10 on average). Average results over 100 runs after 1,000 generations.

Initial EDIs	CE		Length			EDIs		Variations (%)		
$n \times 10$	*mean*	*std.*	*abs.*	*eff.*	*%*	*#*	*%*	*constr.*	*neutral*	*noneff.*
0×	26.1	0.7	185	102	55	—	—	3.6	23	14
1×	25.4	0.7	190	75	40	57	30	3.4	23	16
2×	24.2	0.7	193	67	35	84	44	3.3	23	15
4×	22.2	0.7	195	59	30	100	51	3.3	24	18
max	**18.1**	0.6	200	54	27	121	61	2.7	24	16

The larger the initial programs are, the more quickly the average program size grows to the maximum (see Figure 5.6). This is simply due to the fact that the absolute step size of crossover increases in proportion to absolute program size. As long as programs grow, the step size grows, too. Only after code growth has terminated by reaching maximum length limits, average absolute step size remains constant.

If empty instructions are seeded additionally into the initial population the effective step size decreases for two reasons: First, the more explicit introns are provided initially, the less implicit structural introns have to emerge and the smaller may be the proportion of (structurally) effective code due to less semantic introns. Second, the effective step size may not be indirectly increased by reactivations of introns, if these comprise empty instructions.

Figure 5.6 illustrates the development of average program lengths and average intron rates in the population for different initial amounts of explicit introns. Without using explicit introns the implicit structural introns grow quickly at the beginning of a run until the absolute program length is (almost) maximum. After that point has been reached in about generation 200 the noneffective code decreases slowly towards the end of a run due to the effective code still growing and replacing noneffective instructions. If explicit introns are provided the proportion of implicit introns shrinks. For the maximum initialization, the implicit intron rate reaches only about 10 percent of the maximum possible length at the end of runs with both test problems.

The more explicit introns are provided in initial programs, the smaller the effective code develops. Like implicit structural introns, such introns take away pressure from the effective code to grow and to develop semantic introns (see Section 5.9.1). Recall that semantic introns are in general more difficult to create, depending on the problem configuration. However, since explicit introns are by definition fully independent of *both* the structural and semantic program context they allow the size of effective code to be more independent from the absolute program size.

Explicit introns affect the final effective program size less at the end of a run. Note that the effective size is more strongly determined by a program's ability to solve a certain problem task, i.e., by its fitness. Nevertheless, the effective code grows almost linear over the generations with maximum initialization.

At the beginning of a run implicit structural introns spread within the population about as fast as explicit ones if their initial numbers are the same, see "1×" plots in Figure 5.6. Later both types coexist during the whole run. Since already structural introns emerge easily in linear GP, explicit introns are not favored by evolution. In other words, explicit introns do *not* displace such implicit introns in the course of a run. Thus, it is important to provide a high amount of explicit introns right from the start.

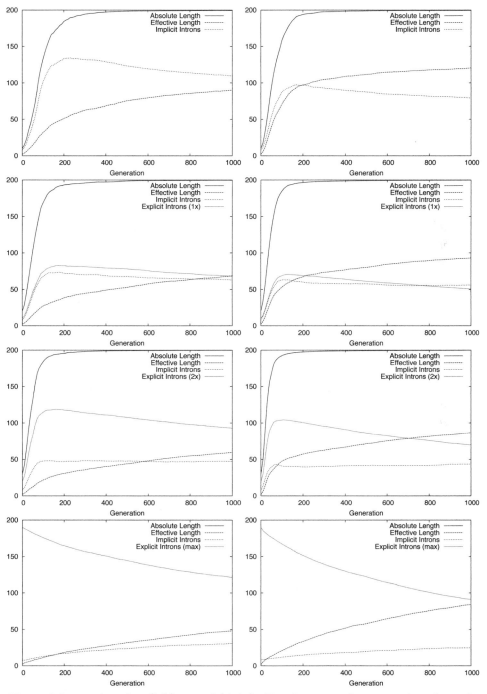

Figure 5.6. *mexican hat* (left), *spiral* (right): Development of program lengths and intron rates over the generations and for different initial amounts of explicit introns ($n \times 10$).

5.10   Summary and Conclusion

In the beginning of this chapter we defined different structural and semantic variation effects and step sizes for the linear program representation. Ten features of variation operators were formulated that we believe are especially desirable for linear GP. A systematic analysis of possible genetic operators was then executed that is based on these concepts. Different operators were introduced and compared with respect to performance and complexity of the resulting prediction models and variation-specific parameters were analyzed.

The most important results may be summarized as follows:

☐ Three basic parameters of linear crossover were identified and analyzed. Either a restriction of segment length or the difference in length between inserted and deleted segments (size fair crossover) led to a better performance. In both cases, the strongest restrictions produced the best results. However, it proved to be more deleterious to limit the distance of crossover points and thus the position of segments.

☐ Unrestricted segment mutation turned out to be at least as powerful as unrestricted recombination and produced less complex solutions. Furthermore, the difference in performance was smaller for two-segment operators than for one-segment operators, in particular for mutations and due to smaller step sizes. Segment mutations operated even more successfully if segments are created fully effective. This resulted from their further reduction of both noneffective variations and program size. The larger effective step size was partly relaxed by the smaller program size which indirectly reduces absolute step size.

☐ As far as segment variations like crossover were concerned, the presence of structural introns reduced the effective step size and took away some of the pressure to grow and to develop semantic introns. For validation purposes, we removed all structural introns from individuals after crossover. Without such an implicit parsimony effect, the (effective) solution size grew much larger than necessary.

☐ Explicit introns provided a more reliable reduction of effective crossover step size than implicit introns because they would not be reactivated. Both a better fitness and a smaller effective size of solutions were achieved depending on the amount of such empty instructions that are seeded into the initial population. Furthermore, implicit introns – including both structural and semantic ones – occurred much less often in the presence of explicit introns.

Chapter 6

LINEAR GENETIC OPERATORS II – INSTRUCTION MUTATIONS

The experimental results from Chapter 5 have confirmed two important assumptions. First, when using recombination best results were obtained with a relatively low limit to segment length. Second, segment recombination has not been found to be more powerful than segment mutation. Both aspects motivate the use of mutations that affect *one* instruction only. The following considerations try to point out why linear programs in particular are likely to be served better by using only minimal mutation operations.

6.1 Minimum Mutation Step Size

Why do small variation steps promise better results in genetic programming? For one reason, small variation steps allow a more precise approximation of a problem by the genetic programs. This is due to the fact that small structural step sizes imply small semantic step sizes, at least with high probability. This is called weak causality (see Section 5.4).

Nevertheless, even changing a genetic program in the smallest possible way might still induce large semantic changes. It is therefore unlikely that the global search progress will slow down substantially by too small of a step size. This must be seen for Genetic Programming in contrast to other evolutionary algorithms, like evolution strategies, that operate on a numeric representation in continuous search space.

Using small variation steps in GP better correspond to the biological example, too: Most mutations in nature affect only small parts of the genotype. Due to very good alignment (homologous crossover) and many identical genes, even the changes caused by crossover of DNA strands are following this pattern of behavior. Otherwise it would not be possible for nature to produce viable offspring with reasonable frequency.

But whereas in nature genotype variations most often result in small changes of the phenotype, crossover in GP has a different behavior: Most crossover operations are highly destructive to both the genotype representations and the resulting phenotypes, i.e., to program behavior. The selection of crossover points in both parents as well as size and structure of the two exchanged substructures are much less constrained in GP. Another reason may be that the functionality of building blocks in programs or sequences of instructions is less dependent on location than is the case with building blocks of DNA, i.e., genes.

The following arguments are put forward in support for a higher potential of mutations in linear GP than would be the case in tree-based GP [23, 11]. In particular, there are some basic reasons that lead us to favor very small mutation step sizes on a linear program structure.

First, already single micro mutations which will exchange a register index in an instruction, might heavily influence the data flow in a linear program (see Section 3.3). For instance, several instructions preceding the mutated instruction may become effective or noneffective. Thus, the effective step size of an instruction mutation (see Definition 5.4) may involve many instructions even if the absolute step size is minimal.

Second, the linear program representation can be manipulated with a *high degree of freedom*. By definition, graph-structured data flow permits a higher variability than a tree-based program would have, due to multiple connections of nodes. This allows for minimal macro variations to be realizable in each position of the program. In a tree-based program it is rather difficult to delete or insert a single node at an arbitrary position. Complete subtrees might need to be removed during such operations in order to satisfy the stronger constraints of the tree structure. A tree structure is therefore less suitable to be varied only by small macro (subtree) mutations, since modification of program parts higher up in the tree usually involve larger parts of code.

Third, substructures in linear GP do not get lost when deleting or inserting an instruction but remain within the imperative representation as inactive code or as non-visited components of the data flow graph, respectively (see Section 3.3). The *existence of structurally noneffective code* in linear genetic programs prevents a loss of genetic material. Code that has become deactivated in a program through a variation may become active again already after the next variation.

Recombination may be less suited for linear GP for the following reasons:

First, in tree-based programs crossover and mutation points can be expected to have a stronger influence on program semantics if they are closer to the root (see Section 5.5). In a linear program, however, each position of an instruction may exert a more comparable influence on program semantics. Recall that the underlying graph representation is restricted in width through the number of registers provided (see Section 3.3).

Second, the contents of many effective registers are often changed simultaneously because of the rather narrow data flow graph of linear genetic programs. Such a graph will be disrupted easily when applying crossover resulting in several program paths to be redirected. As a result, crossover step sizes are, on average, quite large. In tree-based GP, by comparison, crossover only affects a single node in the data flow, the root of the exchanged subtree.

There are, however, facts that mitigate the impact of a crossover event in linear GP. The effective step size of linear crossover is decreased implicitly by increasing the proportion of structural introns (see Section 9.7.2). Inactive instructions may emerge at almost every position in a linear program with virtually the same probability. In tree-based programs the creation of introns is more restricted, especially at higher node levels, because they will always depend on program semantics. A further means to reduce the effect of crossover in linear GP is offered by using a maximum size limit for instruction segments exchanged.

Various researchers have investigated mutation operators for tree-based GP (see Section 5.7.7). Chellapilla [29] defines different types of mutation operators for tree programs ranging from the exchange of a single node (micro mutation) to the exchange of a complete subtree (macro mutation). His main interest, however, was not a general reduction of variation step size. Instead, he applied several operators to the same individual. O'Reilly and Oppacher [98] have minimized the average amount of structural change as far as possible. Nonetheless, only a compromise between a restriction of variation freedom and larger step sizes by loss of code seem to be successful (see also discussion in Section 8.5).

6.2 Instruction Mutation Operators

This section will define all variants of instruction mutations that are considered in this book. We restrict ourselves to the analysis of *macro* instruction mutations. Therefore, unless otherwise stated, the term *instruction mutation* refers to macro instruction mutations.

6.2.1   Macro Mutations

Macro instruction mutations either insert or delete a single instruction. In doing so, they change absolute program length with a minimal effect on program structure. That is, they induce a minimum step size on the level of *full* instructions, the macro level. On the functional level, a single node is inserted in or deleted from the program graph, together with all its connecting edges.

We do not regard macro mutations that *exchange* an instruction or change the *position* of an existing instruction. Both of these variants are on average more destructive, i.e., they imply a larger variation step size, since they include a deletion and an insertion at the same time. A further, but important argument against substitutions of single instructions is that these do not vary program length. If single instructions would only be exchanged there would be no code growth at all.

ALGORITHM 6.1 ((*effective*) *instruction mutation*)
Parameters: linear programs gp; insertion rate p_{ins}; deletion rate p_{del}; maximum program length l_{max}; minimum program length l_{min}.

1. Randomly select macro mutation type *insertion* | *deletion* with probability p_{ins} | p_{del} and with $p_{ins} + p_{del} = 1$.

2. Randomly select an instruction at a position i (mutation point) in program gp.

3. If $l(gp) < l_{max}$ and (*insertion* or $l(gp) = l_{min}$) then

    (a) Insert a random instruction at position i.
    (b) If *effective mutation* then
        i If instruction i is a branch go to the next non-branch instruction at position $i := i + k$ $(k > 0)$.
        ii Run Algorithm 3.1 until program position i.
        iii Randomly select an effective destination register $r_{dest}(i) \in R_{eff}$.

4. If $l(gp) > l_{min}$ and (*deletion* or $l(gp) = l_{max}$) then

    (a) If *effective mutation* then select an effective instruction i (if existent).
    (b) Delete instruction i.

Algorithm 6.1 has a structure similar to Algorithm 5.3. If on average more insertions than deletions of instructions happen ($p_{ins} > p_{del}$), this will be referred to as an *explicit growth bias* of the mutation operator. $(p_{ins} < p_{del})$ will be referred to as an *explicit shrink bias*. In our standard configuration the mutation operator will be bias-free $(p_{ins} = p_{del})$.

6.2.2 Micro Mutations

Macro variations, in general, control program growth by treating instructions as atomic. While variation points of macro operators always fall *between* instructions, micro mutation points always lie *inside* an instruction. Most variation schemes studied in this book apply micro mutations to change a single component of an instruction.

ALGORITHM 6.2 ((*effective*) *micro mutation*)
Parameters: linear programs *gp*; mutation rates for registers p_{regmut}, operators $p_{opermut}$, and constants $p_{constmut}$; rate of instructions with constant p_{const}; mutation step size for constants σ_{const}.

1. Randomly select an (effective) instruction from program *gp*.

2. Randomly select mutation type *register* | *operator* | *constant* with probability p_{regmut} | $p_{opermut}$ | $p_{constmut}$ and with $p_{regmut} + p_{opermut} + p_{constmut} = 1$.

3. If *register mutation* then

   (a) Randomly select a register position *destination* | *operand.*

   (b) If *destination* register then select a different (effective) destination register (applying Algorithm 3.1).

   (c) If *operand* register then select a different *constant* | *register* with probability p_{const} | $1 - p_{const}$.

4. If *operator mutation* then select a different instruction operator randomly.

5. If *constant mutation* then

   (a) Randomly select an (effective) instruction with a constant *c*.

   (b) Change constant *c* through a standard deviation σ_{const} from the current value: $c := c + \mathcal{N}(0, \sigma_{const})$.

In Algorithm 6.2 three basic types of micro variations are discerned – operator mutations, register mutations and constant mutations. Unless otherwise stated, we mutate (exchange) each instruction component with about the same probability. In particular, we make sure that source and destination registers are mutated with the same frequency. The modification of either register type may affect the effective status of preceding instructions. We mentioned in Chapter 3.3.1 that register mutations correspond to a redirection of edges in the functional representation of a linear program. That is, they manipulate the data flow in linear programs.

Constants may be replaced either by a register or by another constant depending on the proportion of instructions p_{const} that hold a constant value. Throughout this book we allow a constant to be set only if there is another register operand used by the same instruction (see Sections 2.1.2 and 7.3). That is, an instruction may not hold more than one constant. Alternatively, separate constant mutations may be applied ($p_{constmut} > 0$). Then a constant is selected explicitly from an instruction before it is modified through a standard deviation (step size) σ_{const} from the current value.

Because we guarantee for each genetic operator that there is a structural variation of the program code, identical replacements of code elements are avoided during micro mutation by Algorithm 6.2.

6.2.3   Effective Mutations

On a statistical basis, fitness neutrality will be more prevalent if macro mutations can change only a single instruction. Because mutation step sizes are small, many mutations will remain noneffective, i.e., do not alter the structurally effective code. To compensate for this tendency we introduce *effective instruction mutations* which apply mutations on the effective parts of a linear genetic program. This is motivated by the assumption that mutations of structurally effective instructions may be less likely to be neutral than mutations of noneffective instructions.

Effective instruction mutations respect the functional structure of a linear program (see Section 3.3) so that only the effective graph component is evolved. In other words, information about the functional program structure is introduced into the genetic operator. The amount of noneffective code may be affected indirectly only through deactivation of depending instructions, i.e., through disconnection of formerly effective subgraphs.

Effective *micro* mutations simply select an effective instruction in Algorithm 6.2. If such an instruction does not exist in the program, the destination register of a random instruction is set effective.

We discern three different approaches to effective *macro* mutation operators [23, 11].

☐ The standard variant of effective mutations (abbr. effmut) allows (single) noneffective instructions to be deleted. In order to guarantee that the effective code is altered at all, an effective (micro) mutation may directly follow such intron deletions. However, this may result in further deactivations of depending instructions and, thus, in more noneffective code. By allowing pure intron deletions, instead, the noneffective code may be definitely reduced in the course of the evolutionary process.

☐ The second variant (effmut2) guarantees that both inserted and deleted instructions always alter the effective code. This implies that noneffective instructions are prohibited from *direct* variation.

☐ In the third variant (effmut3) *all* emerging noneffective instructions are deleted from a program directly *after* applying mutations of variant effmut2.[1] If this would be done after standard instruction mutations, it was only guaranteed that deletions and micro mutations are effective.

The explicit deletion of an effective or noneffective instruction is not complicated. Since the information about the effectiveness or non-effectiveness of an instruction is saved and updated in the linear program representation each time before the fitness calculation, an additional application of Algorithm 3.1 is not necessary, neither for effective micro mutations nor for effective deletions.[2]

If the insertion of an operation is supposed to be effective, however, this has to be assured explicitly in Algorithm 6.1 by choosing a destination register that is effective at the instruction position (see Definition 3.3). Like the detection of effective code, effective registers can be identified efficiently in linear runtime $O(n)$ by terminating Algorithm 3.1 at the respective program position.[3] An inserted branch instruction may be effective only if the following operation is effective, too. Otherwise, this operation will be made effective.

If the program length is minimal, only an insertion is possible. If the program length is maximal, a deletion is applied next in Algorithm 6.1. It must be noted, however, that the latter situation hardly occurs (see Section 6.4). Since programs grow relatively slowly by effective mutations, the maximum program length may easily be chosen sufficiently large such that it is not reached within the observed number of generations.

---

[1] By removing the structurally noneffective code completely linear GP becomes more similar to tree-based GP where such (disconnected) code does not exist because each node must be connected.

[2] After intron deletions, the effective status of instructions does not have to be recalculated anyway.

[3] Then set R_{eff} holds all effective registers for that position.

There is only one situation remaining where an effective deletion or insertion does not change the effective code. This is the case if an instruction that is identical to the deleted/inserted one becomes effective/noneffective at the same position in the resulting *effective* program. However, since this situations occurs only very rarely, it can be neglected.

6.2.4   Minimum Effective Mutations

Effective mutations assure that the structurally effective code is changed. It is, however, not possible to predict whether an effective mutation will change just one or many effective instructions. That is, these genetic operators do not explicitly guarantee that a certain *effective* variation step size (Definition 5.4) is met.

Minimum effective mutations reduce the effective variation distance between parent and offspring to a minimum. For micro mutations this means step size 0, i.e, no program instruction (prior to the mutated one[4]) is allowed to change its status. For macro mutations it is required for all instructions except for the inserted or deleted one, i.e., the minimum effective step size is 1. Therefore, variation operators have to select both the (effective) mutation point and the mutated code in such a way that no preceding program instruction is deactivated or reactivated.

To achieve this goal information about the functional (data flow) dependencies within a linear genetic program are used. Minimum effective mutations develop only one contiguous component of the graph, namely the effective one, while not allowing code to become non-contiguous at all. Since it would be unnecessarily complicated and computationally expensive to calculate a minimum effective mutation deterministically, a probabilistic trial-and-error approach will be used (see Chapter 9). The effective mutation step size is determined *after* the mutation is tried, using a structural distance metric. It will be accepted if the criterion for maximum distance is met. Otherwise, it will be rejected and a new mutation is tried (up to a maximum number of trials).

This probabilistic algorithm does not increase the number of fitness evaluations. Only the structural step size has to be recalculated during each iteration which requires linear costs. In fact, the probabilistic induction of minimum step sizes will turn out to be runtime-efficient in Chapter 9, since the probability that more than one trial is needed decreases over the course of a run.

---

[4]Instructions after the mutation point cannot be affected.

6.2.5 Free Mutations

If we allow both noneffective and effective mutations to occur without imposing any kind of restriction this will be referred to as *free mutation* or *standard mutation* (abbr. mut) in the following. So far we have discussed operators that guarantee a modification of the effective code. Such code-effective mutations reduce the number of neutral variations significantly and more variations become constructive or destructive.

When comparing effective and free mutations on the basis of *generations*, the effective variant is usually superior because evolution will progress faster within the same period of time. The resulting number of effective operations will be significantly lower with the free variant and will depend strongly on the proportion of noneffective instructions in programs.

As mentioned in Section 5.2 fitness does not have to be recalculated after noneffective variations since those are definitely neutral in terms of a fitness change. Hence, only effective variations will cause relevant computational costs. If we compare both mutation variants with respect to number of *evaluations*, i.e., count offspring from effective variations only, the comparison becomes fair in terms of the computational overhead.

The absolute variation step size *between two fitness evaluations*, i.e., two effective variations, increases if several noneffective mutations happen in between.

6.2.6 Explicit Induction of Neutral Mutations

The effective mutation approach has been introduced in Section 6.2.3 to increase the rate of *non-neutral* variations. Another interesting approach that can give insight into the meaning of neutral variations in linear GP, does exactly the opposite: The neutrmut operator transforms most destructive mutations into neutral or constructive ones. Therefore, it explicitly controls the direction in which the fitness of an individual changes after a standard mutation (mut).

The probabilistic Algorithm 6.3 describes a trial-and-error approach to neutrality control. In order to generate more constructive or neutral variations, it repeats an instruction mutation as long as it is destructive. Only after a certain maximum number of trials is a destructive variation tolerated. Unsuccessful trials are discarded. Only the final variation is accepted and the resulting offspring becomes part of the population. Since a destructive variation is necessarily structurally effective, each trial produces extra computational costs in the form of additional fitness calculations. This step is redundant only if the final variation is noneffective.

ALGORITHM 6.3 (*neutral (effective) mutation*)
Parameters: parent program gp_p and offspring gp_o; maximum number of
iterations $n_{maxiter}$.

1. Copy parent program $gp_o := gp_p$. Number of iterations $n := 0$.

2. Apply Algorithm 6.1 to create an (effective) instruction mutation at a
   random position in program gp_o.

3. Apply Algorithm 3.1 to check if the mutation was effective.

4. If the mutation is effective then recalculate fitness $\mathcal{F}(gp_o)$.

5. $n := n + 1$.

6. If the mutation is destructive ($\mathcal{F}(gp_o) > \mathcal{F}(gp_p)$) and $n < n_{maxiter}$
   then $\rightarrow 2$.

7. Stop.

As we said before a better fitness is equivalent to a smaller fitness value $\mathcal{F}$.
Step 3 of the algorithm may be skipped if we apply an effective mutation
operator (effmut*) in Step 2. To explicitly induce neutral variations on
effective code one can apply a certain percentage of effective mutations
(variant effmut2) in Step 3 of the probabilistic algorithm. This mutation
variant is called *effective neutral mutation* (abbr. neutreffmut).

Obviously, the runtime for variations induced by Algorithm 6.3 is not any
more linear in the number of program instructions since the cost for additional fitness evaluations cannot be ignored. Creating a high proportion of
offspring that are neutral may become computationally expensive. On the
other hand, most semantically neutral variations do not alter the effective
code, i.e., are structurally noneffective (see Section 6.4.1).

This motivates an alternative operator (noneffmut) which increases the
proportion of noneffective variations directly. A similar probabilistic control mechanism as described by Algorithm 6.3 may repeat a mutation
(mut) only until it is noneffective (or a maximum number of iterations
has been exceeded). This criterion can be verified efficiently since it only
requires a structural program analysis by Algorithm 3.1. This way, the
control of a semantic variation effect (neutrality) is reduced to the control
of a structural variation effect (non-effectiveness). Through adjusting a
parameter like the maximum number of trials $n_{maxiter}$ the bias towards
noneffective mutations can be varied.

Deterministic calculation of noneffective mutations, as it was applied for effective mutations in Section 6.2.3, is not necessary, since non-effectiveness of a variation is not as simple to guarantee as effectiveness. Noneffective *insertions* of instructions may not be structurally possible if all registers are effective at a certain program position. Instead, there is always at least one effective register depending on our choice of instruction types (see Section 2.1.2). Of course, it would not be reasonable to apply noneffective mutations exclusively, since this would not allow any progress at all.

Not allowing mutations to become destructive may be regarded as an (1+1)-EA selection [119] between parent and offspring. In an (1+1)-EA the offspring replaces the parent only if its fitness is equal or better. This is different from brood selection as proposed in [130] where several offspring of the same parent compete in a (tournament) selection process and only the lucky winner will be allowed into the population. Yu and Miller [143] have found good performance for a Boolean problem (even-3-parity) if neutral mutations are accepted in a modified (1+4)-EA but do not compare their results with an approach that allows destructive variations.

Avoiding both neutral *and* destructive mutations in Algorithm 6.3 has not been found to be a feasible alternative. Too many trials and, thus, too many additional fitness evaluations are necessary until a variation becomes constructive. As a result, freedom of variation will be strongly restricted in the process. Without neutral variations, intermediate variation steps that have not proven to be directly advantageous are not possible, and this severely limits the search success.

For a more general discussion about neutral variations we would like to direct the reader to Section 10.4.

6.3 Experimental Setup

6.3.1 Benchmark Problems

In addition to the two benchmark problems from Section 5.8.1, *mexican hat* and *spiral*, we use two further test problems in this section.

The regression problem *distance* necessitates the Euclidean distance between two points (vectors) $\vec{x}$ and $\vec{y}$ in n-dimensional space to be computed by a genetic program (see Equation 6.1). The higher the dimension (we use $n = 3$) the more difficult this problem becomes.

$$f_{distance}(x_1, y_1, .., x_n, y_n) = \sqrt{(x_1 - y_1)^2 + .. + (x_n - y_n)^2} \qquad (6.1)$$

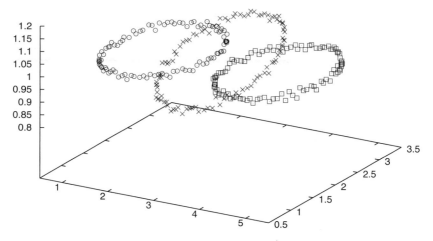

Figure 6.1.   three chains problem.

The *three chains* classification problem concatenates three rings of points that each represent a different data class (see Figure 6.1). Each "ring" is a circle of 100 points in three-dimensional space whose positions are slightly noisy. The rings approach each other in five regions without allowing for intersection. These regions determine the problem difficulty. The problem is easily scalable depending on both the angle of the rings to one another and on the number of rings.

6.3.2   Parameter Settings

Table 6.1 gives an overview of parameter settings specific to the two new problems. Most parameters have already been introduced in Section 5.8.2.

Table 6.1.   Problem-specific parameter settings.

Problem	*distance*	*three chains*
Problem type	regression	classification
Input range	$[0, 1]$	$[0, 5]$
Output range	$[0, 1]$	$\{0, 1, 2\}$
Number of inputs	6	3
Number of outputs	1	1
Number of output classes	—	3
Number of registers	$6 + 6$	$3 + 3$
Number of examples	300	300
Fitness function	SSE	CE
Instruction set	$\{+, +, -, -, \times, \times, /, \sqrt{x}, x^2\}$	$\{+, -, \times, /, x^y, if >\}$
Constants	$\{1, .., 9\}$	$\{1, .., 9\}$

Multiple instances of the same instruction in the instruction set, as used for the *distance* problem, increase the probability that the instruction is selected during initialization and mutation. In this way, the distribution of operator symbols within the population can be manipulated and is not solely determined by fitness selection.

For the *three chains* problem we use *interval classification*. That is, the distance between the problem output and one of the given identifiers for the output classes (0, 1, or 2) must be smaller than 0.5 to be accepted as correct.

Table 6.2 gives an overview of the different explicit bias configurations, i.e., proportions of insertions and deletions, that will be applied with instruction mutation operators. Configuration B1 induces an explicit growth bias by allowing two times more insertions than deletions. The maximum possible bias Bmax uses insertions exclusively. B−1 denotes a shrink bias and B0 is the bias-free standard case.

Table 6.2. Different proportions of insertions and deletions (biases).

Bias	B−1	B0	B1	Bmax
Insertions (%)	33	50	67	100
Deletions (%)	67	50	33	0
Ratio	1:2	1:1	2:1	1:0

Otherwise, the experimental setup is the same as documented in Section 5.8.

6.4 Experiments

The different types of instruction mutations which have been introduced in the previous section will now be compared with regard to prediction performance and (effective) solution size. The influence of several control parameters will also be examined. In particular, the number and the distribution of mutation points will be considered.

6.4.1 Comparison of Instruction Mutations

The following eight Tables 6.3 to 6.10 compare the different mutation operators on the four test problems. We list mean best prediction error and standard deviation over 100 runs, plus the number of hits, i.e., the number of times (out of 100) the optimum has been found. In addition, absolute

Table 6.3. *distance*: Comparison of different instruction mutation operators using bias configuration B1 for effective mutations and B0 otherwise. Average results over 100 runs after 1,000 generations.

Operator	Config.	SSE		#Hits	Length			Variations (%)		
		mean	*std.*		*abs.*	*eff.*	*%*	*constr.*	*neutral*	*noneff.*
mut		6.5	0.3	0	78	32	41	0.5	63	62
noneffmut	maxiter 2	12.0	0.5	0	53	15	29	0.03	84	84
	maxiter 3	16.7	0.4	0	33	6	20	0.005	90	90
neutrmut	maxiter 2	5.4	0.3	1	84	38	45	0.3	81.5	80.9
	maxiter 3	6.0	0.3	0	87	42	48	0.2	89.4	88.6
neutreffmut	effmut 25%	3.7	0.2	0	98	52	53	0.8	70	68
	effmut 100%	**1.4**	0.2	14	60	37	62	13.1	15	0
effmut		2.2	0.2	16	29	24	80	8.2	9.4	4.9
effmut2		2.6	0.3	6	65	36	56	9.6	5.9	0
effmut3		1.9	0.2	15	23	23	100	9.3	6.4	0

Table 6.4. *distance*: Comparison of different instruction mutation operators using bias configuration B0. Average results over 100 runs after 1,000,000 (effective) evaluations.

Operator	Config.	SSE		#Hits
		mean	*std.*	
mut		5.0	0.3	0
noneffmut	maxiter 2	6.3	0.3	0
	maxiter 3	6.2	0.3	1
neutrmut	maxiter 2	4.4	0.3	1
	maxiter 3	5.5	0.3	0
neutreffmut	effmut 25%	4.0	0.3	0
	effmut 100%	**2.7**	0.3	14

and effective program sizes are listed, averaged over all individuals.[5] We also show the distribution of *measured* variation effects, i.e., constructive, neutral, and noneffective variations.

The results of the same runs are compared on the basis of two different scales, number of generations and number of effective evaluations. In the first scale, the number of new individuals in the population (all accepted variations) is counted. In the second scale, *effective* variations – plus those genetic operations that are *not accepted* during neutrality control – are counted. The reader may recall from Section 5.2 that fitness is recal-

---

[5]The size of best solutions is almost identical to the average solution size, because of a small standard deviation in the population (≤ 5 instructions). This is a direct consequence of using minimum step size on the instruction level.

Table 6.5. *mexican hat*: Comparison of different instruction mutation operators using bias configuration B1. Average results over 100 runs after 1,000 generations.

Operator	Config.	SSE		Length			Variations (%)		
		mean	*std.*	*abs.*	*eff.*	*%*	*constr.*	*neutral*	*noneff.*
mut		3.5	0.5	140	60	43	0.8	54	52
noneffmut	maxiter 2	8.6	1.0	146	59	40	0.2	80	79
	maxiter 3	17.6	1.4	131	39	30	0.02	86	86
neutrmut	maxiter 2	1.4	0.2	154	76	49	0.6	72	70
	maxiter 3	1.5	0.2	158	83	53	0.6	82	80
neutreffmut	effmut 25%	0.9	0.11	154	82	53	1.0	66	63
	effmut 100%	**0.3**	0.03	82	58	71	9.8	22	0
effmut		0.9	0.06	39	33	85	6.9	14	3.6
effmut2		1.0	0.06	57	39	69	7.6	12	0
effmut3		1.1	0.07	27	27	100	7.8	11	0.1

Table 6.6. *mexican hat*: Comparison of different instruction mutation operators using bias configuration B1. Average results over 100 runs after 1,000,000 (effective) evaluations.

Operator	Config.	SSE	
		mean	*std.*
mut		2.3	0.4
noneffmut	maxiter 2	3.9	0.5
	maxiter 3	4.5	0.5
neutrmut	maxiter 2	1.2	0.4
	maxiter 3	1.4	0.2
neutreffmut	effmut 25%	1.1	0.13
	effmut 100%	**0.6**	0.06

culated only if the effective code has been changed. Thus, a performance comparison on the level of effective evaluations is a more accurate measure of computational costs. This notwithstanding, a comparison on the level of generations is indispensable for experimental analysis concerning program growth or variation effects.

The results obtained with effective mutations (effmut∗) are listed only for one time measurement (generations). Depending on the implementation the rate of noneffective variations is very small or zero with this operator. Thus, results after 1,000 generations or 1,000,000 effective evaluations (with population size 1,000) differ only very slightly or not at all. In general, the performance of a genetic operator is the more similar with both measurements, the less noneffective variations it produces, and the less variations are rejected during a neutrality control (if used). The

Table 6.7. *three chains*: Comparison of different instruction mutation operators using bias configuration **B1**. Average results over 100 runs after 1,000 generations.

Operator	Config.	CE		#Hits	Length			Variations (%)		
		mean	*std.*		*abs.*	*eff.*	*%*	*constr.*	*neutral*	*noneff.*
mut		15.5	0.6	1	132	57	43	0.2	62	49
noneffmut	maxiter 2	37.6	2.3	0	134	39	29	0.03	87	83
	maxiter 3	68.4	3.1	1	124	24	19	0.007	96	95
neutrmut	maxiter 2	13.4	0.7	2	142	65	46	0.1	82	64
	maxiter 3	10.5	0.6	2	143	70	49	0.1	90	68
neutreffmut	effmut 25%	8.4	0.5	3	143	92	64	0.1	84	41
	effmut 100%	**5.9**	0.4	10	126	110	87	0.4	72	0
effmut		13.9	0.7	2	77	71	92	1.1	38	1.9
effmut2		12.1	0.7	5	96	84	87	1.0	39	0
effmut3		14.0	0.7	1	63	63	100	1.4	34	0

Table 6.8. *three chains*: Comparison of different instruction mutation operators using bias configuration **B1**. Average results over 100 runs after 1,000,000 (effective) evaluations.

Operator	Config.	CE		#Hits
		mean	*std.*	
mut		11.8	0.6	1
noneffmut	maxiter 2	13.3	0.6	1
	maxiter 3	12.3	0.7	4
neutrmut	maxiter 2	11.8	0.6	2
	maxiter 3	9.9	0.6	3
neutreffmut	effmut 25%	**9.3**	0.6	1
	effmut 100%	10.5	0.6	2

effective mutation operator implicitly increases the rate of non-neutral variations including a higher rate of both destructive and constructive events. However, destructive events are by far the dominating variation effect. About 85 percent of all variations are destructive in approximation problems and about 65 percent in classification problems tested.

All three different variants of effective mutation operators (see Section 6.2.3) work almost equally well. Small differences may result either from a slower growth of (effective) code due to a radical removal of all noneffective instructions (effmut3) or from a faster growth due to a higher proportion of such instructions (effmut2).

The effmut2 variant demonstrates that noneffective code remains small even if deletions of noneffective instructions are prohibited (as in effmut). Note that the rate of noneffective variations equals the rate of intron

Table 6.9. *spiral*: Comparison of different instruction mutation operators using bias configuration B1. Average results over 100 runs after 1,000 generations.

Operator	Config.	CE mean	std.	#Hits	Length abs.	eff.	%	Variations (%) constr.	neutral	noneff.
mut		13.6	0.6	0	128	64	50	0.3	50	42
noneffmut	maxiter 2	18.0	0.6	0	139	60	43	0.03	75	72
	maxiter 3	25.5	0.8	0	135	50	37	0.005	89	87
neutrmut	maxiter 2	8.7	0.4	0	143	79	56	0.1	70	57
	maxiter 3	6.0	0.3	1	148	83	56	0.1	83	67
neutreffmut	effmut 25%	2.9	0.2	13	148	101	68	0.2	70	41
	effmut 100%	**2.3**	0.2	20	120	109	91	0.8	55	0
effmut		8.8	0.4	2	74	69	93	1.7	24	2
effmut2		7.2	0.5	1	86	77	90	1.4	25	0
effmut3		9.0	0.4	0	56	56	100	1.9	22	0

Table 6.10. *spiral*: Comparison of different instruction mutation operators using bias configuration B1. Average results over 100 runs after 1,000,000 (effective) evaluations.

Operator	Config.	CE mean	std.	#Hits
mut		9.0	0.4	0
noneffmut	maxiter 2	9.0	0.4	0
	maxiter 3	10.5	0.4	0
neutrmut	maxiter 2	8.4	0.4	0
	maxiter 3	6.7	0.3	1
neutreffmut	effmut 25%	**5.7**	0.3	2
	effmut 100%	7.1	0.4	5

deletions here since all other variations are effective. Depending on the correlation between problem fitness and program length different variants may be superior. For instance, variant effmut2 works better with the classification problems, *three chains* and *spiral*.

The effmut3 results show that the existence of structural introns in linear genetic programs is not so important, at least for the performance of effective instruction mutations. This is due to multiple register usage reflected in the graph-based data flow. It allows the effective code to protect itself against larger deactivation (for more details, see Chapter 9). The use of an explicit growth bias (B1 here) becomes more important with this variant of effective mutations (see also Section 6.4.3). The resulting faster code growth compensates at least partly for the loss of genetic material.

Effective mutations perform better than standard mutations (mut) under the same number of variations (generations). On the level of effective variations (evaluations), however, standard mutations may perform equally well or even better than mutations that vary the effective code exclusively. This situation occurs with the two classification problems and may result either directly from a higher rate of noneffective neutral variations or indirectly from a larger size of solutions.

The neutrmut approach applies an explicit control of neutral variations introduced in Section 6.2.6. After a variation is accepted or a maximum number of trials (2 or 3 here) has been performed the offspring is copied into the population. Otherwise, the operation is repeated. Thus, one variation step may require more than one fitness evaluation, which necessitates a comparison on the basis of evaluations. Neutrality control increases the rate of neutral variations up to about 90 percent. If we compare the rate of noneffective variations we can see that almost all neutral variations are noneffective, too, as far as the approximation problems are concerned.

By comparison, the proportion of noneffective variations is definitely smaller for the classification problems. On the one hand, neutral variations that alter the structurally effective code are induced more easily because discrete fitness functions facilitate the propagation of semantic introns. On the other hand, effective programs may grow larger when using branches because these allow both more semantic introns and a higher specialization onto the training data.

Since about half of the variations turn out to be noneffective and thus neutral already with the standard approach (mut), neutrality control (neutrmut) may affect at most 50 percent of variations that would be destructive otherwise.[6] We found that already two trials are sufficient, on average, for almost all mutations to become neutral. Hence, the number of necessary fitness evaluations is only double that of the standard approach. In other words, only about the same total number of fitness evaluations is required for promoting neutrality of variations as is necessary for avoiding neutrality (effmut).

Concerning the prediction quality Tables 6.3 to 6.10 document that most test problems benefit from an explicit introduction of neutral mutations (neutrmut). Individuals resulting from a neutral variation have a higher survival probability (see Chapter 10). Not surprisingly, improvements in

---

[6]Recall that noneffective variations do not produce computational costs in terms of fitness evaluations.

prediction error compared to standard mutations are more significant on a generational basis than on an evaluation basis.

Can similar improvements be obtained by simply increasing the rate of noneffective variations? Unfortunately, the noneffmut series of experiments demonstrates that by increasing only the rate of noneffective neutral variations, the prediction error is decreased drastically on a generational basis. The lower rate of effective variations leads to a lower rate of constructive operations and, in some cases, to a smaller effective size of programs.

When comparing results after the same number of effective evaluations, this disadvantage is partly compensated. But the performance is still worse than that achieved with the standard variant. Note that the total variation step size increases significantly here because of the high number of noneffective mutations that may happen between two fitness evaluations, i.e., two effective variations. Consequently, if a higher rate of noneffective variations does not improve chances for finding a solution, the slightly larger difference between the proportions of neutral and noneffective variations that occurs with the neutrmut operator seems to be essential.

In order to increase the rate of such effective neutral variations more explicitly the neutreffmut operator applies a neutrality control together with a certain percentage of operator effmut2. Interestingly, this combination improves performance compared to applying both approaches separately, especially on a generational basis. On the basis of evaluations, the difference in average prediction error shrinks between neutreffmut and neutrmut, but is still significant. In addition, neutreffmut still clearly outperforms pure effective mutations (effmut*) for most problems (except for *distance*).

For the two discrete problems less neutral variations are noneffective. Interestingly, even if effective mutations are applied 100 percent of the time (neutreffmut) the resulting rate of neutral variations decreases only slightly. Already 25% of explicitly induced effective mutations allow effective neutral variations to occur significantly more frequently.

In general, we may conclude that increasing the proportion of both neutral *and* effective mutations achieves the highest gain in performance for all test problems. Smaller absolute and effective solutions, however, are achieved by using standard effective mutations which are mostly destructive. Chapter 10 will demonstrate that a small proportion of noneffective code is a direct result of a low rate of noneffective (neutral) variations.

6.4.2   Comparison with Segment Variations

A comparison between standard instruction mutations (mut) and segment mutations (onesegmut) in Section 5.9.2 reveals a significantly better performance in favor of the first approach. This results mostly from the minimum step size of instruction mutations. Standard segment mutations apply an unlimited step size, by comparison.[7]

Figure 6.2 shows fitness development of the current best individual over generations for different macro operators. Early in a GP run much information is gained by the system. Best fitness improves significantly during this period. Towards the end of a run, absolute fitness improvements become smaller. In other words, the convergence speed of the fitness decreases over a run.

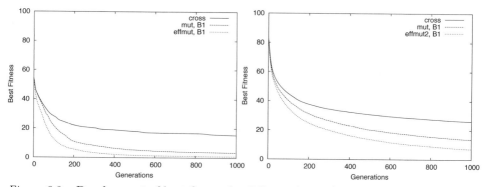

Figure 6.2.   Development of best fitness for different (macro) variation operators with *mexican hat* (left) and *spiral* (right). Average figures over 100 runs.

One can see that (effective) instruction mutations perform better than crossover from early on in a run. The larger absolute step sizes of crossover do not seem to provide an advantage in early generations. In the last 500 generations, on the other hand, fitness difference between operators stops growing.

In particular, the difference between effective and standard instruction mutations does not substantially decrease towards the end of a run. The effectiveness of standard mutations – including insertions and deletions – depends on the ratio of effective code and noneffective code in programs. This ratio stays practically constant during a run as long as the size of programs has not reached the maximum limit (not shown).

---

[7]The size of (effective) solutions differs only slightly.

6.4.3 Explicit Growth Bias

By using macro mutations with a minimum step size of one instruction the speed of code growth is severely restricted. We will test the influence of different growth biases (introduced in Section 6.3) on the performance of instruction mutations. Basically, the speed with which programs may grow during a certain number of generations depends on both the problem and the macro variation operator. While the problem definition determines the correlation between solution size and fitness, an *explicit bias* of the variation operator is semantically independent. In contrast to an *implicit bias* (see Chapter 10), it will influence code growth even without fitness information.

Table 6.11. *mexican hat*: Comparison of free mutations and effective mutations with different bias configurations. Average results over 100 runs after 1,000 generations.

Operator	Config.	SSE		Length			Variations (%)		
		mean	*std.*	*abs.*	*eff.*	*%*	*constr.*	*neutral*	*noneff.*
mut	B−1	1.7	0.2	37	25	68	1.9	37	35
	B0	2.4	0.3	72	41	58	1.3	45	43
	B1	3.5	0.5	140	60	43	0.8	54	52
	Bmax	6.9	0.9	179	75	42	0.8	55	53
effmut	B0	1.3	0.09	26	23	88	7.0	13	4.2
	B1	0.9	0.06	39	33	85	6.9	14	3.6
	Bmax	0.9	0.06	101	72	71	7.3	14	0.6
effmut3	B1	1.1	0.07	27	27	100	7.8	11	0
	Bmax	0.6	0.05	54	54	100	7.3	12	0

In Tables 6.11 and 6.12 the influence of different bias configurations on the best prediction performance and the average program length is compared. For the same bias configuration average program size remains similar for both test problems if we apply standard instruction mutations (mut). Interestingly, this holds for effective size as well. Effective mutations (effmut∗), on the other hand, allow solution sizes to differ considerably between problems, since fewer noneffective code occurs with these variations. Then absolute program length is more subject to fitness selection.

Contrary to Table 6.12, average prediction errors in Table 6.11 show a clear negative influence of growth bias using standard mutations. In fact, the *mexican hat* problem is solved best with a shrink bias. Configuration B−1 reduces absolute and effective code growth almost by half compared to the bias-free configuration B0.

Table 6.12.   *spiral:* Comparison of free mutations and effective mutations with different bias configurations. Average results over 100 runs after 1,000 generations.

Operator	Config.	CE		#Hits	Length			Variations (%)		
		mean	*std.*		*abs.*	*eff.*	*%*	*constr.*	*neutral*	*noneff.*
mut	B0	15.0	0.5	0	75	44	60	0.5	42	36
	B1	13.6	0.6	0	128	64	50	0.3	50	42
	Bmax	13.4	0.6	0	176	88	50	0.2	52	42
effmut2	B0	11.6	0.4	1	55	50	91	2.1	21	0
	B1	7.2	0.4	1	86	77	90	1.4	25	0
	Bmax	6.4	0.3	3	155	136	88	1.1	30	0
effmut3	B1	9.0	0.4	0	56	56	100	1.9	22	0
	Bmax	5.3	0.3	1	122	122	100	1.7	23	0

In contrast to standard mutations, growth bias B1 has been found to improve the performance of the effective mutation operator in both tables. The maximum growth bias Bmax, however, has not turned out to be much more successful than bias level B1, it only produces larger solutions. Clearly effmut3 is improved and performs best, provided only insertions of instructions happen.[8]

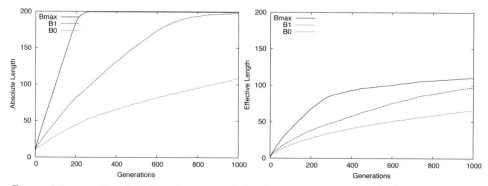

Figure 6.3.   *mexican hat:* Development of absolute program length (left) and effective program length (right). Influence of different growth biases on free mutations (mut). Average figures over 100 runs.

Figure 6.3 illustrates for *mexican hat* the development of absolute and effective length over the generations using standard mutations. The influence of an explicit bias on code growth is relaxed as soon as a genetic program has reached its maximum size. In this case, only instruction deletions are possible (see Algorithm 6.1). Thus, if only insertions are

---

[8]Recall that programs normally grow more slowly with this variant due to a radical deletion of introns (see Section 6.2.3).

otherwise applied (by using Bmax), the rate of insertions and deletions is almost balanced for such programs. This corresponds to applying no bias at all and affects both the absolute program length and the effective length. Note that the growth of effective code slows down in Figures 6.3 as soon as the average absolute size approaches the maximum.

We close this section with a general remark about applying an explicit growth bias in genetic programming. In order to keep structural mutation steps small between fitness evaluations over the entire run, it is required that these are possible at almost all positions of a program representation. In other words, the variability of the representation must be sufficiently high. This is indeed the case for linear genetic programs and their graph-structured data flow (see Section 6.1). Otherwise, a growth bias can only be implemented in such a way that smaller subprograms are replaced with a higher probability by larger subprograms. This, however, would allow larger structural changes to happen as well.

In the following section we will demonstrate that a growth bias – in combination with a minimum mutation step size – may not be outperformed by using larger step sizes in the form of multiple mutations.

6.4.4   Number of Mutation Points

By using an explicit growth bias the evolutionary process can be guided towards regions of search space where the complexity of solutions is more suitable for finding a (near) optimal solution. We have seen in the previous section that, depending on the problem and on the number of generations, this may require code growth to be accelerated or slowed down.

Provided that a problem's fitness benefits from faster growth of programs, it might be argued that a biased operator is not really necessary. Instead, program growth might be accelerated simply by allowing larger absolute step sizes for the variation operator. We will demonstrate in the following that this is not the case and that a minimum mutation step size yields best performance.

Absolute mutation step size is controlled by the maximum number of mutations that may be applied to an individual without exposing the intermediate results to fitness selection. This number is chosen from a uniform distribution over a certain maximum range. Alternatively, mutation step size might be controlled by choosing a maximum segment length in segment mutations. The basic difference between these approaches is that there is either one or a multitude of mutation points. The insertion of an effective segment more likely represents a single contiguous graph component and, thus, may affect less graph nodes on the functional level of the program.

The experiments documented in Tables 6.13 and 6.15 demonstrate that the optimal configuration for both test problems, *mexican hat* and *spiral*, is to mutate, delete, or insert a single effective instruction (effmut). When using standard mutations (mut), it might be expected that the optimal number of mutation points is larger because this increases the chance that the whole variation step becomes effective. Surprisingly, it turns out that already two instructions are optimal, as shown in Table 6.14 and Table 6.16.

Table 6.13.   mexican hat: Multiple effective mutations (effmut2, B0). Average results over 100 runs after 1,000 generations.

Maximum	SSE		Length			Variations (%)		
#Mutations	*mean*	*std.*	*abs.*	*eff.*	*%*	*constr.*	*neutral*	*noneff.*
1	**1.3**	0.1	39	27	70	8.1	10	0
2	1.7	0.1	38	24	63	8.8	11	0
5	2.6	0.2	53	28	53	9.2	14	0
10	3.5	0.2	76	35	46	9.2	15	0
20	7.8	0.4	102	44	43	8.6	16	0

Table 6.14.   mexican hat: Multiple mutations (mut, B0). Average results over 100 runs after 1,000 generations.

Maximum	SSE		Length			Variations (%)		
#Mutations	*mean*	*std.*	*abs.*	*eff.*	*%*	*constr.*	*neutral*	*noneff.*
1	1.6	0.2	72	41	58	1.3	45	43
2	**1.2**	0.1	69	37	53	2.1	37	34
5	1.7	0.2	68	31	46	3.9	26	23
10	2.1	0.2	64	24	37	5.3	23	17
20	4.0	0.4	73	23	32	6.2	22	12

Effective mutations perform better than standard mutations if the mutation number is small, because many standard mutations are noneffective. The more mutations happen simultaneously, however, the higher the probability for a variation step to be noneffective as a whole. As a result, the proportion of noneffective variations decreases together with the difference in prediction error.

The shrinking proportion of effective code observed in all tables may be interpreted as a protective reaction of the system. It reduces the average *effective* step size because a higher proportion of noneffective instructions will cause single mutations to become noneffective (neutral) with a higher probability. We have observed a similar protection mechanism with crossover in Section 5.9.4.

Interestingly, the average effective length of programs decreases if more standard mutations are applied simultaneously while the absolute length remains constant or decreases more slowly (see Tables 6.14 and 6.16). Besides less need for protection, the effective code may grow larger with smaller variation steps because those allow a more precise approximation to solution with a better fitness.

Table 6.15. *spiral*: Multiple effective mutations (**effmut2**, **B1**). Average results over 100 runs after 1,000 generations.

Maximum	CE		#Hits	Length			Variations (%)		
#Mutations	*mean*	*std.*		*abs.*	*eff.*	%	*constr.*	*neutral*	*noneff.*
1	**7.6**	0.4	2	86	78	91	1.7	25	0
2	10.4	0.5	0	81	71	87	2.6	19	0
5	16.4	0.5	0	79	63	80	4.8	14	0
10	21.8	0.6	0	80	59	73	6.0	15	0
20	28.5	0.6	0	88	58	66	6.3	20	0

Table 6.16. *spiral*: Multiple mutations (**mut**, **B0**). Average results over 100 runs after 1,000 generations.

Maximum	CE		#Hits	Length			Variations (%)		
#Mutations	*mean*	*std.*		*abs.*	*eff.*	%	*constr.*	*neutral*	*noneff.*
1	15.0	0.4	0	75	44	60	0.5	42	36
2	**13.9**	0.5	0	76	44	58	1.0	34	27
5	16.7	0.6	0	76	39	51	2.3	24	13
10	22.0	0.6	1	66	31	46	4.0	18	12
20	25.6	0.7	0	58	23	40	5.3	18	8

It is important to note in this context that an explicit growth bias (which has been used only for the experiment documented in Table 6.15 here) is not reinforced by using multiple instruction mutations per variation step. That is, the absolute variation step size does not affect the ratio of inserted and deleted instructions here.

Two conclusions are in order: (1) A non-minimal number of instruction mutations does not improve performance in linear GP, at least if mutations are effective. In other words, a fitness evaluation after each instruction mutation is essential and cannot be spared. Minimum structural step sizes still induce semantic step sizes that are large enough, on average, to escape from local minima. (2) A higher mutation step size may not be regarded as an alternative to an explicit growth bias. The prediction error does not improve by using several effective mutation points, neither does the length of programs grow necessarily.

6.4.5   Self-Adaptation

The principle of self-adaptation (see discussion in Section 5.4.1) can be applied for the coevolution of structural step sizes in linear GP. This may either concern the number of mutation points in instruction mutations or the segment length in segment mutations. Here the self-adaptation of the number of effective instruction mutations is discussed. Only one parameter has to be encoded into each individual, the *maximum* mutation step size n. Actual step sizes may then be selected from a uniform or normal distribution over the maximum range.[9] For this discussion we choose a uniform distribution. The variation of the individual parameter value is controlled by a mutation probability p and a constant mutation step size of ± 1.

Results in the previous section have demonstrated that the optimum performance is obtained with a (constantly) minimal number of effective mutation points, namely one. This does not automatically imply that varying the number of effective mutation points during runtime cannot be advantageous. For instance, it would be interesting to know, whether a higher mutation step size at the beginning of a run is more beneficial. Perhaps a higher diversity in initial generations renders the evolutionary algorithm less dependent on the composition of the genetic material in the initial population. At least self-adaptation will provide us with information about how precisely and how fast the optimal setting of mutation parameters is approached.

Figure 6.4 shows how mutation step size develops over generations when using self-adaptation. As one can see, the average individual step size in the population converges to the minimum step size 1 for both problems, *mexican hat* and *spiral*. The higher the mutation probability is set for the step size parameter the more quickly the minimum is reached. We made sure that no convergence occurs without fitness (selection). In this case, the average mutation step size during a run oscillates around the value that has been provided initially (10 here).

The prediction performance of these runs (not shown here) comes very close to the performance obtained with constant step size 1 in Tables 6.13 and 6.15. In other words, varying a maximum step size on the symbol

---

[9]Only positive integer values are permitted as step sizes.

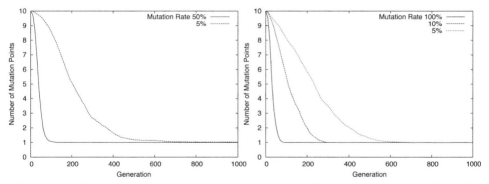

Figure 6.4. Development of the maximum number of mutation points with self-adaptation for different parameter mutation rates using *mexican hat* (left) and *spiral* (right). Numbers averaged over all parameter values in the population Initial setting is 10. Average figures over 100 runs.

structures during runtime has not been found to perform better than using constant step size 1 from the beginning. It appears that larger variation steps on the linear program structure are not more successful.

6.4.6 Distribution of Mutation Points

The final series of experiments on mutation investigates the role of the mutation point. In the standard case each instruction is chosen with the same probability. But is such a uniform distribution of mutation points really close to the optimum? At first sight, we might expect it to be true for an imperative representation composed of a linear sequence of instructions.

Figure 6.5 shows how the functional structure of an *effective* linear program is built by applying the three analysis algorithms from Section 3.4. For each program position, the structural information is averaged over all effective programs of the final generation that hold an instruction at that position. The average effective length is about 55 instructions for *mexican hat* and 110 instructions for *spiral*, with standard deviation of effective lengths being below 5 instructions.

How does the average number of effective registers and the average effectiveness degree depend on the effective instruction positions? Over the first half of the program length the number of effective registers stays almost constant while decreasing over the second half, until it becomes 1 at the last effective instruction in a program.[10] The effectiveness of instruc-

---

[10] The average value is larger due to variable program length.

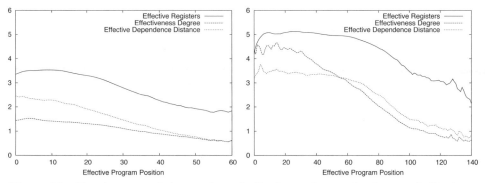

Figure 6.5. Development of the number of effective registers, the degree of effectiveness, and the effective dependence distance over effective program positions using effective mutations (**effmut**). Position 0 holds the first instruction of a program. Average figures over all programs of the final (1,000th) generation and over 100 runs. Results for *mexican hat* (left) and *spiral* (right).

tions decreases more regularly towards the end of a linear program, by comparison. Both the effectiveness degree and the effective dependence distance are 0 at the last effective instruction.

These observations can be explained if we recall from Chapter 3.3 that the last effective instruction of a linear program corresponds to the root of the underlying (effective) graph component. The number of effective registers at an instruction position in the program is an approximation of the graph width at that position. It appears that this width grows quickly to a certain maximum (starting form the graph root) and stays rather constant then because it is restricted by the total number of available registers. Among other things, a restriction is necessary in order to not unnecessarily increase the search space of programs (see also Section 7.1). A wider graph requires a longer imperative representation. Correspondingly, the distance of depending (effective) instructions increases in Figure 6.5 together with the number of effective registers.

We can test the effective mutation operator with two alternatives to a uniform distribution of mutation points over the effective program length. Basically, the selection frequency is either increased towards the beginning of a program (graph sinks) or towards the end of a program (graph root).

Tables 6.17 and 6.18 compare the performance of the three different distributions. Performance decreases if the mutation probability is higher at the end of a linear program, and is almost not affected (*mexican hat* problem) or increased (*spiral* problem) if mutation probability is higher at the beginning. These effects directly follow from the functional structure of the genetic programs:

An instruction close to the program end is most likely located high up in the graph structure where the graph width (number of effective registers) is rather small. Mutations are more destructive in this region since more calculation paths lead through instruction nodes. In turn, mutation effects in central and lower graph regions (where graph width is more constant) are less destructive.

Table 6.17. mexican hat: Comparison of different frequency distributions of mutation points over the effective program length n (**effmut**). $\mathcal{U}(n)$ calculates a uniformly distributed integer number within range $[0, n)$. $\mathcal{N}(0, 0.33n)$ calculates a normally distributed random number from range $(-n, n)$ with expectation 0 and standard deviation $0.33 \times n$. Average results over 100 runs after 1,000 generations.

Mutation	SSE		Length			Variations (%)		
Distribution	*mean*	*std.*	*abs.*	*eff.*	*%*	*constr.*	*neutral*	*noneff.*
$\mathcal{U}(n)$	0.9	0.06	39	33	85	6.9	14	3.6
$\lvert\mathcal{N}(0, 0.33n)\rvert$	0.8	0.07	44	37	84	5.6	18	3.5
$n - 1 - \lvert\mathcal{N}(0, 0.33n)\rvert$	12.8	1.5	39	31	79	8.3	12	4.5

Table 6.18. spiral: Comparison of different frequency distributions of mutation points over the effective program length n (**effmut**). Average results over 100 runs after 1,000 generations.

Mutation	CE		#Hits	Length			Variations (%)		
Distribution	*mean*	*std.*		*abs.*	*eff.*	*%*	*constr.*	*neutral*	*noneff.*
$\mathcal{U}(n)$	8.8	0.4	2	74	69	93	1.7	24	1.7
$\lvert\mathcal{N}(0, 0.33n)\rvert$	4.5	0.3	10	86	79	91	1.3	33	1.7
$n - 1 - \lvert\mathcal{N}(0, 0.33n)\rvert$	14.8	0.8	0	79	72	91	1.8	27	1.6

Note that a higher mutation frequency at the beginning of a linear program may have an even more positive influence on the evolutionary search if a larger number of registers is used. As we will see in Section 7.1 the functional program structure becomes more tree-like then.

A second explanation for the above results may be found in the effectiveness degree which decreases approximately linearly over the program length in Figure 6.5. A high connectivity of graph nodes reduces the probability that effective subgraphs are disconnected. One may expect now that the effective step size increases continuously the closer the mutation point is located to the program end (the graph root). At least this it true to a certain extent, as will be demonstrated in Section 9.7.2.

6.5   Summary and Conclusion

The most important results of this chapter can be summarized as follows:

☐ In general, better fitness values occur with smaller mutation step sizes. The best performance as well as the the smallest solutions were obtained by using a minimum mutation step size of one instruction, in combination with a guaranteed effectiveness of the variation. It appears that even smallest changes of the program structure induce semantic step sizes that are sufficiently large, on average, to escape from local minima (see also Chapter 9).

Effective instruction mutations performed even better when coupled with an explicit bias to code growth. Such a performance gain was not possible with a larger mutation step size. Moreover, we found that the effective program length may shrink by using multiple instruction mutations.

☐ An additional gain in performance, but larger solutions, were obtained by increasing the proportion of neutral instruction mutations on the effective code. This particularly emphasizes the importance of neutral variations for the evolutionary progress. In general, the induction of neutral variations requires that we obtain information about program semantics by means of multiple fitness evaluations. These extra computational costs cannot be neglected even if one needs to recalculate fitness only after (structurally) effective code has been altered. Nonetheless, an explicit control of neutrality has been found computationally affordable on the basis of (effective) evaluations.

☐ If only single effective instructions are varied, the existence of structurally noneffective code in programs has not been found to be absolutely essential for producing high quality solutions. The same is true for noneffective variations. That does not mean, however, that structural introns may not contribute to evolutionary progress at all (see Section 10.7.5).

Other noneffective code turned out to be more clearly beneficial. Since effective neutral variations were highly profitable this must be valid for semantic introns, too, which tend to result from these variations.

For a summary of results concerning the influence of the different genetic operators on the solution size, the reader is directed to Section 10.8.1. Moreover, Chapter 10 will discuss several causes for code growth in linear GP. Again neutral variations will play an important role.

Chapter 7

ANALYSIS OF CONTROL PARAMETERS

In the previous two chapters parameters have been analyzed that are closely related to one of the variation operators. In this chapter we analyze influences of more general system parameters that are relevant in linear genetic programming. In particular, the number of registers, the number of constants, the population size, and the maximum program length will be studied. Additionally, we compare different initialization techniques for linear genetic programs. Test problems are again the approximation problem *mexican hat* and the classification problem *spiral* introduced in Section 5.8.1.[1]

7.1 Number of Registers

In linear genetic programming saving local information in registers is an implicit part of the imperative representation. Each operation on registers or constants is combined with an assignment of the result to another register that may again serve as an operand in succeeding instructions. For the following considerations we assume that all registers can be written into.

The number of registers is crucial for determining performance of linear GP. If the number of inputs is low and only a few calculation registers are provided, register content will be overwritten frequently. This makes complex calculations and the emergence of complex problem solutions quite difficult. If too many calculation registers are provided, on the other

---

[1] The only difference to the configuration in Section 5.8.2 is that *mexican hat* is treated with a complete function set $\{+, -, \times, /, x^2, e^x\}$ that allows the optimum solution to be found.

hand, the search space is unnecessarily expanded. Furthermore, many programs may be semantically identical in the initial population since the probability is low that instructions manipulate effective registers, given that there are so many registers to choose from (see also Section 2.3.1). Hence, an optimal number of registers can be expected for each problem which will represent the best trade-off. Certainly, this optimal number of calculation registers will depend on the problem structure as is the case for the maximum program length. As we have seen earlier, both parameters determine size and shape of the program graph.

Table 7.1. *spiral*: Effects of different register numbers using effective mutations (eff-mut2, B1). Number of input registers is 2. Calculation registers are initialized with constant 1. Average results over 100 runs after 1,000 generations.

#Calculation	CE		#Hits	Length			Variations (%)		
Registers	*mean*	*std.*		*abs.*	*eff.*	%	*constr.*	*neutral*	*noneff.*
0	24.7	0.5	0	77	73	96	1.8	30	0
2	10.8	0.6	0	82	76	92	1.9	26	0
4	7.6	0.4	2	86	78	91	1.7	25	0
8	6.8	0.3	3	97	86	89	1.4	26	0
16	**6.1**	0.3	3	111	96	86	1.0	30	0
32	8.8	0.4	0	132	110	83	0.6	35	0
64	11.9	0.5	0	144	113	78	0.4	41	0
128	17.2	0.6	0	153	108	70	0.3	49	0

#Calculation	#Eff.	Eff.	Eff.Dep.
Registers	Registers	Degree	Distance
0	1.9	5.5	1.4
2	3.4	4.0	2.3
4	4.7	3.3	3.1
8	7.1	2.6	4.5
16	10.8	2.1	6.6
32	15.7	1.7	9.0
64	20.9	1.4	11.2
128	25.1	1.2	12.5

Additional registers may not be beneficial for problems that feature a high number of inputs. Because not all inputs may be relevant for a solution, calculations may not require additional registers for a better performance at all. Instead, irrelevant inputs could simply be overwritten.

In this section we investigate how the number of (calculation) registers affects the system behavior. Prediction quality, program length and variation effects, together with the functional structure of *effective* linear programs is analyzed. The latter requires a look at the number of effective registers, effectiveness of instructions, and distance of depending effective instructions (see Section 3.4).

If mutations are generated with the effmut operator, good solutions may still be found, even with the highest number of registers (see Table 7.1). In contrast, by using standard mutation (mut) the prediction error increases significantly beyond a certain register number (cf. Tables 7.2 and 7.3).

Table 7.2. *spiral:* Effects of different register numbers using free mutations (mut, B1). Number of input registers is 2. Calculation registers are initialized with constant 1. Average results over 100 runs after 1,000 generations.

#Calculation	CE		Length			Variations (%)		
Registers	*mean*	*std.*	*abs.*	*eff.*	*%*	*constr.*	*neutral*	*noneff.*
0	26.9	0.5	105	59	56	0.6	47	33
2	14.8	0.5	120	63	52	0.4	48	38
4	12.5	0.4	128	66	52	0.3	49	41
8	**10.5**	0.4	136	67	49	0.2	53	45
16	11.8	0.4	145	68	47	0.1	58	50
32	17.2	0.6	148	59	40	0.1	68	61
64	40.4	1.2	142	26	18	0.0	86	82
128	66.5	1.2	135	8	6	0.0	94	93

#Calculation	#Eff.	Eff.	Eff.Dep.
Registers	Registers	Degree	Distance
0	1.8	3.5	1.2
2	3.1	2.9	2.1
4	4.4	2.7	2.8
8	6.5	2.3	4.1
16	9.7	1.9	6.0
32	12.7	1.5	7.2
64	9.3	1.0	4.5
128	4.7	0.6	1.7

Since the effective mutation operator selects the destination register of newly inserted instructions effectively (see Section 6.2.3) the evolutionary process becomes somewhat independent of the total number of registers. The drawback of a larger search space can thus be counterbalanced. With standard mutations the probability of selecting an effective register decreases directly with the number of registers provided. The resulting higher rate of noneffective variations promotes the emergence of more noneffective instructions.

As we know from Section 3.3, the number of effective registers corresponds to the width of the (effective) program graph. The more registers that are available, the wider this graph may become. Concurrently, the connectivity of graph nodes, or, more precisely, the number of incoming edges per node (indegree) decreases with higher register numbers. A constant indegree of 1 means that the graph represents a tree program. Remember that the connectivity of nodes corresponds to the effectiveness degree of instructions in the imperative program which provides information about how often the result of an effective instruction is used to calculate the program output.

Figure 7.1 shows the average distribution of effective registers over the effective program positions. Obviously, the functional structure becomes more and more tree-shaped with a higher number of registers if we take into account that the average effectiveness degree over all program instructions in Table 7.1 converges to 1. With standard mutation and many registers, this value may even become smaller than 1 (see Tables 7.2 and 7.3). In this case, the rate of effective instructions is so low, on average, that many programs do not even hold a single effective instruction, i.e., have effective length 0.

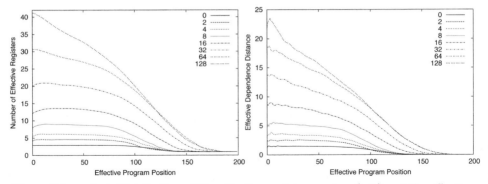

Figure 7.1. *spiral:* Distribution of the effective register number (left) and the effective dependence distance (right) over the (effective) program positions using effective mutations (**effmut**) with different numbers of calculation registers. Average figures over all programs of the final (1,000th) generation and over 100 runs. The standard deviation of program lengths ranges between 5 instructions (0 calculation registers) and 10 instructions (128 calculation registers).

The number of registers also influences the length of linear genetic programs. Note that in Table 7.1 the effective size grows continuously with the register number. Larger and wider program graphs are required to represent the same solution if nodes are only weakly connected. That means more (effective) instructions are needed in the imperative program. This, in turn, increases the average distance between two depending instructions in the effective program (see also Figure 7.1). As we know two

Table 7.3. mexican hat: Effects of different register numbers using effective mutations (**mut, B0**). Number of input registers is 2. Calculation registers are initialized with constant 1. Average results over 100 runs after 1,000 generations.

#Calculation	SSE		Length			Variations (%)		
Registers	*mean*	*std.*	*abs.*	*eff.*	*%*	*constr.*	*neutral*	*noneff.*
0	7.6	0.9	52	37	71	3.2	29	26
2	6.0	0.9	66	39	59	1.7	41	39
4	3.0	0.5	73	39	53	1.1	49	47
8	**1.3**	0.2	80	35	44	0.6	59	58
16	3.6	0.5	78	25	32	0.2	73	72
32	21.1	1.0	68	12	18	0.0	86	85
64	42.1	1.2	61	5	8	0.0	92	91

#Calculation	#Eff.	Eff.	Eff.Dep.
Registers	Registers	Degree	Distance
0	1.7	1.4	1.1
2	2.7	1.3	1.6
4	3.3	1.3	2.0
8	4.3	1.2	2.5
16	4.4	1.1	2.3
32	3.4	0.9	1.6
64	2.5	0.7	1.0

depending instructions correspond to two directly connected instruction nodes in the graph representation.

It has to be mentioned, however, that the program length is not always affected by the register number in evolutionary runs with effective mutations. For the *mexican hat* problem we found hardly any change in the amounts of effective code and noneffective code, not even with very many registers. Nevertheless, similar developments over the number of registers were observed in terms of the structural program analysis.

Similar developments as those found for effective mutations can be observed with standard mutations until a certain number of registers (see Tables 7.2 and 7.3). Beyond that point the complexity of solutions – including the size and proportion of effective code, the average number of effective registers, as well as the average effective dependence distance – decrease again.

7.1.1 Initialization of Registers

The results in Table 7.1 are obtained by using as many input registers as there are input values. Calculation registers are initialized with a constant value 1. We have seen that beyond a certain register number the performance starts to decrease again. At that point, the probability for selecting an input register during mutation becomes simply too low. This problem can be overcome by initializing more registers with input values.

As a side effect, input values are less likely to be lost by overwriting in calculations. The same input value may be *used* more frequently as an operand in a genetic program if it is held in more than one register. As indicated in Section 3.3, such operand registers label variable sink nodes (terminals) in the functional representation. More input registers mean more variable terminals that share the same label.

In the following experiments, we assign an input value to each register such that each input occupies about the same number of registers. As one can see in Table 7.4, the average prediction error stays approximately the same even above the optimal number of registers. Apparently, the problem with a larger search space by more registers is counterbalanced by registers being initialized with input values, as opposed to the situation with constant initialization in Table 7.1. Moreover, the best prediction error has been found to be half its former size while the hit rate is significantly higher.

Table 7.4.   spiral: Effects of different register numbers using effective mutations (eff-mut2, B1). Number of input registers is 2. Calculation registers are initialized with input values. Average results over 100 runs after 1,000 generations.

#Calculation	CE		#Hits	Length			Variations (%)		
Registers	*mean*	*std.*		*abs.*	*eff.*	%	*constr.*	*neutral*	*noneff.*
0	24.7	0.5	0	77	73	96	1.8	30	0
2	9.5	0.4	1	82	76	92	1.9	25	0
4	5.5	0.3	3	84	76	91	1.8	24	0
8	3.4	0.3	16	91	80	88	1.6	25	0
16	**3.0**	0.2	9	103	89	86	1.3	26	0
32	3.4	0.3	15	113	95	84	1.0	29	0
64	3.6	0.3	11	126	102	81	0.9	32	0
128	3.9	0.3	7	133	103	77	0.7	34	0

The average number of effective registers is quite similar to that of standard initialization (undocumented). In other words, calculations do not involve a larger number of effective registers only because more registers are initialized with input data. The size of resulting (effective) solutions is also comparable to that of standard initialization runs.

The behavior described here has not been observed with the approximation problem. The *mexican hat* performance improves only slightly and gets worse again for higher register numbers, similar to the situation where calculation registers are initialized with constants.

We will now analyze how crossover results are influenced by the number of registers holding input values. Table 7.5 and Table 7.6 show that the average prediction error improves to a certain extent by using more calculation registers. Especially the *mexican hat* problem is much better solved if compared to a constant initialization of 4 calculation registers (see baseline results at maximum length 200 in Tables 7.13 and 7.14).

Table 7.5. mexican hat: Effects of different register numbers using crossover (cross). Number of input registers is 2. Calculation registers are initialized with input values. Average results over 100 runs after 1,000 generations.

#Calculation	SSE		Length			Variations (%)		
Registers	*mean*	*std.*	*abs.*	*eff.*	*%*	*constr.*	*neutral*	*noneff.*
0	11.4	0.9	144	71	49	6.4	21	14
2	5.9	0.8	167	65	39	5.3	24	19
4	2.8	0.5	177	59	33	4.6	27	23
8	**1.7**	0.2	184	52	28	3.8	30	26
16	1.7	0.2	187	43	23	3.1	34	31
32	4.5	0.4	186	34	18	2.6	45	41
64	10.2	1.3	187	25	13	1.8	51	49

Table 7.6. spiral: Effects of different register numbers using crossover (cross). Number of input registers is 2. Calculation registers are initialized with input values. Average results over 100 runs after 1,000 generations.

#Calculation	CE		Length			Variations (%)		
Registers	*mean*	*std.*	*abs.*	*eff.*	*%*	*constr.*	*neutral*	*noneff.*
2	23.8	0.7	186	109	58	3.5	24	13
4	19.0	0.6	187	102	55	3.2	24	15
8	15.3	0.5	187	101	54	2.8	23	15
16	**13.0**	0.4	190	98	52	2.2	23	15
32	15.1	0.5	192	87	45	1.8	25	17
64	18.2	0.5	192	77	40	1.5	30	20
128	22.7	0.5	192	67	35	1.2	35	24

A lower proportion of effective code, i.e., a higher proportion of structural introns, may be maintained by using more registers. This results mostly from the fact that a smaller *proportion* of registers is effective, on average. If only a small number of additional registers is provided, the effective length of programs depends strongly on their absolute length. It is interesting to note that the absolute length grows larger over the number of registers while the effective length grows smaller. In Table 7.6 the absolute length is virtually the same for all register configurations due to both a faster code growth and the maximum length bound.

A smaller proportion of effective code is correlated with a higher number of noneffective variations because it reduces the effective step size of segment variations like crossover. Crossover performance is improved until the rate of effective operations and the effective code are reduced so much that better solutions cannot be produced any more (on average).

We will demonstrate in Section 9.7.2 that the register number on its own has a negative influence on the effective step size, independent of the applied variation operator: A decreasing effectiveness degree of instructions by more registers renders the deactivation of larger segments of code more likely and the effective code more brittle.

7.1.2 Constant Registers

An effective way to protect input information of programs is to forbid overwriting input registers as destination registers in instructions. *Constant input registers* could be considered unchangeable over the run. In the graph interpretation of linear programs constant input registers are constant sinks that may be direct successors of many more nodes.

For the two problems under investigation this technique has not been found to produce better results than those obtained with the standard configuration. In contrast to the approach from Section 7.1.1 the probability for selecting an input register decreases with the total number of registers. Moreover, if all input registers are constant, extra variable (writable) registers have to be provided for calculation and for storing the program output(s). These additional registers increase the search space of programs.

7.2 Number of Output Registers

In the standard case, a single register is explicitly designated in linear GP for holding the output of a program after execution.[2] Alternatively, one can check the fitness separately for *multiple output registers*. Recall that output registers may be any writable register, including input registers.

If the fitness of an individual program is calculated it is executed once for each fitness case. The content of all registers is saved after each program execution. This allows the program fitness to be calculated efficiently

---

[2]Let us assume that there is only one output defined by the problem to be solved.

multiple times without further execution while each time the content of another register may be used as the program output. The output register with which a program performs best during training is saved with the program and determines its fitness value. Note that this register may not be changed any more when the program is applied to unknown test data.

Each output register or, more precisely, the last instruction in a program that manipulates it, labels the root of a contiguous subgraph in the functional interpretation (see Section 3.3). These subprograms may be considered as *multiple solutions*. If the output register is static exactly one contiguous component is effective and tested. If the output register is dynamic, a different component becomes effective for each designated output register. Correspondingly, in the imperative code the distinction between effective and noneffective instructions depends on the definition of the output register.[3]

For both test problems, *mexican hat* and *spiral*, the performance has not been found to improve with multiple output registers over a single output register. While crossover (cross) results were almost unchanged in both test cases, instruction mutation (mut) results were more restricted. In general, the output register that is saved with the best-fit individual changed mostly at the beginning of a run. After a while one output register dominated the population. This experiment not only shows that the output register is better fixed, but also encourages the exclusive development of a single graph component, as it is possible with effective mutations.

In addition, the content of registers may be saved not only after the entire program has finished, but after the execution of each instruction. Then fitness can be checked for each program register and each program position. Oltean *et al.* [97] report on a better performance for simple regression problems when comparing this method on the basis of uniform crossover, allowing multiple crossover points and segments.

In Section 11.6 we will discuss the combination of multiple output registers.

7.3 Rate of Constants

Besides instruction operators and registers, constants represent the third basic component of linear genetic programs. The reader may recall from Section 2.1.2 that we allow only one of two operands of an instruction to

---

[3]There still may exist program instructions that are noneffective for all (potential output) registers.

hold a constant. In this way, assignments of constant values are avoided. For instance, instructions like $r_0 := 1 + 2$ or $r_0 := sin(1)$ would not be possible. There is thus at least one register for each program position whose manipulation may influence the effective code. Otherwise, if the number of effective registers becomes zero, effective variations would not be possible at each program position.

The same arguments hold for constant register operands, like inputs that have been discussed in Section 7.1.2.[4] While number and range of constants (we use $\{0, .., 9\}$) in the terminal set are problem-dependent parameters, we examine the number of operands *in programs* that represent constants. This number equals the number of instructions holding a constant and is controlled by the probability by which constants are created in programs during mutation and initialization. At standard configuration a probability of 50 percent is used in most experiments. This has been found to be a good choice, in general. Note that the composition of programs, i.e., the distribution of program elements in the population, is strongly influenced by fitness selection.

Table 7.7. mexican hat: Effects of different proportions of instructions holding a constant (**effmut, B1**). Average results over 100 runs after 1,000 generations.

Constants (%)	SSE		Length			#Eff.	Eff.	Eff.Dep.
	mean	*std.*	*abs.*	*eff.*	%	Registers	Degree	Distance
0	1.2	0.2	41	36	88	3.7	1.5	2.0
50	0.6	0.06	33	28	85	2.8	1.2	1.6
100	33.8	0.01	18	11	60	1.0	0.9	0.9

Table 7.8. spiral: Effects of different proportions of instructions holding a constant (**effmut, B1**). Average results over 100 runs after 1,000 generations.

Constants (%)	CE		Length			#Eff.	Eff.	Eff.Dep.
	mean	*std.*	*abs.*	*eff.*	%	Registers	Degree	Distance
0	10.1	0.5	62	59	96	5.0	3.7	2.7
50	8.4	0.4	66	62	95	4.6	3.3	3.1
100	12.8	0.5	69	63	91	4.1	2.5	3.9

For the *mexican hat* problem, Table 7.7 compares prediction performance, program size and program characteristics for different rates of constants. Interestingly, prediction error increases significantly less from the baseline

---

[4]In our implementation, constant values are saved in registers (see Section 2.1.1). Instead of holding constants directly in instructions they are addressed via register indices. These "registers" differ from what is referred to as a constant (input) register in that their value may not change between two executions of the same program.

case of 50% if constants are completely forbidden, than if each instruction includes a constant value. Moreover, both absolute and effective program size become smaller the more instructions hold a single register operand.

These results may be explained by having a look at the functional structure of programs. If all instructions use the result of only one other instruction the graph is reduced to a linear list of operator nodes. Such a restriction makes the emergence of successful solutions for complex problems impossible or, at least, substantially more difficult. As a result, the average number of effective registers, the average degree of effectiveness and the average effective dependence distance are constantly 1 for all effective programs.[5]

The results in Table 7.8 show, by contrast, that the *spiral* classification is less influenced by the rate of constants in linear programs, as can be seen for almost all observed features. This behavior can be attributed to the fact that branches are used for this problem. With branches, the data flow is not restricted to a linear list of nodes even if all instructions operate on a single register only.

7.4 Population Size

The evolutionary algorithm that is used throughout the book (see Section 2.3.2) operates on a steady-state population. Population size is an important parameter when comparing mutation-based with recombination-based variation.

The performance of recombination depends by definition on the composition of the genetic material in the population. The genotype diversity of a population influences innovation in a positive way, while larger populations allow a higher diversity than smaller ones.

On the other hand, population size may have a smaller influence on the performance of mutations which generate diversity by continuously introducing new genetic material into the population. It has to be noted, however, that diversity is not the only system attribute that is influenced by the population size. Even a pure mutation-based approach may still benefit from the higher parallelism of the search in larger populations. Moreover, as we will see below, population size has an influence on the complexity of solutions.

---

[5]The last two parameters in Table 7.7 are slightly smaller due to programs with effective length 0. The first parameter calculates 1 for these programs because at least the output register stays effective.

If solution quality is compared for different population sizes on the basis of a constant number of generations, larger populations always produce better results. More evaluations are performed per generation while average number of evaluations (and variations) _per individual_ remains the same. The number of evaluations equals the number of variations since newly created individuals are the only ones evaluated. A fair comparison can only be guaranteed if runtime is measured on the basis of fitness evaluations.

The smaller the population size, the more often an individual is selected for variation and the more variations occur within a certain number of generations. If a population does not have enough individuals in relation to the number of evaluations, performance will depend more strongly on the composition of the initial genetic material and code diversity may be quite low.

With a larger population, more solutions may be developed in parallel. However, if a population has too many individuals in relation to the number of evaluations, the number of variations per individual may not be sufficient to develop successful solutions. Then success will depend more on random events than on real evolutionary progress.

Table 7.9. _mexican hat_: Effects of population size on crossover (cross). Average results over 100 runs after 1,000,000 evaluations.

Population Size	#Generations	SSE		Length			Variations (%)		
		mean	_std._	_abs._	_eff._	_%_	_constr._	_neutral_	_noneff._
10	100,000	23.2	2.4	143	74	52	4.5	39	24
100	10,000	12.4	1.4	196	91	46	5.6	24	18
1,000	1,000	16.1	1.5	180	60	33	4.5	28	25
10,000	100	11.9	1.3	97	21	22	4.4	36	33

Table 7.10. _spiral_: Effects of population size on crossover (cross). Average results over 100 runs after 1,000,000 evaluations.

Population Size	#Generations	CE		Length			Variations (%)		
		mean	_std._	_abs._	_eff._	_%_	_constr._	_neutral_	_noneff._
10	100,000	45.3	3.6	109	83	76	2.9	41	31
100	10,000	23.5	0.7	196	125	64	3.8	18	11
1,000	1,000	26.1	0.7	185	102	55	3.6	23	14
10,000	100	24.7	0.4	125	53	42	3.0	38	23

Table 7.9 and Table 7.10 demonstrate that crossover performs worst in very small populations. It is interesting to see that the relative difference in performance is rather low with larger population sizes after the

same number of evaluations. When using effective mutations, the situation is less clear. For the *spiral* problem best solutions are obtained with the smallest population size (see Table 7.12). The *mexican hat* problem, instead, is solved most successfully with a medium population size (see Table 7.11). Only if the number of generations falls below a certain minimum, the performance decreases again. This example demonstrates that a pure mutation-based approach does not automatically perform better with a smaller population size. In general, crossover performance seems to depend less on the relation of population size and generation number than instruction mutations.

Table 7.11.   mexican hat: Effects of population size on effective mutations (effmut2, B0). Average results over 100 runs after 1,000,000 evaluations.

Population	#Generations	SSE		Length			Variations (%)		
Size		*mean*	*std.*	*abs.*	*eff.*	*%*	*constr.*	*neutral*	*noneff.*
10	100,000	1.8	0.3	119	66	56	8.2	5.2	0
100	10,000	1.1	0.1	70	43	62	9.0	6.3	0
1,000	1,000	**0.7**	0.05	39	25	64	8.4	9.9	0
10,000	100	2.8	0.2	21	12	55	9.0	16.6	0

Table 7.12.   spiral: Effects of population size on effective mutations (effmut2, B0). Average results over 100 runs after 1,000,000 evaluations.

Population	#Generations	CE		Length			Variations (%)		
Size		*mean*	*std.*	*abs.*	*eff.*	*%*	*constr.*	*neutral*	*noneff.*
10	100,000	**5.7**	0.3	122	105	86	1.5	16	0
100	10,000	7.5	0.4	96	88	92	1.4	29	0
1,000	1,000	11.6	0.4	51	47	92	2.2	20	0
10,000	100	25.5	0.5	24	18	76	3.4	31	0

The different optimal population sizes found for the two test problems may result from a different correlation between solution quality and solution size. Population size clearly influences code growth, especially when using effective mutations. But why do programs become larger in smaller population? As long as larger solutions show a better fitness, an individual may grow larger in a smaller population because it is selected and varied more frequently. Likewise, causes of code growth other than fitness may be reinforced (see Chapter 10). In particular, more neutral variations per individual may create more neutral code.

The small absolute step size of instruction mutations may lead programs to grow only insufficiently in larger populations if only a few generations are observed.

7.5   Maximum Program Length

The simplest form of growth control in genetic programming is to keep
the maximum size limit of programs as small as necessary for representing successful solutions. In tree-based GP this is the maximum number of
nodes or the maximum tree depth [64]. In linear GP we restrict the maximum number of program instructions. In this section the influence of the
maximum program length is examined for unlimited linear crossover. In
contrast to crossover, effective mutations control complexity of programs
themselves. For effective mutations, the upper bound of program length
may be chosen sufficiently large to not be reached within an observed
period of generations.

Table 7.13. *mexican hat*: Effects of maximum program length on crossover (cross).
Average results over 100 runs after 1,000 generations.

Maximum	SSE		Length			Variations (%)		
Length	*mean*	*std.*	*abs.*	*eff.*	%	*constr.*	*neutral*	*noneff.*
25	10.3	1.2	25	15	62	5.6	24	22
50	**4.8**	0.8	48	26	54	5.3	24	22
100	8.4	1.2	94	40	43	5.0	26	23
200	16.1	1.5	180	60	33	4.5	28	25
500	20.4	1.5	410	97	24	4.1	32	28
1,000	21.0	1.5	751	145	19	3.9	35	31

Table 7.14. *spiral*: Effects of maximum program length on crossover (cross). Average
results over 100 runs after 1,000 generations.

Maximum	CE		Length			Variations (%)		
Length	*mean*	*std.*	*abs.*	*eff.*	%	*constr.*	*neutral*	*noneff.*
20	37.7	0.7	20	16	78	4.5	19	13
50	30.2	0.8	49	34	69	3.9	20	14
100	27.9	0.7	96	59	61	3.8	22	15
200	26.1	0.7	185	102	55	3.6	23	14
500	23.3	0.7	446	216	48	3.5	26	16
1,000	**21.7**	0.6	858	392	46	3.3	27	16

Tables 7.13 and 7.14 show exactly the opposite effect on the performance
of our two test problems. While *mexican hat* benefits from a small maximum size of solutions, *spiral* does not. Most successful solutions for the
regression problem may be assumed in low-dimensional regions of the
search space, while for the classification task even very large effective solutions perform better. In other words, fitness is positively correlated with
program size for the latter problem. For the former problem there is a

similar behavior until a sufficiently large maximum size has been reached. Beyond that point, the correlation becomes negative.

One important general conclusion can be drawn from the fact that even very long linear programs still improve results: the underlying graph representation is not restricted in scalability, neither the graph depth nor the graph width.

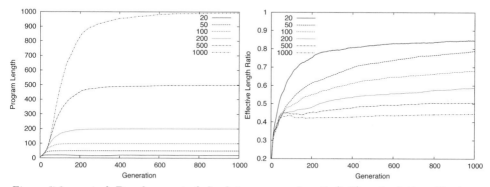

Figure 7.2. *spiral*: Development of absolute program length (left) and relative effective length (right) for different maximum bounds using crossover (**cross**). The less code growth is restricted by the maximum complexity bound, the smaller the proportion of effective code and the less it increases over a run. Average figures over 100 runs.

In both tables, absolute length and effective length increase with the maximum bound. Simultaneously, the proportion of effective code decreases. Figure 7.2 shows the development of both the absolute program length and the proportion of effective code (*relative effective length*) over an exemplary run for different bounds on maximum length. Absolute length in the population converges quickly to the maximum during a run. This development can only be delayed depending on how large a maximum bound is configured and is characterized by an explosive increase of program length in early generations. Unlimited exchange of instruction segments during crossover causes this behavior. Another cause is that noneffective code may grow almost without restrictions in linear GP since it does not directly influence program fitness and emerges relatively easily.

The rate of effective code increases because this type of code may still grow even if the absolute length of a program is already maximal. In this way, noneffective code is replaced by effective code. Interestingly, the proportion of effective code remains mostly constant over a run with the highest maximum bound (1,000 instructions).

In general, a lower proportion of effective instructions in programs reduces the effective step size of crossover, meaning that less effective instructions are exchanged. This is, however, not the case here for a higher maximum program bound which leads to a larger absolute step size, on average, as well as an increasing *amount* of effective code.[6] As a result, *more* effective instructions are exchanged.

For the same reason, the proportion of noneffective variations increases only slightly compared to the proportion of noneffective code in Tables 7.13 and 7.14. We only note here that this is different for free instruction mutations where a minimum step size causes the effectiveness of operations to depend more directly on the proportion of effective instructions.

7.6 Initialization of Linear Programs

The initialization of individuals is the first step of an evolutionary algorithm. In genetic programming it determines the size, shape, and diversity of programs in the initial population. Depending on the type of program representation, different strategies may be developed. Popular methods for initializing tree populations will be discussed in Section 8.1.2. In this section we define and compare different initialization methods for the linear representation. Basically, the following forms are available:

☐ *Free initialization* creates initial programs randomly (standard case).

☐ *(Fully) effective initialization* builds initial programs completely from structurally effective code, starting with the last instruction of a program (see Section 6.2.3).

☐ *Maximum initialization* lets the absolute length of all initial programs equal the maximum program length parameter.

☐ *Variable-length initialization* selects initial program lengths from a uniform distribution within a predefined range.

☐ *Constant-length initialization* enforces the same initial length for all programs in a population.

These different strategies make reference to the *initial absolute length* of programs. The *initial effective length* may vary freely and is controlled indirectly through the initial absolute length. A fully effective initialization allows higher effective diversity of initial programs without increasing the total amount of genetic material.

---

[6]Recall that a larger amount of noneffective code implies a larger amount of effective code, especially if only a few program registers are available.

If programs are initialized with too large a size they may be less flexible during evolutionary search, especially if the average step size of macro variations is small. The minimum step size of instruction mutations lends itself well to achieving best prediction quality by starting with relatively small initial programs (see Tables 7.15 and 7.17). Moreover, both the absolute size and the effective size of solutions will increase clearly by effective mutations if a longer initial size is chosen. In general, it seems to be more difficult for the evolutionary algorithm to follow a search path from a complex region of the search space to another complex region with better programs than it would be to start with programs of low complexity and evolve them into programs with high complexity.

Table 7.15. mexican hat: Effects of initial program length on effective mutations (eff-mut2, B0) using free initialization. Maximum program length is 200. Average results over 100 runs after 1,000 generations.

Initial	SSE		Length			Variations (%)		
Length	*mean*	*std.*	*abs.*	*eff.*	*%*	*constr.*	*neutral*	*noneff.*
5	**0.6**	0.06	39	26	67	8.3	10	0
10	0.7	0.1	39	26	65	8.5	10	0
50	0.9	0.1	70	38	54	8.7	9	0
100	1.2	0.1	115	54	47	8.6	9	0
200	3.5	0.4	196	79	40	8.6	11	0

Table 7.16. mexican hat: Effects of initial program length on effective mutations (eff-mut2, B0) using effective initialization. Maximum program length is 200. Average results over 100 runs after 1,000 generations.

Initial	SSE		Length			Variations (%)		
Length	*mean*	*std.*	*abs.*	*eff.*	*%*	*constr.*	*neutral*	*noneff.*
5	0.6	0.06	36	25	69	8.5	10	0
10	**0.4**	0.05	40	28	69	8.6	9	0
50	1.0	0.1	72	48	67	8.6	9	0
100	2.5	0.2	120	77	64	8.4	11	0
200	6.0	0.5	196	118	60	7.7	16	0

Figure 7.4 shows for the example of the *mexican hat* problem, how the program length develops when applying effective mutations with different initial lengths. The effective length continuously increases during a run in almost the same amount. Therefore, it strongly depends on the initialization, how large programs may become in the end. Apparently, maximum mutation steps of one instruction are too small to be able to sufficiently break up larger initial structures.

Table 7.17. *spiral*: Effects of initial program length on effective mutations (effmut2, B0) using free initialization. Maximum program length is 200. Average results over 100 runs after 1,000 generations.

Initial	CE		Length			Variations (%)		
Length	*mean*	*std.*	*abs.*	*eff.*	*%*	*constr.*	*neutral*	*noneff.*
5	**10.1**	0.5	50	46	92	2.1	20	0
10	11.3	0.5	55	50	91	2.1	20	0
50	14.2	0.6	82	69	85	1.9	21	0
100	16.8	0.6	128	100	78	1.7	24	0
200	22.3	0.6	197	136	69	2.0	23	0

Table 7.18. *spiral*: Effects of initial program length on effective mutations (effmut2, B0) using effective initialization. Maximum program length is 200. Average results over 100 runs after 1,000 generations.

Initial	CE		Length			Variations (%)		
Length	*mean*	*std.*	*abs.*	*eff.*	*%*	*constr.*	*neutral*	*noneff.*
5	10.0	0.5	50	46	92	2.2	20	0
10	**8.6**	0.5	53	48	91	2.1	21	0
50	16.4	0.6	83	74	89	2.2	21	0
100	22.7	0.6	132	116	87	2.2	22	0
200	31.0	0.5	198	175	88	3.4	19	0

In Figure 7.3 we can see, by comparison, that the more (effective) code exists initially, the less the (effective) length grows in the course of the evolutionary algorithm with unrestricted linear crossover, i.e., in standard linear GP. Interestingly, the effective size converges to almost the same value in the final generation, no matter how large the initial programs were. Similar results have been observed with (unrestricted) segment mutation. Apparently, larger step sizes allow (effective) programs to grow almost independent of their initial (effective) size.

After a free initialization, neither with crossover nor with effective mutation the effective length falls below its initial level. But a rapid drop of effective length occurs at the beginning of runs in Figure 7.5 if longer individuals were initialized fully effectively. This decrease has been found with both benchmark problems and results from early deactivation of code. However, the absence of inactive, that is noneffective, code in the initial population reduces the emergence of such code during a run. As a consequence, the effective code remains larger than with standard initialization.

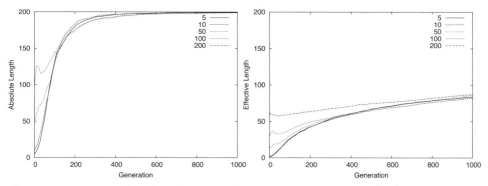

Figure 7.3. *mexican hat*: Development of absolute program length (left) and effective program length (right) for different inital lengths using free initialization and crossover (**cross**). Average figures over 100 runs.

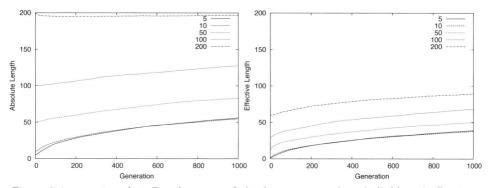

Figure 7.4. *mexican hat*: Development of absolute program length (left) and effective program length (right) for different initial lengths using free initialization and effective mutations (**effmut2, B0**). Average figures over 100 runs.

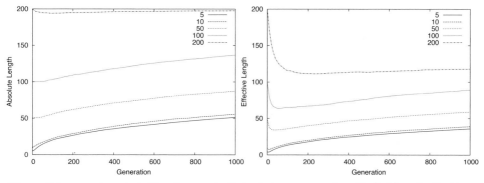

Figure 7.5. *mexican hat*: Development of absolute program length (left) and effective program length (right) for different initial lengths using fully effective initialization and effective mutations (**effmut2, B0**). Average figures over 100 runs. (Similar figures found for the *spiral* problem.)

From the comparison of Table 7.15 with Table 7.16 we can see that effective initialization results in worse performance for larger initial programs than standard initialization, as is confirmed by a comparison of Table 7.17 with Table 7.18. A slightly better performance is obtained only with constant initial length 10, probably due to a higher diversity of initial effective solutions.

If the initial lengths are too small, many programs may be identical in both their effective structure and their semantics. In particular, many initial programs may have an effective length of zero. Initialization influences diversity in such a way that both *more* or *longer* programs allow a higher diversity. If variation is dominated by recombination the composition of the initial population has a stronger influence on the success of solutions (see also Section 7.4). This is another reason, besides its larger absolute step size, why crossover may perform better with a higher amount of initial genetic material. At least the *mexican hat* problem is better solved with longer initial programs (see Tables 7.19 and 7.20).

Table 7.19. *mexican hat*: Effects of initial program length on crossover (cross) using free initialization. Maximum program length is 200. Average results over 100 runs after 1,000 generations.

Initial	SSE		Length			Variations (%)		
Length	*mean*	*std.*	*abs.*	*eff.*	%	*constr.*	*neutral*	*noneff.*
5	15.0	1.5	179	60	33	4.7	29	25
10	15.5	1.4	180	58	32	4.4	29	25
50	7.4	1.0	180	61	34	4.8	26	23
100	**5.4**	0.6	184	63	34	5.1	25	21
200	6.9	0.6	200	73	37	5.3	25	19

Table 7.20. *spiral*: Effects of initial program length on crossover (cross) using free initialization. Maximum program length is 200. Average results over 100 runs after 1,000 generations.

Initial	CE		Length			Variations (%)		
Length	*mean*	*std.*	*abs.*	*eff.*	%	*constr.*	*neutral*	*noneff.*
5	28.1	0.6	187	113	61	4.1	22	12
10	**25.7**	0.6	186	101	54	3.6	24	15
50	26.0	0.7	187	97	52	3.3	24	16
100	30.1	0.7	188	94	50	3.4	24	16
200	36.1	0.7	200	103	52	4.1	24	14

We have seen in Section 5.9.5 that smaller effective length may be maintained in linear programs by initializing programs partially with empty instructions (explicit introns). Furthermore, the proportion of implicit introns is significantly reduced in this way and, thus, reactivations are much less likely. For both reasons, crossover steps become smaller in terms of the effective code. Figure 7.3 demonstrates that this may not be achieved simply by increasing the initial program length. If program size is doubled only, effective size will double, too.

In the experiments described above, all initial programs share the same absolute length. One remaining question is whether variable-length programs can produce significantly better results. In general, we found that a variable-length initialization changes prediction error and program size only slightly if compared to a constant-length initialization with the same average length. This is mostly due to the fact that random programs may still differ in their effective length even if their absolute length is constant. Also note that there is no relevant difference in performance if the initial length is small. Only if initial programs are large enough and fully-effective, variable length may outperform constant length.

7.7 Constant Program Length

Genetic programming usually evolves programs of a variable-length representation. Typically, the population is initialized with small programs that grow in the course of the evolutionary process. The traditional tree representation requires that programs change size and shape for creating successful solutions. Otherwise, if valid programs would be restricted to a constant number of nodes or a certain shape of trees, variability and chances of finding a solution may be quite small.

The imperative representation used in linear GP contains inactive code that emerges almost independent of the composition of the set of program components provided (see Section 3.2). The only precondition for this special type of intron code is that the number of registers the program can write into is larger than one. The existence of structurally inactive code, together with the fact that data flow between registers is organized as a graph, allows evolution of genetic programs without changing their absolute size. Programs may thus be initialized with a certain absolute length which remains constant during the entire run while the effective length of the program may change.

The evolution of fixed-length programs requires that absolute program length is determined by the user instead of being subject of the evolutionary algorithm. This is a drawback first because the absolute length may have a significant influence on prediction performance, and second because programs have their maximum size already from the beginning of a run. Thus, using a constant absolute program size is a combination of maximum initialization and a restriction of program length. Both techniques have been investigated separately in the two previous sections.

As it might have been expected, we have not found constant program length to be a feasible alternative to a growing program length. With effective instruction mutation, results were generally worse or at least not better. With standard crossover, performance improved only for the *mexican hat* problem and smaller fixed-length programs (undocumented). Recall that this problem gained in both partial experiments above, i.e., a complexity control by a smaller maximum program size and a higher diversity by longer initial code.

7.8 Summary and Conclusion

Different control parameters were examined in this chapter with respect to their influence on linear GP. Some important results are summarized in the following.

☐ The performance of linear GP strongly depends on the number of calculation registers. Smaller register numbers will restrict the expressiveness of programs while larger numbers may increase the search space unnecessarily. The more registers are provided the more registers may be effective and the lower will be the effectiveness degree of instructions. For functional structure this means wider graphs with less connections per node. An intermediate register number produced the best prediction results. More tree-like structures, as may result from higher register numbers, were usually not optimal.

☐ An initialization of all registers with input values achieved better results in general than initializing additional calculation registers to constant values or write-protecting the input registers.

☐ The question of whether a smaller or a larger population size leads to more successful solutions could not be answered clearly (if compared on the basis of the same number of evaluations). Instruction mutation showed a significantly better performance in small populations for certain problems. Basically, this depends on the size of the optimum solution. In a smaller population programs grew larger, especially if the variation step size was small.

☐ The relation of program size and fitness determines how much a problem solution benefits from a higher bound on complexity. When using unrestricted recombination, linear programs grow quickly until the maximum length is reached. This happens for both effective and noneffective code, even if a larger upper bound led to a smaller *proportion* of effective code.

Because a large maximum program length can still produce better results, the graph-based linear representation is not restricted in scalability.

☐ Finally, we compared possible initialization methods for linear genetic programs, including *maximum* and *fully effective*. In general, effective instruction mutation performed worse with a larger initial size of programs. Apparently, small absolute step size of the operator is less suitable to transform larger random structures. This was different for unrestricted segment variation which can perform better with more initial code.

Chapter 8

A COMPARISON WITH TREE-BASED GENETIC PROGRAMMING

In this chapter a comparison between the linear representation and the traditional tree representation of genetic programming is performed. The comparison examines prediction performance and model size based on two collections of benchmark problems that have been composed of artificial test problems and of real-world applications from bioinformatics, respectively. Both linear GP and tree-based GP use crossover for macro variations. Additionally, we apply the linear GP variant from Section 6.2.3 which works exclusively with (effective) instruction mutations to compare its performance for a larger number of problems. But first of all, we introduce tree-based GP in some further detail.

8.1 Tree-Based Genetic Programming

The earliest and most commonly used approach to genetic programming is the evolution of tree structures represented by variable-length expressions from a functional programming language, like S-expressions in LISP [64]. This classic approach is referred to as *tree-based genetic programming* (TGP). The inner nodes of such program trees hold *functions* (*instructions*). The leaves hold *terminals* which are input variables or constants.

Pure functional programs, by definition, do not include assignments to memory variables as is the case in imperative programs. These have to be incorporated explicitly by means of special functions which realize read and write access to an external memory [64, 134]. Such "imperative" extensions are, however, not in common use because they do not necessarily provide a significant increase in expressiveness of functional programs.

However, memory – usually in the form of a stack – is needed during the interpretation of program trees in order to save intermediate results of evaluated subtrees (see also Section 3.3.3). While a program tree is evaluated the nodes are traversed in a predefined order (preorder or postorder). The value of a node is calculated by applying its function to the results of its child nodes (subtrees) which have to be evaluated first. Then the value is returned to the parent node. At the end of execution the root node holds the final program output.

Assignments to an external memory may be used if a program solution is supposed to return more than one output. Otherwise, multiple outputs could be read from a tree program at specially designated inner nodes, apart from the tree root [79]. Finally, multiple program outputs may be implemented such that individuals are multiple expressions (trees) which calculate one output each.

8.1.1   Tree Genetic Operators

Crossover is traditionally the genetic operator of choice used for recombining old solutions into new and potentially better solutions. Figure 8.1 illustrates program representation and *subtree crossover* in tree-based GP. In each parent individual the crossover operator selects a node (*crossover point*) randomly and swaps the two corresponding subtrees to create two offspring individuals. Function (inner) nodes might be chosen as crossover points with a higher probability than terminal nodes. Koza proposes a 90 percent selection of inner nodes [64].

The mutation operator exchanges single terminals or function identifiers. Each tree node may be selected as a mutation point with the same probability. A *node mutation* replaces a random function by a legal alternative from the function set that requires the same number of operands. In doing so, loss or creation of complete subtrees is avoided. Functions may not be exchanged with terminals. A certain amount of constants is maintained in programs by fixing user-defined probabilities for constant and variable terminals.

Alternatively, a *subtree mutation* replaces a complete subtree by a random subtree. For creation of a new subtree the same method may be applied that is used for initialization of programs. In contrast to crossover, however, it has to be explicitly guaranteed that subtree mutation is bias-free. This will be the case if inserted subtrees are on average the same size as deleted subtrees.

In standard TGP crossover is aborted and its effects are reversed, if one of the offspring exceeds the maximum complexity bound. Since the parent

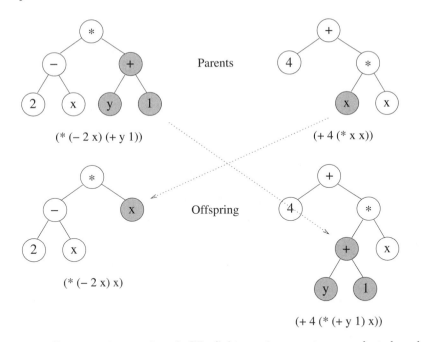

Figure 8.1. Crossover in tree-based GP. Subtrees in parents are selected and exchanged.

individuals are not modified in this case, they neither have to be reproduced in a steady-state population nor have their fitness re-evaluated. The *maximum depth* parameter limits the maximum length of a path from the root to a leaf. If only depth is limited, as practiced in [64] (using a maximum depth of 17) programs may still become extremely large in number of nodes, especially if a larger number of generations is considered. In order to tighten the bound a maximum limit may be placed on both the number of nodes *and* the depth of tree programs.

In order for tree crossover to remain executable after parent individuals have reached their maximum complexity, one method may exchange equally large subtrees. This, however, restricts the free selection of variation points drastically. For the comparison of this chapter we decided to use a variant that limits the freedom of variation the least by executing the crossover operation in any case. If an offspring tree becomes too large in the number of nodes, the node at the crossover point is replaced by one of its direct successors (*after* crossover). The old node and all its other subtrees are deleted. This step is repeated until the total tree size falls below the maximum bound. Note that in contrast to selecting valid subtrees already in the parent individuals (*before* crossover) the positions of crossover points can be selected more freely here.

Recall from Section 5.7.1 that crossover in linear GP is always possible by exchanging equally long instruction segments if otherwise the maximum program length would be exceeded. This is mostly due to a higher variability (weaker constraints) of the imperative representation which allows the existence of noneffective code not connected to the root in the equivalent functional program.

In general, using genetic programming without any complexity bound is rather uncommon since unnecessarily large solutions are not desirable. First, they are less flexible during genetic manipulations. Within a certain number of generations reasonable progress may only be made up to a certain complexity of solutions. Otherwise, too complex variations might be necessary to find improvements. Second, larger programs increase the processing time both during and after the search. Third, interpretation of larger solutions is potentially more difficult. Finally, the principle of Occam's Razor states that shorter (equally fit) solutions are more general than longer ones. For these reasons low complexity is an important quality of genetic programs, besides a high prediction performance.

8.1.2   Initialization of Tree Programs

Genetic programs are created randomly from elements of the function and terminal set. Different initialization methods are applied in tree-based GP that control the composition of genetic material in the initial population.

☐ The *full method* generates only full trees, i.e., trees with all terminal nodes on the same level. In other words, the path length from any terminal node to the root of the tree is the same.

☐ The *grow method* chooses any node (function or terminal) for the root, then recursively calls itself to generate child trees if these are needed. If the tree reaches the maximum depth, all further nodes are restricted to be terminals and growth will stop. The shape and size of trees strongly depends on the probabilities by which a terminal node or a function node is selected.

☐ The *half-and-half method* merely chooses the full method 50 percent of the time and the grow method the other 50 percent.

All of these generation methods can be specified with a "ramp" of initial depth values instead of using the same depth. For instance, if the ramp is 2–5, then 25 percent of the trees will be generated with depth 2, 25 percent will be generated with depth 3, and so on. *Ramped half-and-half* is typically the method of choice for initialization since it produces a wide variety of tree shapes and sizes.

8.2   Benchmark Problems

The benchmark problems that are used in this chapter for a comparison with tree-based GP comprise three problem classes. These are classification, regression, and Boolean functions.

In general, a GP benchmark may be regarded as a combination of problem (data set) and instruction set. The difficulty of a problem strongly depends on the composition of the function set in GP since this set may, in principle, hold any function – including the optimal solution of a problem should this be known (trivial case). For artificial benchmark problems for which the optimal solution is already known in advance the absolute best configuration is not always desired. Instead, the problem difficulty is scaled over the set of elementary functions provided. An optimization of the function set may be interesting in more application-oriented research or if one wanted to compare the performance of GP with other methods.

8.2.1   GP Benchmarks (GPPROBEN)

The first set of problems tested is referred to as GPPROBEN. Some problems became popular benchmarks in the GP community or in the machine learning community, respectively. Others have already been used in experiments of this document, but not necessarily with the same configuration. Table 8.1 summarizes all relevant problem characteristics and problem-specific configurations. These comprise dimensions of data set, fitness function, and function set.

Table 8.1. Complexity and configuration of GPPROBEN problems. Maximum input and output ranges are rounded. Set of constants is $\{0,1\}$ for Boolean problems and $\{1,..,9\}$ otherwise.

Problem	#Inputs	Input Range	Output Range	#Samples	Fitness	Function Set
11multiplexer	11	$\{0,1\}$	$\{0,1\}$	2048	SE	$\{\wedge, \vee, \neg, if\}$
even5parity	5	$\{0,1\}$	$\{0,1\}$	32	SE	$\{\wedge, \vee, \neg\}$
even8parity	8	$\{0,1\}$	$\{0,1\}$	256	SE	$\{\wedge, \vee, \neg, if\}$
two chains	3	$[-2,2]$	$\{0,1\}$	500	CE	$\{+, -, \times, /, sin, cos, if >\}$
spiral	2	$[-2\pi, 2\pi]$	$\{0,1\}$	194	CE	$\{+, -, \times, /, sin, cos, if >\}$
double sine	1	$[0, 2\pi]$	$[-1,1]$	100	SSE	$\{+, -, \times, /\}$
distance	6	$[0,1]$	$[0,1]$	300	SSE	$\{+, -, \times, /, \sqrt{x}, x^2\}$
mexican hat	2	$[-4,4]$	$[-1,1]$	256	SSE	$\{+, -, \times, /, e^x, x^2\}$

Among Boolean functions, the **11multiplexer** function calculates 1 of 8 input bits as output value that is singled out by 3 address bits [64]. The **evenNparity** functions compute 1 if the number of set input bits is even, otherwise the output is 0. Note that the lower-dimensional parity problem even5parity is treated without using Boolean branches here. Fitness function for Boolean problems is the sum of output errors (SE).

The two classification problems, spiral and two chains, are described in Section 5.8.1 and Section 11.4.1, respectively. For all classification problems in this chapter the classification error (CE) defines program fitness. The classification method is always *interval classification* which holds a program output $gp(\vec{i_k})$ to be correct for an input vector $\vec{i_k}$ as long as the distance to the defined class identifier $o_k \in \{0, .., m\}$ is smaller than 0.5, i.e., $|gp(\vec{i_k}) - o_k| < 0.5$.

The one-dimensional regression problem double sine requires a sine function to be approximated by arithmetic functions over an input range of two periods. For a description of the two-dimensional regression mexican hat and the six-dimensional distance problem see Sections 5.8.1 and 11.4.1.

8.2.2 Bioinformatics Problems (BIOPROBEN)

The second set of benchmarks BIOPROBEN contains real-world classification problems. Most problems originate from the *UCI Repository of Machine Learning Databases* [88], and all have a biological background. Typically, such problems feature high dimensional input data. The original data sets have been edited slightly.

Table 8.2. Complexity of BIOPROBEN data sets. For all these classifications problems a common fitness function (CE) and function set $\{+, -, \times, /, x^y, if >, if \leq\}$ are used.

Problem	#Inputs	#Classes	Input Range	Output Range	#Samples
splice junction	60	3	$\{1, .., 4\}$	$\{0, 1, 2\}$	1594
splice junction 2	60	2	$\{0, .., 3\}$	$\{0, 1\}$	768
promoters	57	2	$\{0, .., 3\}$	$\{0, 1\}$	106
ecoli	7	8	$[0, 1]$	$\{0, .., 7\}$	336
helicases	25	2	$[0, 1]$	$\{0, 1\}$	78
soybean	35	19	$\{0, .., 6\}$	$\{1, .., 19\}$	307
wine	13	3	*continuous*	$\{1, .., 3\}$	178
dermatology	34	6	$\{0, .., 3\}$	$\{1, .., 6\}$	366

Table 8.2 summarizes all features of the BIOPROBEN data sets, including input dimension, number of output classes, and number of (training) samples. Most input ranges are discrete and comprise possible states of attributes.

☐ Splice junctions are points on a DNA sequence at which "superfluous" DNA is removed during the process of protein creation in higher organisms. The **splice junction** data set is composed of sequences of 60 nucleotide positions extracted from the DNA of primates. The problem represented by this data set is to recognize boundaries between exons (the parts of DNA sequence retained after splicing) and introns (the parts of DNA sequence spliced out). The problem consists of two subtasks: recognizing exon/intron boundaries (called EI sites), and recognizing the inverse, intron/exon boundaries (IE sites). In the biological community, IE borders are also referred to as *acceptors* while EI borders are referred to as *donors*. About 50 percent of the data comprise non-splice examples that have been taken from sequences known to not include a splicing site at all. The nominal attribute values A, G, T, and C – representing the four nucleotide bases from which DNA is built – have been replaced by numeric values (see Table 8.2). Some unknown or uncertain characters are represented by 0. The problem comes with three data sets, one for each class. The first half of each set is used for training, the following quarter of the set for validation, and the last quarter for test purposes (see below). A second data set **splice junction 2** is derived by excluding all non-splice examples. This results in the simpler task to distinguish IE sites from EI sites only.

☐ Another problem that deals with the classification of DNA sequences is **promoters**. A *promoter* initiates the process of gene expression, i.e., the biosynthesis of a protein. The task is to predict whether subsequences of *E. coli* DNA belong to a region with biological promoter activity or not. Each subsequence holds 57 nucleotides.

☐ The **ecoli** data require the cellular localization sites of proteins in *E. coli* bacteria to be predicted from several values measured. In doing so, eight classes which correspond to localization sites have to be discriminated.

☐ **Helicases** is an image classification problem. Two different structures of hexametric helicases of DNA strands [28] need to be discerned from electron microscopy images.

☐ A diagnosis of 19 different soybean diseases has to be learned from the **soybean** data. 13 percent of the data samples suffer from missing input values (completed here by constant value 7).

☐ The task described by the **wine** data set is to discern three sorts of wine by their constituents resulting from chemical analysis.

☐ The last problem comes from the medical domain, more precisely the differential diagnosis of erythemato-squamous diseases is a **dermatology** task. The difficulty of this problem results from the fact that all six

Linear Genetic Programming

diseases share most clinical and histopathological features of erythema with only very little differences.

8.2.3 Generalization Data

The most important capability of a prediction model is its ability to generalize from a given set of input-output examples to unknown (unlabeled) data inputs. The generalization ability strongly depends on the correlation of training data to generalization data. As far as possible, both data sets should cover the same region of the data space. In general, the problem definition defines the domains of input and output data, including dimensions and attribute ranges. Especially in complex or higher dimensional data spaces, however, there is a higher probability that the correlation between two randomly selected sets of data points is poor. Moreover, generalization performance depends on the size of the training data set and how regularly training data are distributed over data space.

These problems occur in particular when dealing with data derived from a real problem domain. Often it comprises much more data points than may be sufficiently represented in the training set. On the other hand, the available amount of data samples is very often limited. But even if both are not the case, data samples may be difficult to select uniformly distributed if the structure of the data space is unknown. As a result, correlation of training data and generalization data may be low.

The use of artificial test problems may give a better understanding for what types of problems a method is suitable and for what types it is not. Moreover, since the problem structure is known, artificial benchmarks give a better idea of the problem difficulty. The difficulty is often scalable over slight modifications of the problem definition.

The identification of generalization data is straightforward for the regression problems. For these problems generalization can be called interpolation. For the mexican hat problem, for instance, test data points are selected randomly between the regular grid of training data points (see Figure 5.2). For the distance problem generalization data are created in the same way as the training data by calculating the Euclidean distance for different random pairs of 3-dimensional points from the same input ranges.

Since we do not want to separate two "clouds" of fixed data points only in the case of the two chains problem (see Figure 11.5), the data space is supposed to include all points that lie within a certain distance from two virtual circles in three-dimensional space.

In some data sets of the BIOPROBEN collection, e.g., in ecoli, the distribution of data samples over the output classes is rather non-uniform with some classes under-represented. In other data sets the total number of samples is relatively small compared to the number of inputs, e.g., in promoters.

In both cases it is difficult to split a data set for training, validation and testing. Results might leave too much to chance to be general. One possibility to get more reliable generalization results with relatively small data sets is to apply *n-fold cross validation*, a method that divides data into *n* disjoint subsets and repeats the training process *n* times while each time another subset is excluded from training and is used instead for validation. We have not done this here. Instead, we restrict ourselves to the problems with sufficient amounts of data, like splice junction.

Following the evolutionary algorithm of Section 2.3 the generalization ability of best-so-far individuals is checked during training by recalculating their error on a validation set. At the end of a run the individual with minimal validation error is applied again on the test set. Except for the spice junction problem, the validation and the test set contain about as many examples each as the training set (see Table 8.1).

8.3   Experimental Setup

A comparison between completely different methods, as performed for neural networks and genetic programming in Chapter 4, may be based on prediction performance only. In this case, simply the best or nearly the best configuration may be selected for each approach. If the approaches tested are more related, however, similar parameters should be configured similarly to guarantee a fair comparison. This is more important, the less two approaches differ. Otherwise, their main differences can hardly be made responsible for a potential difference in performance. For the same reason comparing results from the literature may be crucial. Comparability of results can be guaranteed best within the same system environment.

8.3.1   A Multi-Representation GP System

Experiments in this chapter have been performed with the multi-representation GP system [20] that comprises different representation forms for genetic programs, including trees and linear structures. Such a platform allows the user to test different representation types with minimal implementation overhead, i.e., without changing the adaptation of the system to a certain problem. The fairest comparison of GP representations is achieved by using the same system environment as far as possible. Among other things, this includes a common evolutionary algorithm, a common selection method, and a general definition of instruction set and terminal set. In this way, the probability is reduced that slightly differing implementation details or parameter configurations may influence the results.

8.3.2   Complexity of Programs

The following comparison between a tree representation and a linear representation of genetic programs tries to be as fair as possible, especially in terms of the maximum complexity of programs. If we assume that all program parts are executed this is true for the evaluation time as well. In particular, the same maximum number of instructions (200) is allowed in both kinds of programs. For program trees this is the number of inner (non-terminal) nodes while for linear programs the number of lines is counted. The lower bound of absolute program size corresponds to one instruction (node).

Alternatively, it may be taken into account that not all instructions of the linear representation – in contrast to a tree representation – are structurally effective (after Definition 3.4). Remember that such noneffective instructions may always be removed completely from a linear program before it is executed and, therefore, do not cause computation costs (see Section 3.2.1). Thus, the actual solution is represented by the effective program only.

From that point of view, it may be a realistic alternative to restrict the *effective* length of a linear program instead of its absolute length. This can be realized, for instance, by repeating a crossover operation until a maximum number of effective instructions is met. In so doing, a maximum of n inner tree nodes is regarded as being equivalent to n effective instructions. Such a comparison would still be fair in terms of the same maximum number of *executed* instructions.

The maximum absolute length may not be left completely unrestricted, however. First, a higher amount of noneffective code usually implies larger effective code (see e.g. Section 7.5). Second, absolute (and effective) crossover step sizes are increased because longer segments are exchanged.

We know from Section 5.9.1 that there is another important argument for restricting the absolute program length and leaving the effective length to be influenced only indirectly by this. The structurally noneffective code takes away pressure from the effective code to grow and to develop semantic introns as a protection against larger crossover steps. In other words, the presence of noneffective code puts an *implicit parsimony pressure*[1] on effective code size. Therefore, the structurally noneffective code is also one reason why effective LGP solutions may be more compact in size than TGP solutions.

The second reason why linear genetic programs can manage with a smaller number of instructions is that their functional structure describes a directed acyclic graph (DAG) and is not as restricted as a tree structure. Among other things, the higher freedom of connections between the program functions allows the result of subsolutions (subgraphs) to be reused multiple times. Therefore, the same maximum number of instructions will allow imperative programs to express more complex solutions than tree programs.

8.3.3 Parameter Settings

Table 8.3 lists the parameter settings for both GP approaches. All choices are supposed to be general and have not been adapted to a specific problem. Problem-dependent parameters like the fitness function and the function set have been introduced already, together with the benchmark problems in Section 8.2.

Table 8.3. General parameter settings for linear GP (left) and tree-based GP (right).

LGP		TGP	
Parameter	Setting	Parameter	Setting
Number of generations	500 (1,000)	Number of generations	500 (1,000)
Population size	500	Population size	500
Maximum program length	200	Maximum operator nodes	200
Initial program length	10–30	Maximum tree depth	17
Initialization method	random	Initial tree depth	4–7
Number of registers	#inputs+10	Initialization method	ramped
Macro variation rate	90%	Crossover rate	90%
Micro mutation rate	10% (100%)	Node mutation rate	10% (100%)
Tournament size	2	Tournament size	2
Instructions with constant	50%	Constant Terminals	25%

General conclusions can be drawn about the performance of the two GP variants only, if parameters special for one variant are not explicitly optimized for each problem. For linear GP we allow 10 additional registers besides the required minimum number of (writable) registers that hold inputs. All registers are uniformly initialized with input data such that

---

[1] For an *explicit* parsimony pressure see Section 10.8.3.

each input value is assigned to about the same number of registers. Only if the number of inputs is already much larger than 10, as in case of most BIOPROBEN tasks, additional registers are not provided. In this case, the total number of registers may be sufficiently high already.

The average initial size of programs is around 20 instructions in all experiments. In particular, as many instructions that are used on average in initial linear programs as (inner) nodes, are used in initial tree programs. In linear GP this is realized simply by choosing the initial program lengths uniformly distributed in an appropriate range. In tree-based GP we apply the ramped-half-and-half method (see Section 8.1.2) which is controlled by a maximum and a minimum depth of initial trees. This results in a more probabilistic configuration of the initial program size in terms of the number of operator nodes. Note that the maximum possible number of nodes in a tree of a certain depth depends on the arity of nodes.

A balanced ratio of population size and generations has been chosen to guarantee a sufficient number of evaluations per individual, evolutionary progress, and diversity (see Section 7.4).

With similar complexity bounds, the same steady state EA has been chosen, described in Section 2.3, including the same selection method, tournament selection. Of course, the genetic operators are highly specific for a representation type. Both linear crossover and tree crossover are unrestricted in terms of the maximum size of exchanged subprograms.

As mentioned before, linear crossover, while operating on the imperative code, may affect multiple crossover points on the functional level. Tree crossover, however, always affects one crossover point. Hence crossover may be supposed to be more destructive in linear GP. On the other hand, small pieces of code may be exchanged at all parts of the linear representation and (structural) introns may be easily created at each position in a linear program to reduce the effective step size. For the tree representation, both are more difficult to achieve or involves stronger restrictions on the variation freedom (see Section 8.5).

All variations including both crossover and mutations are induced effectively for linear GP. That is, each genetic operation alters at least one effective instruction. Remember that operations on program trees are always fully effective in this sense, because structurally noneffective code is not defined (see Section 3.2). For linear crossover it is sufficient to guarantee the effectiveness of deleted segments (effdel, see Section 5.7.4). Then noneffective crossover might only be the result of exchanges of effectively identical code, which is very unlikely. In addition, we compare a pure mutation-based variant of LGP that applies effective mutations (effmut2,

B1, see Section 6.2.3) as a macro operator with a minimum segment length of one instruction.

There are only two differences between the parameter configurations used for GPPROBEN and BIOPROBEN. First, twice as large a population size (of 1,000 individuals) is used in the latter collection of benchmark problems. Second, since the average input dimension is significantly higher for most BIOPROBEN tasks, micro (node) mutations are always applied in combination with crossover. For GPPROBEN tasks only one genetic operation is executed per individual. Both a larger population size and a high mutation rate guarantee a higher code diversity in the population.

8.4 Experiments and Comparison

8.4.1 Prediction Quality and Complexity

Tables 8.4 and 8.5 show the best and the average prediction performance of 100 best-of-run solutions that have been found with tree-based GP and with linear GP, respectively, for the GPPROBEN problems. Program size is given by both the number of operator nodes and the tree depth in TGP. In LGP the absolute and effective program length are distinguished. Each complexity measure is averaged over all programs of a run (and over 100 independent runs). Because the execution of programs during fitness calculations is by far the most time-consuming step, average effective complexity is directly related to computational overhead of each GP variant.

When comparing the prediction errors of both GP approaches, most test problems are better solved by linear GP (except for distance). In general, the difference is clearest for discrete problems, including Boolean functions and classifications. In particular, much higher hit rates have been found with 11multiplexer, even8parity and two chains. Among the continuous (regression) problems, the difference in error is most significant for the difficult mexican hat problem.

In all test cases the size of tree programs is much larger in Table 8.4 than the effective program length in Table 8.5. Because both measurements count the number of executed instructions, they may be directly compared. The average absolute length of linear programs is similar for all problems and comes typically close to the maximum limit of 200 instructions.

Table 8.6 documents a much higher prediction quality in linear GP for all eight test problems when using instruction mutations instead of unrestricted linear crossover. Especially for most discrete problems we ob-

Table 8.4. GPPROBEN: Prediction quality and program size using crossover-based TGP. Average results over 100 runs after 500 generations. Average program size given in operator nodes.

Problem	Error			#Hits	Size	Depth
	best	*mean*	*std.*			
11multiplexer	0.0	186.0	12.1	10	138	15
even5parity	2.0	8.3	0.2	0	143	15
even8parity	0.0	68.6	2.1	1	179	11
two chains	0.0	13.4	1.1	5	146	15
spiral	17.0	36.0	0.9	0	152	15
double sine	0.2	8.7	0.8	0	147	15
distance	0.0	6.8	0.5	0	68	13
mexican hat	0.5	11.6	1.1	0	81	14

Table 8.5. GPPROBEN: Prediction quality and program size using crossover-based LGP. Average results over 100 runs after 500 generations.

Problem	Error			#Hits	Length		
	best	*mean*	*std.*		*abs.*	*eff.*	%
11multiplexer	0.0	92.0	9.1	31	189	88	46
even5parity	1.0	8.4	0.3	0	173	46	26
even8parity	0.0	25.9	2.2	22	167	88	52
two chains	0.0	4.7	0.5	24	186	79	42
spiral	7.0	24.6	0.5	0	187	87	46
double sine	0.6	7.7	0.7	0	181	48	27
distance	0.6	8.7	0.3	0	185	31	17
mexican hat	0.05	3.2	0.3	0	189	37	19

Table 8.6. GPPROBEN: Prediction quality and program size using mutation-based LGP. Average results over 100 runs after 500 generations.

Problem	Error			#Hits	Length		
	best	*mean*	*std.*		*abs.*	*eff.*	%
11multiplexer	0.0	2.3	1.1	94	101	83	82
even5parity	0.0	1.3	0.1	38	77	43	55
even8parity	0.0	1.6	0.3	68	101	85	84
two chains	0.0	0.8	0.1	50	96	77	80
spiral	0.0	10.4	0.4	1	93	80	86
double sine	0.04	2.9	0.3	0	76	45	59
distance	0.0	2.9	0.2	1	74	36	48
mexican hat	0.01	1.0	0.1	0	79	39	49

Table 8.7. BIOPROBEN: Prediction quality and program size using crossover-based TGP. Average results over 50 runs after 500 generations. Average program size given in operator nodes.

Problem	Error			#Hits	Size	Depth
	best	*mean*	*std.*			
splice junction	211.0	386.0	8.2	0	138	15
splice junction 2	14.0	36.1	2.2	0	137	15
promoters	0.0	5.8	0.6	2	142	15
ecoli	37.0	73.2	2.2	0	151	15
helicases	0.0	2.1	0.1	6	148	14
soybean	79.0	153.5	6.3	0	134	14
wine	0.0	17.4	1.5	2	147	14
dermatology	4.0	57.4	4.8	0	134	14

Table 8.8. BIOPROBEN: Prediction quality and program size using crossover-based LGP. Average results over 50 runs after 500 generations.

Problem	Error			#Hits	Length		
	best	*mean*	*std.*		*abs.*	*eff.*	%
splice junction	78.0	189.1	10.6	0	160	58	36
splice junction 2	6.0	18.4	1.1	0	163	66	40
promoters	0.0	1.7	0.2	8	181	54	30
ecoli	36.0	54.0	1.4	0	180	77	43
helicases	0.0	1.4	0.1	12	184	79	43
soybean	67.0	95.3	2.2	0	186	70	38
wine	0.0	2.5	0.2	3	138	87	63
dermatology	4.0	14.3	1.3	0	186	69	37

Table 8.9. BIOPROBEN: Prediction quality and program size using mutation-based LGP. Average results over 50 runs after 500 generations.

Problem	Error			#Hits	Length		
	best	*mean*	*std.*		*abs.*	*eff.*	%
splice junction	52.0	97.4	5.2	0	140	110	78
splice junction 2	5.0	11.9	0.7	0	127	104	82
promoters	0.0	0.3	0.1	30	111	89	80
ecoli	22.0	32.2	0.8	0	98	86	88
helicases	0.0	0.7	0.1	36	105	87	83
soybean	30.0	55.6	2.4	0	111	94	84
wine	0.0	1.2	0.1	9	118	103	87
dermatology	2.0	4.3	0.3	0	112	92	82

serve: Not only is the average prediction error significantly smaller, but the optimal solution has been found in many more runs, which is indicated by significantly higher hit rates. Since all variations are effective, the difference in performance may be accredited mostly to the difference in variation step size.

A parsimony effect of both maximum program length and noneffective code is responsible for a very similar *effective* size of solutions that has been found with crossover in Table 8.5 and with instruction mutations in Table 8.6. This might be evidence that the proportion of semantic introns in effective programs is rather small. At least it shows that a difference in (effective) program size may hardly be responsible for the large difference in prediction quality here.

The corresponding results for the BIOPROBEN collection of (classification) problems are printed in Tables 8.7 to 8.9. For all BIOPROBEN problems the average performance is higher with LGP. Concerning the quality of best solutions this is only true for the splice junction. In all other problem cases best results are similar.

The better performance in best and average prediction that has been found with effective mutations shows again – for a wider range of problems than in Chapter 6 – that this operator clearly outperforms linear crossover.

For some problems average effective length is significantly larger when using instruction mutations than has been found with linear crossover (cf. Tables 8.8 and 8.9). We can explain this by the fact that a certain amount of noneffective code will always emerge with crossover since the survivability of programs depends on this type of code. Together with a maximum bound, this restricts the growth of effective code, as discussed above. Another argument is the relatively high input dimension of BIOPROBEN problems. This requires the use of many registers in programs. Since the applied mutation operator creates each new instruction effectively, the proportion of effective code is almost independent of the number of registers (see Section 7.1).

8.4.2 Generalization Ability

The generalization results for regression problems in Tables 8.10 to 8.12 demonstrate that both validation error and test error come close to the training error (in Tables 8.4 to 8.6). That is, a variation operator that improves training performance improves generalization performance in almost the same amount. We therefore may safely assume that correlation between training data and generalization data is high.

Table 8.10. Generalization ability using crossover-based TGP.

Problem	Validation Error			#Hits	Test Error			#Hits
	best	*mean*	*std.*		*best*	*mean*	*std.*	
two chains	0.0	10.9	0.6	1	1.0	11.9	0.6	0
splice junction	130.0	208.3	3.7	0	144.0	212.2	3.4	0
distance	0.0	6.9	0.6	0	0.0	7.3	0.5	0
mexican hat	0.4	15.9	1.5	0	0.4	16.2	1.4	0

Table 8.11. Generalization ability using crossover-based LGP.

Problem	Validation Error			#Hits	Test Error			#Hits
	best	*mean*	*std.*		*best*	*mean*	*std.*	
two chains	0.0	7.9	0.5	2	2.0	8.4	0.4	0
splice junction	69.0	120.3	5.6	0	55.0	123.8	5.9	0
distance	1.4	10.3	0.3	0	1.2	9.6	0.3	0
mexican hat	0.03	3.3	0.4	0	0.03	3.6	0.5	0

Table 8.12. Generalization ability using mutation-based LGP.

Problem	Validation Error			#Hits	Test Error			#Hits
	best	*mean*	*std.*		*best*	*mean*	*std.*	
two chains	0.0	4.6	0.3	6	2.0	5.1	0.3	0
splice junction	59.0	88.7	3.1	0	57.0	89.7	3.2	0
distance	0.0	3.5	0.3	1	0.0	4.0	0.3	1
mexican hat	0.006	1.1	0.1	0	0.006	1.3	0.1	0

Generalization errors of the classification problems tested are more different from training error,[2] especially when using effective mutations. This may be attributed to the fact that both problem solutions apply branches. On the whole, branches improve training performance such that they support a specialization to the training examples. Without using branches the three prediction errors become more similar (undocumented), but all are worse than with branches. If branches are essential for finding the optimal solution or allow a significantly higher fitness during training, they may not lead to a worse generalization.

The generalization errors are slightly more similar than the training errors when comparing different representations, on the one hand, or different genetic operators, on the other hand. Obviously, a genetic operator that performs better on the training set may not necessarily do the same on

---

[2]Note that validation set and test set of splice junction are half as large as the training set.

unknown data if this originates from a different part of the data space. Note that it is training fitness that is influenced most directly by the performance of a genetic operator.

8.5   Discussion

Instruction mutations vary the length of imperative programs in minimal steps. In the functional equivalent of a program only one operator node is inserted in or deleted from the corresponding program graph, together with its incoming and outgoing edges. First, the imperative representation allows insertions or deletions of code to be permanently small at each position, because the degree of freedom is higher in a directed acyclic graph than in a tree, by definition.

Second, structurally noneffective code parts in linear programs may be temporarily disconnected from the effective graph component (see Section 3.3). Effective instruction mutations do not prohibit such disconnections (deactivations) of code (see also Section 6.2.4). On the one hand, the coexistence of inactive (disconnected) code in programs avoids an irrecoverable loss of code and allows its reactivation (reconnection). On the other hand, multiple connections of nodes in the graph structure reduce the probability for disconnections. Also, disconnections decrease implicitly in the course of a run as a result of an increasing connectivity of instruction nodes, as will be demonstrated in Section 9.7.2.

Both are different in traditional tree-based GP. Due to higher constraints of the tree structure, deletions or insertions of subtrees are not possible as separate operations. A tree structure requires a removed subtree to be directly replaced at the same position. In linear GP the register identifiers (pointers) are encoded in the imperative instructions. If those are disconnected by deactivation, they are either automatically reconnected to other instructions or represent a terminal (in the graph structure).

Lopez *et al.* [79] extended the traditional GP approach by inactive subtrees that remain part of the representation. Special (inner) nodes do not execute their subtrees but hold a pointer that redirects the data flow to another part of the (effective) program. Such *structural introns* may be reactivated after variation when being reconnected to the result-producing code.

(Macro) mutations changing size and shape of trees are less likely to have small effects on higher tree levels. At least deletions of larger subtrees may not be avoided without significantly restricting the freedom of variation. In a tree each node is connected only by one edge on a unique path to the root. Since the tree representation does not allow unconnected components, a disconnection of code always means its loss. Nevertheless, the probability for such larger mutation steps may be reduced as far as possible in TGP. Therefore, three elementary tree operations may be distinguished – insertion, deletion and substitution of a single node [98]:

(1) If an operator node is inserted in a tree it replaces a random node which becomes a successor of the new node. All remaining successors of the newly inserted node become terminals. Since most instructions usually require more than one operand, almost each insertion will create a new terminal node in this way.

(2) Accordingly, if a random inner node is selected for deletion it is replaced by one of its successors, e.g., the largest subtree. All other successors of the deleted node will be lost, including the corresponding subtrees.

(3) A node may be substituted by another node of the same arity only. In particular, terminal nodes are exchanged only by other terminals then. Alternatively, nodes may be substituted freely while supernumerary subtrees are completed by a terminal or deleted, respectively.

In [98] these *minimum tree mutations* are applied in combination with search techniques like *simulated annealing* and *hill climbing* that are both operating with a single search point (individual program). In [99] the authors combine these search techniques with a standard population-based search by tree crossover. Unfortunately, the performance of these mutations is not compared with crossover while using the same search method.

8.6   Summary and Conclusion

After an introduction to tree-based GP, we compared this more traditional approach with linear GP by using two collections of benchmark problems. The comparison was supposed to be fair particularly with regard to the (maximum) complexity of genetic programs.

□ With unrestricted crossover, LGP performed better than TGP and produced more compact solutions in terms of the number of executed instructions. Especially for (real-world) classification problems, the difference in performance between a tree representation and a linear representation was significant.

□ Even better prediction results were obtained for linear GP by means of effective instruction mutations. This was especially clear for the applied GP benchmarks. Results showed a smaller difference in performance between the two representation forms than between the two linear genetic operators applying maximum (unrestricted) or minimum step sizes. This recommends a general use of minimum mutation steps in linear genetic programming and confirms our results from Chapter 5 and Chapter 6 for a wider range of applications.

☐ We also argued why, first, LGP allows smaller solutions and, second, a minimization of growth and shrink operations may be incomplete in TGP. Both may be reduced to the two fundamental differences of representations that have been outlined already in Chapter 1. In the first case, this means that effective linear programs may be more compact in size because of a multiple usage of register content and an implicit parsimony pressure by structurally noneffective code. In the second case, stronger constraints of the tree structure and the lack of non-contiguous components prohibit that structural step sizes can be minimal.

PART III

ADVANCED TECHNIQUES AND PHENOMENA

Chapter 9

CONTROL OF DIVERSITY AND VARIATION STEP SIZE

In this chapter we will investigate structural and semantic distance metrics for linear genetic programs. A causal connection between changes of genotypes and of phenotypes form a necessary condition for being able to control differences between genetic programs. The two objectives of this chapter are to show (1) how distance information between individuals can be used to control structural diversity of individuals and (2) how variation distance on effective code can be controlled probabilistically with different linear genetic operators.

9.1 Introduction

Like other evolutionary search algorithms, genetic programming cannot (completely) fulfill the principle of *strong causality*, i.e., small variations in genotype space imply small variations in phenotype space [110, 116]. Obviously, changing just a small program component may lead to almost arbitrary changes in program behavior. However, it seems to be intuitive that the probability of a large fitness change grows with more instructions being modified. In other words, a *weak causality* principle might still be in effect.

As discussed in Section 5.4, a *fitness landscape* on the search space of programs is defined by a structural distance metric between programs and a fitness function that reflects the quality of programs. The application of a genetic operator corresponds to performing a *step* from one point to another in this landscape. In general, variation step size should be correlated with the distance on the fitness landscape.

The *edit distance*, sometimes referred to as *Levenshtein distance* [118, 44], between varying length character strings has been proposed as a metric for representations in genetic programming [59, 100]. Such a measure not only permits an analysis of genotype diversity within a population, but it offers the possibility to control the step size of variation operators more precisely. In [52] a correlation between edit distance and fitness change of tree programs has been demonstrated for different test problems. A comparison of different diversity measures for genetic programs in terms of their information content and their correlation with fitness may be found in [27].

This chapter is an extension of our previous work [24]. It first introduces efficient structural distance metrics that operate selectively on substructures of the linear program representation. Correlation between structural and semantic distance as well as distribution of distances are examined for different types of variation.

One objective is the explicit control of structural diversity, i.e., the average program distance, in LGP populations. To that end, we introduce a two-level tournament method that selects for fitness on the first level and for diversity on the second level. We will see that this is less motivated by a better *preservation* of diversity during a run but by a control of a diversity *level* that depends on the configuration of the selection method. We will also see that prediction improves significantly if the diversity level of a population is increased.

The simplest form of diversity control might be to regularly inject random individuals into the population during runtime. In [59] a more explicit maintenance of diversity is proposed by creating and injecting individuals that fill "gaps" of under-represented areas in genotype space. However, a full experimental account is still missing for this computationally expensive approach. De Jong *et al.* [55] could improve parsimony pressure through Pareto-selection of fitness and tree size by adding a third diversity objective. An explicit diversity control that is based on fitness sharing and an efficient distance metric for tree programs may be found in [34]. Burke *et al.* [26] maintain diversity by selecting individuals with different genetic lineage for recombination. This happens independently from fitness selection.

A more implicit control of genetic diversity is offered by semi-isolated subpopulations, called *demes*, that are widely used in different areas of evolutionary computation (see also Section 4.3.2). There, only a certain percentage of individuals is allowed to migrate from one deme to another during each generation.

The second objective of this chapter is to examine and control the structural distance between a parent program and its offspring, i.e., the variation step size. While the effect of variation on the absolute program structure, i.e., the absolute variation distance (see Definition 5.3), may be controlled by the genetic operators, as demonstrated in Chapter 5, the amount of change induced on the effective code, i.e., the effective variation distance (see Definition 5.4), may differ significantly from the absolute change. By monitoring effective variation distance, structural step sizes can be controlled more precisely in relation to their effect on program semantics. We will demonstrate that even strong restrictions of the maximally allowed effective mutation distance do not imply a real restriction of the freedom of variation.

Here we apply two different variants of linear GP that we already know from Chapters 5 and 6: Variant (1) uses recombination by standard linear crossover and variant (2) uses effective instruction mutation. In (1) the absolute variation distance is unlimited while in (2) it is restricted to a minimum.

9.2 Structural Program Distance

9.2.1 Effective Edit Distance

The *string edit distance* [118, 44] calculates the distance between two arbitrarily long character strings by counting the number of basic operations – including insertion, deletion, and substitution of single characters – that are necessary to transform one string into another. Usually each operation is assigned the same unit costs 1, independent of which character is affected. The standard algorithm for calculating string edit distance needs time $O(n^2)$ where n denotes the maximum number of components compared between two individual programs. More efficient algorithms are discussed in [87].

In general, the correlation between semantic and structural distance is lower, the higher the proportion of noneffective code that occurs with a certain variation operator or parameter configuration. We apply edit distance to determine the structural distance between effective parts of programs (*effective distance*).

A difference in effective code can be expected to be directly related to a difference in program behavior (semantic distance). It is important to recall that the effective distance is not part of the absolute distance. Actually, two programs may have a small absolute distance while their effective distance is comparatively large (see Section 9.5). On the other hand, two programs with equal effective parts might differ significantly in their noneffective code.

```
void gp(r)
  double r[5];
{  ...
// r[4] = r[2] * r[4];
   r[4] = r[2] / r[0];
// r[0] = r[3] - 1;
// r[1] = r[2] * r[4];
// r[1] = r[0] + r[1];
// r[0] = r[3] - 5;
// r[2] = pow(r[1], r[0]);
   r[2] = r[3] - r[4];
   r[4] = r[2] - 1;
   r[0] = r[4] * r[3];
// r[4] = pow(r[0], 2);
// r[1] = r[0] / r[3];
   r[3] = r[2] + r[3];
   r[4] = r[2] / 7;
// r[2] = r[2] * r[4];
   r[0] = r[0] + r[4];
   r[0] = r[0] - r[3];
}
```

Example 9.1. Linear genetic program. Noneffective instructions are commented. Register r[0] holds the final program output.

Our *selective* distance metric concentrates on representative substructures of linear programs and considers simply the sequence of operators of effective instructions. For instance, this sequence can be written for Example 9.1 as $(-, +, /, +, *, -, -, /)$ where parsing started at the last effective instruction. Although this distance detects fewer differences, it has been found accurate enough to differentiate between program structures, provided that the operator set (function set) used is not too small. In most cases the modification of an effective register changes the effectiveness status of at least one instruction and thus the effective operator sequence.[1]

Because the exchange of identical program components is not allowed, changing one constant into another constant is the only type of variation that is not registered at all by this method.

By including program registers into distance calculation the distance measure might become more ambiguous because most registers are used only

---

[1] Note that the absolute operator sequence would never be altered by the exchange of registers.

temporarily during calculation. As such, they may be replaced by others without altering the behavior of the underlying program. In reality, it is only the last assignment to an output register and all readings of input registers before their content is overwritten that are invariable. In addition to that, the distance between operator sequences is not unique since the order of instructions may be changed without changing program behavior, as indicated in Section 3.3.3. In linear GP, functional dependencies between the instruction nodes usually form a rather narrow ("linear") graph structure. The narrower this graph structure is, the more similar the position of a node to the position of the corresponding instruction in the program, i.e., the smaller the effective dependence distance (see Section 3.4). The upshot of this is that a linear program may be represented to a sufficient degree by its operator sequence.

We are also motivated by the fact that restricting the number of components in the comparison significantly reduces the time needed for calculating the edit distance between two programs. Calculation time only depends on the number n of effective instructions. If we would include the noneffective instructions there are m more components to compare, resulting in costs $O((n + m)^2)$ with $m \geq n$ in many scenarios. Extending the distance calculation further to include registers and constants of instructions, a factor of 4 has to be taken into account (see Section 2.1.1). Thus, computational costs would increase by a total factor of 64, if we assume $m \approx n$.

9.2.2 Alternative Distance Metrics

In all of the following experiments we will apply the edit distance metric described above. However, even though the reduction of program elements to be identified accelerates distance calculation, there are other, more efficient metrics possible on linear genetic programs.

For example, one could give up the order of operators and compare only the frequency with which an operator is applied. Program distance may therefore be reduced to the distance between two pattern vectors v and w of equal length n (n = size of operator set). Each vector position v_i represents the frequency of an operator type in the genetic program corresponding to v. The *Manhattan distance* simply calculates the sum of absolute differences between equal vector positions, i.e., $\delta_{man}(v, w) = \sum_{i=1}^{n} |v_i - w_i|$. This requires a runtime $O(n)$ while n will be much smaller here, because it is not related to the length of programs. In other words, computation costs are constant in terms of program length. Although the accuracy of this structural distance is definitely lower than the edit distance, it has proven to be sufficient for an explicit control of diversity.

Another distance metric that is more efficient than the edit distance can be applied for controlling step sizes of (effective) instruction mutation. If an instruction at a certain program position is varied, this measure calculates how many of the *previous* instructions depending on it in the program (including the mutation point) have changed their effectiveness status. Operationally, this is the *Hamming distance* between the status flags of instructions and takes time $O(n)$ in the worst case where n is the maximum program length.

We will see later that the efficiency of a distance calculation is more important for controlling diversity than for controlling variation distance.

9.3   Semantic Program Distance

The most obvious metric for evaluation of the behavior of a genetic program is the fitness function $\mathcal{F}$. This usually calculates the distance of the predicted outputs $gp(\vec{i_k})$ returned by a program and the desired outputs given by n fitness cases, i.e., input-output examples $(\vec{i_k}, o_k)$, $k = 1, .., n$. For example, in Equation 9.1 this is simply the Manhattan distance between the two output vectors:

$$\mathcal{F}(gp) = \sum_{k=1}^{n} |gp(\vec{i_k}) - o_k| \qquad (9.1)$$

Correspondingly, the semantic differences between two genetic programs may be expressed by their *fitness distance*:

$$\delta_{fit}(gp_1, gp_2) = |\mathcal{F}(gp_1) - \mathcal{F}(gp_2)| \qquad (9.2)$$

In this case, the quality of solving the overall problem is considered. Another possibility is to compare the outputs of two programs directly. The same distance metric as in the fitness function may be used for computing the distance between the output vectors of programs (see Equation 9.3). In the following this will be referred to as *output distance*.

$$\delta_{out}(gp_1, gp_2) = \sum_{k=1}^{n} |gp_1(\vec{i_k}) - gp_2(\vec{i_k})| \qquad (9.3)$$

Note that the relative output distance between two programs is independent from their performance in terms of solving a prediction task. Actually, two programs may have a similar fitness while their output behavior differs significantly, i.e., different subsets of the training data may be approximated with different accuracy.

For discrete problems like classifications the fitness function calculates a classification error (see Equation 2.2). Then the output distance is defined as follows:

$$\delta_{boolout}(gp_1, gp_2) = \sum_{k=1}^{n}\{1 \mid class(gp_1(\vec{i_k})) \neq class(gp_2(\vec{i_k}))\} \qquad (9.4)$$

Function *class* in Equation 9.4 hides the classification method used to map continuous program outputs to discrete class identifiers.

9.4 Control of Diversity

In GP the *diversity* Δ of a population may be defined as the average distance of k randomly selected pairs of programs using a distance metric δ:

$$\Delta = \frac{1}{k}\sum_{i=1}^{k}\delta(gp_{1i}, gp_{2i}) \qquad (9.5)$$

The *genotype diversity* (or *structural diversity*) of programs is measured by means of a structural distance metric. Since we apply the edit distance between effective programs we refer to the *effective diversity*.

We introduce the two-level tournament selection shown in Figure 9.1 for explicit control of diversity. On the first level, three tournaments of two individuals each select winners by fitness. On the second level, a tournament among these three winners determines the two individuals with *maximum* distance. While an absolute measure, such as fitness, may be used to compare between two individuals, selection by a relative measure, such as distance or diversity, necessarily requires a minimum of three individuals. In general, two out of k individuals are selected with the greatest sum of distances to the $k - 1$ other individuals. Selection pressure on the first level depends on the *size* of fitness tournaments. Pressure of diversity selection on the second level is controlled by the *number* of these tournaments. Additionally, a selection rate controls how often diversity selection takes place at all and, thus, fine-tunes the selection pressure on the second level.

The number of fitness calculations and the processing time do not increase with the number of (first-level) tournaments if the fitness values of all individuals are saved and only updated after variation. Only diversity selection on the second level becomes more computationally expensive the more individuals participate in it. Because k selected individuals require $\binom{k}{2}$ distance calculations, an efficient distance metric is important.

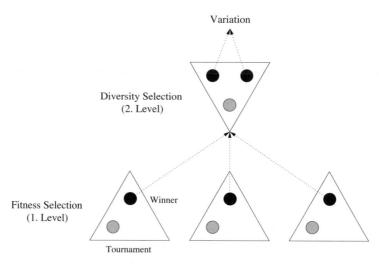

Figure 9.1. Two-level tournament selection.

The two-level tournament selection constitutes a multi-objective selection method that finds individuals that are fitter *and* more diverse in relation to others. One advantage over applying fitness selection *or* diversity selection independent from each other on the *same* level is that the proportion of fitness selection is not reduced. Moreover, selecting individuals only by diversity with a certain probability does not result in more diversity among *better* solutions in the population.

Selection for a linear combination of both objectives, fitness and diversity, as is often practiced with fitness and size (parsimony pressure) has some drawbacks: (1) It requires an appropriate weighting which is, in general, rather difficult to find. (2) The influence of program size or distance depends directly on its absolute value which changes over a run. With a two-level selection this is a local rank, relative to other programs. (3) Fitness and diversity have approximately the same priority. With our approach, instead, fitness selection is not only decoupled from diversity selection but always has a higher priority.

An explicit control of effective diversity increases the average distance of individuals. The population spreads more widely over the fitness land-scape and the probability is lower that the evolutionary process gets stuck in a local minimum. A too high diversity, instead, has potentially negative effects on population convergence and fitness improvement.

While increasing the effective distance between programs affects the diversity of a population, selection for absolute distance has also been found to improve results, but to a lesser extent. Apart from the fact that it is a more time-consuming process, this finding confirms that the absolute distance inaccurately measures the effective program distance (see Section 9.2).

Increasing the average distance between programs by diversity selection has the side effect of accelerating the growth of (effective) program length. In order to avoid an impact on results, we select for the effective edit distance δ_{eff} minus the distance in effective length, i.e., $\delta_{eff}(gp_1, gp_2) - |l_{eff}(gp_1) - l_{eff}(gp_2)|$. This is possible because both edit distance and length distance operate on the instruction level. A difference in length is thus no longer rewarded directly during selection. To further reduce the influence of code growth one might select for the *relative effective distance*:

$$\delta_{releff} = \frac{\delta_{eff}(gp_1, gp_2)}{\max(l_{eff}(gp_1), l_{eff}(gp_2))} \tag{9.6}$$

Note here that the size of the longest pattern string (effective program) determines the maximum effective distance possible.

Controlling *phenotype* or *semantic diversity* can be done by a selection for a maximum *semantic distance* of individuals using the output distance defined in Section 9.3. Fitness distance has been found less suitable for this purpose. Obviously, relative output distance between programs is able to measure semantic differences more precisely. Moreover, selection by fitness distance may be less effective for discrete problems if the number of fitness values is small.

9.5 Control of Variation Step Size

Already the smallest variations of a symbolic program structure may affect its program behavior enormously. In linear GP these variations especially include the exchange of (effective) registers. Several instructions that precede a varied instruction in a program may become effective or noneffective (see also Section 3.3.1). In this way, mutations can not only affect fitness, i.e., program semantics, but the flow of data in linear genetic programs represented by a directed acyclic graph (see Section 3.3). Even though larger variations of program behavior are less likely by using small structural variation steps, this effect is undesirable.

An *implicit control* of structural variation distance has been employed in Chapter 6 by imposing corresponding restrictions on different types of mutation operators. However, genetic operators may only guarantee for the *absolute* program structure that a certain maximum step size is not exceeded. Variation steps on the *effective* code, instead, may still be much larger although they might appear with a lower probability.

A major concern of this chapter is an *explicit control* of the *effective* variation distance. The variation of a parent program is repeated until its effective distance to the offspring falls below a maximum threshold. Therefore, the structural distance between parent and offspring is measured explicitly by applying the effective distance metric as defined above.

In the following extract of a linear program, commented instructions are noneffective if we assume that the output is held in register r[0] at the end of execution. The program status on the right represents the result of applying an effective micro mutation to instruction number 8 (from the top). The first operand register r[3] is exchanged with register r[2]. As a consequence, 5 preceding (formerly noneffective) instructions become effective which corresponds to an effective mutation distance of 5.

```
void gp(r)                              void gp(r)
   double r[5];                            double r[5];
{  ...                                  {  ...
// r[4] = r[2] * r[4];                  // r[4] = r[2] * r[4];
   r[4] = r[2] / r[0];                     r[4] = r[2] / r[0];
// r[0] = r[3] - 1;                        r[0] = r[3] - 1;
// r[1] = r[2] * r[4];                     r[1] = r[2] * r[4];
// r[1] = r[0] + r[1];                     r[1] = r[0] + r[1];
// r[0] = r[3] - 5;                        r[0] = r[3] - 5;
// r[2] = pow(r[1], r[0]);                 r[2] = pow(r[1], r[0]);
   r[2] = r[3] - r[4];                     r[2] = r[2] - r[4];
   r[4] = r[2] - 1;                        r[4] = r[2] - 1;
   r[0] = r[4] * r[3];                     r[0] = r[4] * r[3];
// r[4] = pow(r[0], 2);                 // r[4] = pow(r[0], 2);
// r[1] = r[0] / r[3];                  // r[1] = r[0] / r[3];
   r[3] = r[2] + r[3];                     r[3] = r[2] + r[3];
   r[4] = r[2] / 7;                        r[4] = r[2] / 7;
// r[2] = r[2] * r[4];                  // r[2] = r[2] * r[4];
   r[0] = r[0] + r[4];                     r[0] = r[0] + r[4];
   r[0] = r[0] - r[3];                     r[0] = r[0] - r[3];
}                                       }
```

Example 9.2. Change of effective code (right program) after effective register mutation (in line 8 of left program).

Since exchange of identical instruction elements – including registers, operators, and constants – is avoided, operator mutations will always change the operator sequence. But operator mutations may also induce a variation distance that is larger than 1, if the new operator requires a different number of parameters than the former operator. As a consequence, registers have to be either added to or removed from the particular instruction. Preceding instructions in program that depend on such a register operand may be reactivated or deactivated, respectively.

Using an explicit control of the *fitness* distance between parent and offspring, instead, requires an additional fitness calculation after each variation tried, and can become computationally expensive, especially if a larger number of fitness cases is involved. By comparison, a structural distance like edit distance has to be recalculated only once after each variation while its computational costs do not directly depend on the number of fitness cases. While it is not really motivated to restrict *positive* fitness changes (fitness improvement) at all, it is rather difficult to find appropriate maximum thresholds for the fitness distance because those are usually problem-specific.

9.6 Experimental Setup

All techniques discussed above have been tested with three benchmark problems, an approximation, a classification, and a Boolean problem. Table 9.1 summarizes problem attributes and problem-specific parameter settings of our LGP system.

Table 9.1. Problem-specific parameter settings

Problem	*sinepoly*	*iris*	*even8parity*
Problem type	regression	classification	Boolean function
Problem function	$sin(x) \times x + 5$	—	even8parity
Input range	$[-5, 5]$	$[0, 8)$	$\{0, 1\}$
Output range	$[0, 7)$	$\{0, 1, 2\}$	$\{0, 1\}$
Number of inputs	1	4	8
Number of outputs	1	1	1
Number of registers	1+4	4+2	8+0
Number of examples	100	150	256
Fitness function	SSE	CE	SE
Instruction set	$\{+, -, \times, /, x^y\}$	$\{+, -, \times, /, if >, if \leq\}$	$\{\wedge, \vee, \neg, if\}$
Constants	$\{1, .., 9\}$	$\{1, .., 9\}$	$\{0, 1\}$

The first problem is referred to as *sinepoly* and denotes an approximation of the sine polynomial $sin(x) \times x + 5$ by non-trigonomic functions. Thus, given that the maximum length of genetic programs is limited and that the *sine* function is defined by an infinite Taylor-series, the optimum cannot be found. In addition to the input register – that is identical to the output register – there are four further calculation registers used in this problem. Recall that this additional program memory is important in linear GP, especially if input dimension is low. With only one register the calculation potential would be very restricted indeed. Fitness is measured by the *sum of square errors* (SSE). 100 fitness cases have been uniformly distributed over the input range $[-5, 5]$.

The second problem *iris* is a popular classification data set that originates from the *UCI Machine Learning Repository* [88]. These real-world data contain 3 classes of 50 instances each, with the class label referring to a type of iris plant. Fitness is calculated by the *classification error* (CE), i.e., the number of wrongly classified inputs. A program output $gp(\vec{i_k})$ is considered correct for an input vector $\vec{i_k}$ if the distance of the output value to the desired class identifier $o_k \in \{0, 1, 2\}$ is smaller than 0.1, i.e., $|gp(\vec{i_k}) - o_k| < 0.1$. Note that finding a solution would be easier if the error threshold would be extended to the maximum (0.5 here).

The last problem tested is a parity function of dimension eight (*even8parity*). The Boolean branch in the instruction set is essential for a high number of successful runs with this problem. The sum of output errors (SE), i.e., the number of wrong output bits, defines the fitness.

Table 9.2. General parameter settings.

Parameter	Setting
Population size	2,000
Fitness tournament size	4
Maximum program length	200
Initial program length	10
Reproduction rate	100%
Micro mutation rate	25%
Macro mutation rate	75%
Instruction deletion	33%
Instruction insertion	67%
Crossover rate	75%

Problem-independent parameter configurations are given in Table 9.2. Only one genetic operator is selected at a time to vary an individual. Either linear crossover (cross, see Section 5.7.1) or (effective) instruction mutation ((eff)mut, see Section 6.2.3) are used as macro operator. A doubled insertion rate than deletion rate (explicit growth bias B1, see Section 5.8) guarantees a sufficient growth of programs when using smallest mutation step sizes.

9.7 Experiments

9.7.1 Distance Distribution and Correlation

First of all, we demonstrate that there is a causal connection between structural distance and semantic distance (fitness distance) of linear genetic programs. We do this by applying the effective edit distance defined in Section 9.2. Causality forms a necessary precondition for the success of evolutionary algorithms. Although already small variations of the program structure may lead to almost arbitrary changes in program behavior, small differences in genotype should correspond to small differences in phenotype, at least with a higher probability (see also Section 5.4).

In the first experiment distances of 2,000 pairs of *randomly* selected individuals have been observed in each generation. Figures 9.2 to 9.4 visualize the resulting relation of (effective) program distance and fitness distance together with the corresponding distributions of program distances. For all test problems there is a clear positive correlation between program distance and fitness distance for most of the measured distances. The phenomena are somewhat similar for the crossover-based and the mutation-based variant of linear GP.

In a second experiment, we investigate the structural *variation* distance, i.e., the distance between parent and offspring or, more precisely, the distance of a modified individual from its original state. Figures 9.5 to 9.7 again demonstrate a positive correlation between program distance and fitness distance, which means at least a weak causality. However, smallest structural step sizes on the effective code still induce relatively large semantic step sizes on average. We will demonstrate in Section 9.7.7 that even if the effective step size is set to the minimum of 1 for macro mutations, evolutionary progress is not slowed down.

The distance distributions reveal that, in general, shorter effective distances occur with a higher frequency than longer distances. As one might expect, the distribution of crossover distances is substantially wider than the distribution of distances induced by instruction mutations. The distribution range of distances is significantly smaller than in the first experiment because the individuals in the second experiment are related. That the structural distance between parent and offspring is significantly smaller, on average, than between two arbitrary individuals is an important property of evolutionary algorithms to work efficiently.

The distance distributions of Figures 9.5 to 9.7 also show that more than two thirds of all effective mutations induce effective distance 1. Even though macro mutations insert or delete full effective instructions in the majority of cases, effective distances larger than 1 occur in less than one third of these cases. Hence it can be suspected that the effectiveness of preceding instructions changes with a relatively low probability.

In crossover runs a high amount of operations results in effective distance 0. A high proliferation of structural introns (see Section 3.2) occurring with the crossover operation produces this result, together with the 25

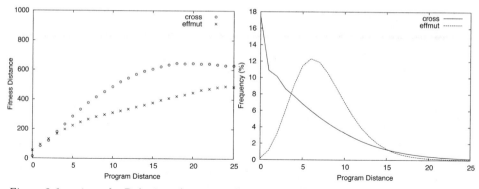

Figure 9.2. *sinepoly:* Relation of program distance and fitness distance (left) and distribution of program distances (right) in crossover runs (**cross**) and in runs using effective mutations (**effmut**). Average figures over 100 runs.

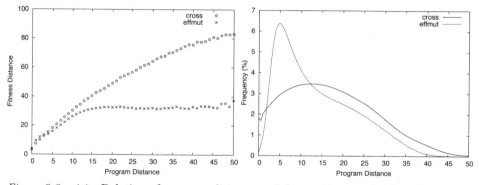

Figure 9.3. *iris:* Relation of program distance and fitness distance (left) and distribution of program distances (right).

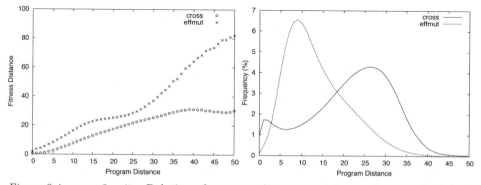

Figure 9.4. *even8parity:* Relation of program distance and fitness distance (left) and distribution of program distances (right).

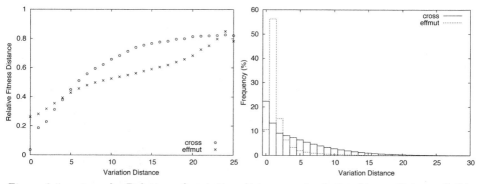

Figure 9.5. *sinepoly:* Relation of variation distance and relative fitness distance (left) and distribution of variation distances (right) in crossover runs (**cross**) and in runs using effective mutations (**effmut**). Average figures over 100 runs.

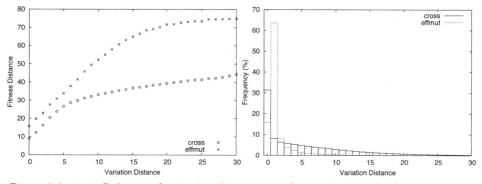

Figure 9.6. *iris:* Relation of variation distance and fitness distance (left) and distance of variation distribution (right).

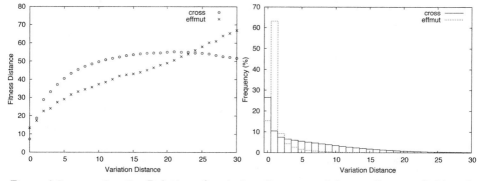

Figure 9.7. *even8parity:* Relation of variation distance and fitness distance (left) and distance of variation distribution (right).

percent micro mutations used in all experiments which are not explicitly effective.

9.7.2   Development of Effective Step Size

The 3D plot in Figure 9.8 shows how, for the *iris* problem, the distribution of effective step sizes develops over the course of a run with effective mutations (effmut). The distribution is changing such that step sizes 1 and 0 increase in frequency while larger step sizes decrease in frequency. So after about 100 generations, changes are caused almost exclusively with mutations that act on one instruction only, rather than by deactivation of depending effective code. Deactivation is mostly responsible for effective distances larger than 1. Reactivation of (structurally) noneffective code, instead, is much less likely because the proportion of this code remains low due to the effmut operator (see Section 6.4.1).

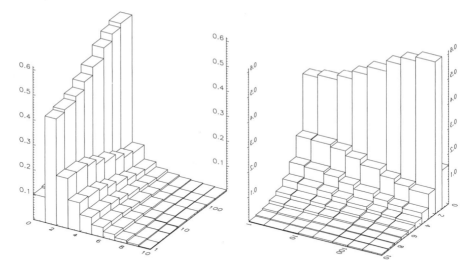

Figure 9.8.   iris: Development of the frequency distribution of effective step sizes over 500 generations (approximately logarithmic scale) when using effective mutations (effmut). Step sizes range from 0 to 9 here. Frequency of step size 1 increases clearly. Right figure same as left figure but rotated by 90 degrees.

It appears that evolution favors effective program structures that are less fragile against stronger variation. In other words, more robust individuals are preferred over brittle ones. We found that the effectiveness of an instruction is often guaranteed by more than one (succeeding) instruction. Figure 9.9 shows the average effectiveness degree or dependence degree (see Section 3.4) of a program instruction to grow continuously during a run. On the functional level this can be interpreted to mean that the number of connections increases between nodes of the effective graph component. Thus, the graph-shaped structure allows the effective code to protect itself against larger disconnections (deactivations). Smaller step sizes on the effective program structure will result in offspring with potentially higher fitness, no matter whether this *self-protection effect* is an implicit evolutionary phenomenon or simply a consequence of the increasing power and complexity of solutions. Reducing the probability of deactivations by multiple node connections offers linear GP a fundamental advantage over tree programs where each node is connected to the root by only one edge (cf. Section 8.5).

When investigating the evolution of effective step sizes, it has to be considered that this depends on the development of (effective) program length. The larger programs become, the larger step sizes are possible, in principle. Although programs grow over a run, the frequency of step sizes that are larger than 1 instruction, decreases in Figure 9.8 when a distance range of 0 to 9 is observed. Variation distances significantly larger than 10 instructions do not occur at the beginning of a run due to rather small initial program lengths (see Section 9.6). Even if the *maximum* step size increases continuously with program length in the course of a run, the accumulated proportion of distances larger than 10 comprises only about 2 percent. Nevertheless, such events may have an influence on the *average* step size.

Figure 9.9 shows a clear dependence of the average variation distance on the number of additional (calculation) registers. While a small register number (plus 2 in the example) results in a virtually constant average effective step size over generations, larger numbers of registers lead to an increase. Such behavior can be explained again by the effectiveness degree of instructions that turns out to be lower in Figure 9.9 if more registers are available (see also Section 7.1). Then deactivations of code become more likely and affect larger parts of a program. Nevertheless, the average step size remains relatively small even for large numbers of registers. We should point out that the fundamental development of step sizes, as shown in Figure 9.8, for 2 calculation registers is similar for larger numbers of registers.

Larger step sizes also do not result simply from larger programs. Neither the size of effective code nor the size of noneffective code have been found to be significantly different for larger register numbers.

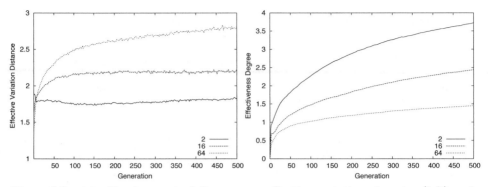

Figure 9.9. *iris*: Development of the average effective mutation step size (left) and the average degree of effectiveness (right) over the generations for different numbers of additional calculation registers (2, 16, 64) using effective mutations (**effmut**). Average figures over 50 runs.

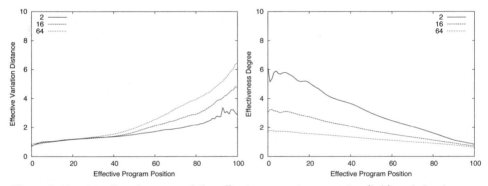

Figure 9.10. *iris*: Development of the effective mutation step size (left) and the degree of effectiveness (right) over the effective program positions. Position 0 holds the first instruction of a program. Average figures over 50 runs.

Figure 9.10 compares the effective step size and the effectiveness degree for different (effective) program positions. Because a higher absolute number of registers involves wider but not necessarily larger program graphs, the number of connections between the instruction nodes decreases (see also Section 7.1). At the beginning of a program step sizes are similarly small for different register numbers. This part typically features the highest effectiveness, especially if the number of registers is small. Towards the end of a program the effectiveness decreases while the effective step size increases. Larger step sizes are correlated with higher register numbers even though the effectiveness is similarly small. As noted earlier, the effective step size not only depends on the effectiveness of the mutated instruction, but also on the effectiveness of the (depending) preceding instructions in a program. Instruction nodes closer to the root, near the last effective instruction in a program, have less connections, especially with many calculation registers, and are, therefore, less protected against disconnections.

When using random instruction mutations, the amount of noneffective instructions in programs continuously increases during a run, while this amount remains mostly constant with effective instruction mutations (see Figure 9.11). At the same time, the number of effective instructions is smaller with mut than can be observed with effmut (not shown). The higher proportion of noneffective code comes along with more noneffective variations (effective step size 0) and, thus, a smaller average effective step size. If noneffective variations are excluded, however, there is a clear linear increase in average step size for mut in Figure 9.11. Apparently, a higher number of noneffective instructions increases the likelihood for reactivations.

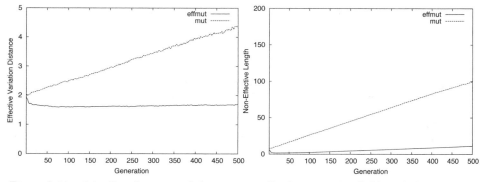

Figure 9.11. *iris*: Development of the average effective step size (left) and the number of noneffective instructions (right) for effective mutations (effmut) and free mutations (mut). Noneffective variations not regarded. Effective step size increases proportionally to the amount of noneffective code. Average figures over 100 runs.

It has to be noted, however, that the increase in step size is still small compared to the increase in noneffective code. Thus we may conclude that the dependence between intron instructions increases over a run as well. The self-protection effect may be supposed to be weaker than for effective code, but still present. Noneffective instructions may be much more loosely connected via register dependencies since they are not directly influenced by fitness selection. The reader may recall that this code can form several disconnected graph components (see Section 3.3). Our experiment has thus identified larger effective step sizes as a second reason for the worse performance of free instruction mutations compared to effective mutations, in addition to the higher rate of noneffective variations.

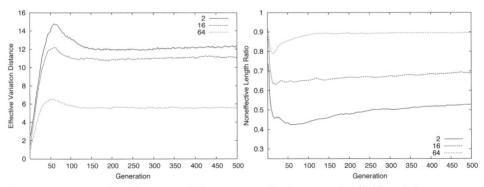

Figure 9.12. *iris*: Development of the average effective step size (left) and the proportion of noneffective length (right) over the generations for different numbers of additional calculation registers (2, 16, 64) using linear crossover (**cross**). Higher proportion
of noneffective code leads to smaller effective step sizes. Average figures over 50 runs.

Finally, we compare the development of effective step size for linear
crossover (**cross**) in Figure 9.12. In contrast to the results found with
instructions mutations, the step size *decreases* with a larger number of
registers, even though the average effectiveness degree remains similar to
that in Figure 9.9. This is because a higher number of registers implies a
higher proportion of noneffective code when using segment variations, as
shown in Figure 9.12 and in Section 7.1. As already noted, the proportion
of noneffective instructions in a program may act as a second implicit
protection mechanism that reduces the effective step size, besides the self-
protection effect described. A higher robustness of effective code seems to
have a smaller influence on the effective step size than a higher proportion
of noneffective code for segment variation.

9.7.3   Structural Diversity Selection

For the three test problems introduced in Section 9.6, Table 9.3 shows
average error rates obtained with and without selecting for structural
diversity. Different selection pressures have been tested. For the minimum
number of fitness tournaments (three) necessary for a diversity selection
on the second level (see Section 9.4) we discern selection probabilities of
50 percent and 100 percent. Higher selection pressures are induced by
increasing the number of tournaments (up to 4 or 8 here).

Diversity selection is examined under a crossover and a mutation approach. For each problem and both forms of variation, the performance
increases continuously with the influence of diversity selection in Table
9.3. The highest selection pressure tested results in a two-fold or higher
improvement of prediction error. This clearly shows, among other things,

that not only population-dependent operators like crossover, but even pure mutation-based variation may benefit from a higher code diversity.

It is notable that in all test cases, linear GP works significantly better by using (effective) mutations instead of crossover. As already demonstrated in previous chapters, the linear program representation is more amenable for small mutations, especially if those are directed towards effective instructions.

Table 9.3. Second-level selection for *structural* diversity with different selection pressures. Selection pressure controlled by selection probability and number of fitness tournaments (T). Average error over 200 runs. Statistical standard error in parenthesis.

Variation	Selection		*sinepoly* SSE		*iris* CE		*even8parity* SE	
	%	#T	*mean*	*std.*	*mean*	*std.*	*mean*	*std.*
cross	0	2	3.01	0.35	2.11	0.10	58	3.4
	50	3	2.89	0.34	1.42	0.08	35	2.4
	100	3	2.77	0.34	1.17	0.07	27	2.2
	100	4	1.96	0.22	**1.09**	0.07	**19**	1.8
	100	8	**0.69**	0.06	—		—	
effmut	0	2	0.45	0.04	0.84	0.06	15	1.2
	50	3	0.43	0.03	0.63	0.05	12	1.0
	100	3	0.30	0.02	0.60	0.05	10	1.1
	100	4	0.23	0.02	**0.33**	0.04	**7**	0.8
	100	8	**0.17**	0.01	—		—	

9.7.4 Development of Effective Diversity

In Section 9.4 we defined the (structural) diversity of a population as the average effective distance between two randomly selected individuals. Figure 9.13 illustrates, exemplary for the *iris* problem,[2] the development of diversity during runs for different selection pressures and variation operators. The higher the selection pressure chosen, the higher the diversity. Instead of a premature loss of diversity we observe an increase of structural diversity over the generations. While effective diversity increases with crossover until a certain level and stays rather constant then, it increases almost linearly with effective mutation. This behavior might find its explanation in the variable-length representation in genetic programming. The longer effective programs develop during a run, the larger effective distances can become.

---

[2] *even8parity* and *sinepoly* have yielded similar results.

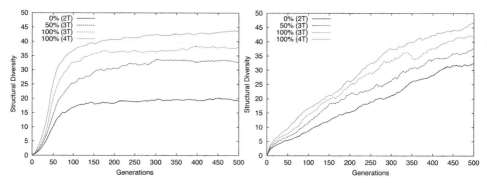

Figure 9.13.   *iris*: Structural diversity (average effective distance) with different selection pressures. Selection pressure controlled by selection probability and number of fitness tournaments (T). Average figures over 100 runs. Macro variation by **cross** (left) or **effmut** (right).

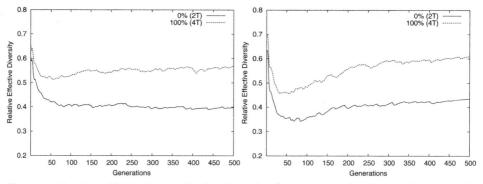

Figure 9.14.   *iris*: Normalized effective diversity (average relative distance) with and without diversity selection. 100 percent macro variation.

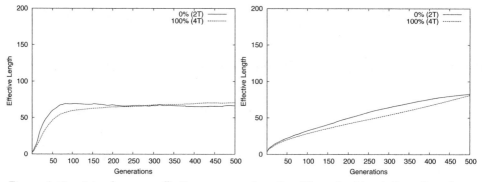

Figure 9.15.   *iris*: Average effective program length with and without diversity selection. Difference in program lengths negligibly small compared to difference in diversity.

Therefore, we compare a diversity control that applies the *relative* effective distance metric (see Equation 9.6). Figure 9.14 shows the development of this *normalized effective diversity* with and without an explicit diversity control. In addition, Figure 9.15 confirms that growth of effective code is hardly affected by diversity selection and that thus the influence of program length on the distance calculation can be neglected. Apart from an early drop during the first 50 generations there is no further decrease of diversity in later generations. Both forms of variation, linear crossover and effective mutation, maintain diversity over a run, even without an explicit distance control. This is especially interesting because crossover is applied exclusively for variation here, together with a 100 percent reproduction rate. The disruptive nature of linear crossover as well as the high amount of noneffective code in programs (see Chapters 5 and 6) may be responsible for this phenomenon.

With effective mutation the normalized diversity may even increase again with effective mutation, but then levels off and remains at an almost constant level.

It is clear that mutations continuously introduce a high degree of innovation into the population. The success of recombination, instead, depends only on the composition of the genetic material in the population. The more different two recombined solutions are, the higher the expected innovation of their offspring.

9.7.5 Semantic Diversity Selection

The computational overhead of a structural distance control has been found affordable for linear genetic programs, especially if the order of instructions is not considered (see Section 9.2). Here we test a semantic diversity selection for comparison. Semantic diversity is defined as the average *output* distance of two individuals that have been randomly selected from the population (see Section 9.3). For each problem the same distance metric has been used like in the corresponding fitness function (see Table 9.1).

Comparing results in Table 9.4 with results in Table 9.3 we conclude that semantic diversity selection has a much smaller effect on the prediction quality than selection for structural diversity. The continuous problem *sinepoly* could not be solved more successfully by semantic diversity selection. For the two discrete problems one can detect a significant influence only in runs with effective mutation.

A possible explanation is that program semantics is related to the unique optimum of the problem, in contrast to program structure. For the program outputs the optimum is the set of desired outputs given in fitness cases. Hence, the number of possibly different output patterns decreases when fitness approaches its optimum value 0. Structural diversity, instead, is relatively independent from fitness.

Table 9.4. Second-level selection for *semantic* diversity with different selection pressures. Selection pressure controlled by selection probability and number of fitness tournaments (T). Average error over 200 runs. Statistical standard error in parenthesis.

Variation	Selection		sinepoly SSE		iris CE		even8parity SE	
	%	#T	mean	std.	mean	std.	mean	std.
cross	0	2	3.01	0.35	2.11	0.10	58	3.4
	50	3	2.40	0.22	1.82	0.09	40	2.5
	100	3	3.51	0.36	1.62	0.08	46	3.1
	100	4	3.42	0.33	1.80	0.09	42	2.8
effmut	0	2	0.45	0.04	0.84	0.06	15	1.2
	50	3	0.33	0.02	0.77	0.06	13	1.2
	100	3	0.43	0.03	0.68	0.05	12	1.1
	100	4	0.49	0.05	0.42	0.05	9	0.9

9.7.6   Diversity and Fitness Progress

Further interesting observations can be made when comparing the convergence of best fitness and population diversity over a *single* run. Fitness of the current best individual reflects the progress of the evolutionary search. Two typical example runs in Figures 9.17 and 9.18 reveal that there is no continuous increase in the average effective distance as one might expect from averaging results over multiple runs (see Figure 9.13). The growth of structural diversity is interrupted rather by sudden rapid drops (*diversity waves*). Simultaneously, periods of fast fitness convergence can be observed where the current best individual is replaced once or several times in a row. Code diversity decreases quickly because a new best individual spreads in the population within a few generations. How quickly program diversity recovers after such an event depends on how many generations have elapsed so far. The higher the diversity level that has been reached before the drop, the sharper the increase. Structural diversity increases on fitness plateaus, i.e., during periods where the best fitness stagnates. During those times the population spreads over the fitness landscape to explore the search space of programs more widely. Comparable results have been found with runs using both kinds of macro variations.

A different behavior has been observed with the continuous problem (*sinepoly*). Structural diversity also progresses wave-like, but with a higher

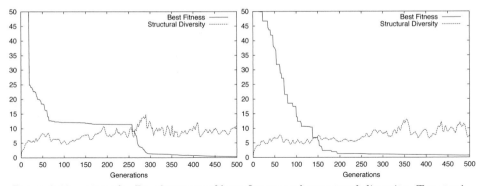

Figure 9.16. *sinepoly*: Development of best fitness and structural diversity. Two typical example runs.

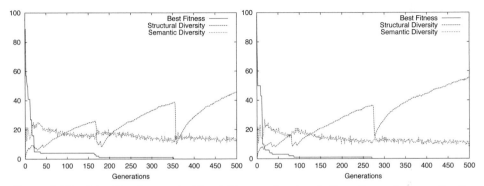

Figure 9.17. *iris*: Development of best fitness, structural diversity, and semantic diversity. Structural diversity grows during phases of fitness stagnation. Two typical example runs.

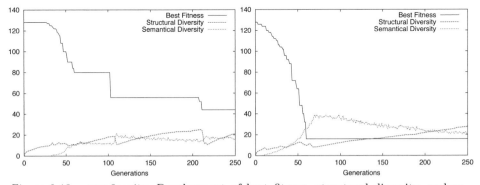

Figure 9.18. *even8parity*: Development of best fitness, structural diversity, and semantic diversity. Structural diversity grows during phases of fitness stagnation. Two typical example runs.

frequency and a smaller amplitude (see Figure 9.16). Correlation with best fitness is less clear and phases of fitness stagnation are shorter. Results in [27] confirm that correlation between diversity and best fitness is comparatively weak for regressions.

While structural diversity decreases quickly in our discrete problems (*iris* and *even8parity*) when the best fitness improves, a sudden increase of semantic diversity (average fitness distance) can be observed. This phenomenon can be explained by a fast propagation of the new best fitness value in the population. During periods where best fitness stagnates, average fitness distance decreases again.

It is important to note that the increase in structural diversity on fitness plateaus happens implicitly, i.e., without applying an explicit control of diversity. Diversity selection only increases the structural distance between individuals on fitness plateaus. Radical drops of diversity as a consequence of a sudden acceleration of convergence speed, however, are just as possible as without diversity selection. This demonstrates that increasing structural diversity does not slow down convergence to the best fitness over a run. On the contrary, much smaller prediction errors have been observed with diversity selection in Table 9.3.

9.7.7   Control of Effective Mutation Step Size

In Section 9.5 we motivated the explicit control of the *effective* distance between parent and offspring. We will restrict ourselves to instruction mutations here. Recall that our distance metric regards instructions (operators) as the smallest units. Variation is accordingly dominated by macro mutations with an *absolute* step size that is set at its permanent minimum of 1 instruction. *Effective* step size may become significantly larger than 1, however, as demonstrated in Section 9.7.1.

What we want to find out in particular is, whether solution quality may be further improved by reducing effective mutation distances probabilistically. In the following experiments, a program is mutated repeatedly until the distance between parent and offspring falls below a maximum threshold. Each time a mutation is not accepted its effect on the program is reversed while the choice of the mutation point is free in every iteration. After a predetermined number of unsuccessful trials, the procedure is terminated and the last variation is executed without restrictions.

Table 9.5 compares average prediction errors for different maximum mutation distances. We consider the maximum program length (200 instructions) to be the maximal possible distance. For all three benchmark problems, best results are obtained with maximum effective distance 1. Thus, at most one instruction may change its effectiveness status, i.e., one node of the effective graph component may be added or removed (see Section 3.3). It is interesting to note that in this case insertions or deletions of full instructions do not create noneffective code at all.

Table 9.5. Maximum restriction of effective mutation distance. Average error over 200 runs. Statistical standard error in parenthesis.

Variation	Maximum Distance	*sinepoly* SSE		*iris* CE		*even8parity* SE	
		mean	*std.*	*mean*	*std.*	*mean*	*std.*
effmut	—	0.46	0.06	0.90	0.06	16	1.3
	20	0.41	0.05	0.83	0.06	15	1.2
	10	0.35	0.04	0.72	0.06	13	1.2
	2	0.28	0.03	0.68	0.05	11	1.1
	1	**0.26**	0.03	**0.54**	0.05	**9**	0.9

This result is all the more interesting if we consider that a restriction in variation distance always implies a restriction in variation freedom. More specifically, certain modifications might not be executed at certain program positions because too many other instructions would be affected. It is important in this context to watch the number of iterations required until a mutation gets accepted. On the one hand, the average number of iterations reveals how strongly the variation freedom is restricted. On the other hand, multiple recalculations of the effective distance may produce computational costs that cannot be neglected.

Table 9.6. Average number of iterations until a maximum mutation distance is met.

Variation	Maximum Distance	#Iterations *sinepoly*	*iris*	*even8parity*
effmut	—	1.00	1.00	1.00
	10	1.02	1.02	1.02
	5	1.06	1.05	1.05
	2	1.18	1.12	1.12
	1	1.37	1.18	1.20

As we can learn from Table 9.6, the average number of iterations until a maximum distance criterion is met, increases only slightly when we lower the threshold. Not even one and a half iterations are necessary, on average, with the lowest maximum bound (1 instruction) while the maximum number of iterations (10 here) has hardly ever been reached. Both aspects, together with the results from Table 9.5 emphasize that freedom of variation is restricted only slightly and that the computational overhead of controlling effective mutation distances is affordable.

Results in Table 9.6 correspond to the distance distributions in Figures 9.5 to 9.7 where only about 20 to 35 percent of all measured effective step sizes are larger than 1. By turning these larger disruptions explicitly into step size 1 (through further trials), there is less need for an implicit step size control during the evolutionary process, i.e., a self-protection of effective code as reported in Section 9.7.2. In particular, no higher effectiveness degree of instructions has to emerge just for protection purposes, but only if it is advantageous for reaching better solutions. Thus we have seen that even though the average effective step size has turned out to be small already implicitly, an explicit minimization leads to an even better performance.

9.8   Alternative Selection Criteria

A two-level tournament selection may also be used for implementing *complexity (growth) control*, as will be applied in Section 10.8.4. The separation of linear genetic programs into effective and noneffective instructions offers the possibility for a *selective* complexity selection. In other words, one may select specifically for the smallest *effective, noneffective,* or *absolute* program length. Diversity selection and complexity selection can also be applied in combination by adding a third selection level.

Besides smaller length or larger distance there are other properties of linear genetic programs that may be selected for. For instance, one might want to select for a smaller or larger *average number* of effective registers. Like the length of the imperative program, the width of the functional program structure may vary with the problem to be solved. Another possible alternative might be to select for a higher effectiveness degree of instructions, i.e., for a higher connectivity of nodes.

Active selection for more diverse individuals may also be used to reduce the population size without sacrificing performance. By maintaining the same level of diversity, even a small population may cover a wide area of the search space. Smaller population sizes mean less fitness evaluations per generation which, in turn, results in computational speedup. This is especially interesting for time-critical applications. In [85] population size is reduced actively by removing individuals that are structurally very similar to other individuals with equal fitness.

9.9 Summary and Conclusion

In this chapter we measured and controlled the diversity of effective programs and the effective step size of different variation operators explicitly for three different benchmark problems. We proposed different metrics to calculate structural or semantic distance between linear genetic programs. The following major conclusions can be drawn from the various experiments performed:

☐ A clear positive correlation between structural distance and fitness distance of programs was demonstrated. In particular, measuring structural differences between subcomponents of effective programs has demonstrated (weak) causality of variation step sizes.

☐ An explicit control of code diversity was introduced in terms of a two-level tournament selection that compares fitness on the first level and diversity on the second level. Fitness selection always has higher priority with this multi-objective selection method. By increasing structural distance between effective programs (effective diversity) in the population, performance improved significantly. This was the case for both crossover-based and pure mutation-based variation.

☐ The level of effective diversity has been found to stabilize early during a run even if crossover is applied exclusively and even without applying an explicit diversity control. This level is directly adjustable by the selection pressure applied on diversity.

☐ Instruction mutations were introduced in Chapter 6 to cause minimal structural variations on linear genetic programs. Only one instruction was varied to let programs grow or shrink. In this chapter we tried to achieve the same on the level of effective code. In particular, it turned out to be best if not more than one effective instruction in a program changes its effectiveness status through mutation. On the functional level only one node of the effective graph component may be added or removed. The average number of mutations iterated to fulfill this condition was small.

☐ Effective mutation step sizes were measured much smaller than expected. Effective program structures emerged that were quite robust against larger destructions (deactivations) in the course of evolution. An increasing degree of effectiveness of instructions is responsible for this self-protection effect or implicit control of effective step size. In this way, multiple connections of instruction nodes (on the functional level) offer a fundamental advantage of linear programs over tree programs.

Chapter 10

CODE GROWTH AND NEUTRAL VARIATIONS

This chapter brings together theories about neutral variations and code growth in genetic programming. We argue that neutral variations are important for the growth of code in GP runs. Other existing theories about code growth are verified for linear GP and are partly reevaluated from a different perspective.

In evolutionary computation neutral variations are argued to explore flat regions of the fitness landscape while non-neutral variations exploit regions with gradient information. We investigate the influence of different variation effects on growth of code and the prediction quality for different kinds of variation operators. It is well known that a high proportion of neutral code (introns) in genetic programs may increase the probability for variations to be neutral. But which type of variation creates the introns in the first place? For linear GP with minimum mutation, step size results show that neutral variations almost exclusively represent a cause for (rather than a result of) the emergence and growth of intron code. This part of the chapter is a continuation of our earlier studies [25].

We also examine different linear genetic operators regarding an implicit length bias. In contrast to an explicit bias, implicit bias does not result from the dynamics of the operator alone, but requires the existence of a fitness pressure.

We will close this chapter with a discussion about how to control code growth in linear GP. Different approaches are reviewed including variation-based methods and selection-based methods. Both may be applied specifically to effective code and/or to noneffective code.

10.1   Code Growth in GP

One characteristic of genetic programming is that variable-length individuals grow in size. To a certain extent this growth is necessary to direct the evolutionary search into regions of the search space where sufficiently complex solutions exist with high fitness. It is not recommended, however, to initiate evolutionary algorithms with programs of very large or even maximal size (see Section 7.6). If the initial complexity of programs is too high the population may be not flexible enough to move towards a region of the search space with highly fit programs.

Through the influence of variation operators – especially their variation step size – and through other effects that will be discussed in this chapter, genetic programs may grow too quickly. The size of those programs may thus significantly exceed the minimum size required to solve the problem. As a result, finding a solution may become more difficult. This negative effect of code growth, i.e., programs becoming larger than necessary without corresponding fitness improvements, became known as the *bloat effect*. Code growth has been widely investigated in the GP literature [64, 2, 16, 91, 124, 70, 125, 71, 10, 128].

In general, a high complexity of GP programs causes an increase of evaluation time and reduces the flexibility of genetic operations in the course of the evolutionary process. The situation is aggravated by the fact that even if unnecessarily large solutions are found of acceptable quality, they are more difficult to analyze and may show worse generalization performance [117].

Depending on the proportion of noneffective code occurring with a certain combination of variation operators, the problem of longer processing time may be solved in linear GP by removing structural introns from the genetic program prior to fitness calculation (see Section 3.2.1). Thus, only effective code imposes relevant computational costs during execution. Computational costs, however, are only one aspect of the problem.

The complexity of a linear genetic program is measured by the number of instructions it contains. As already noted, we distinguish between *absolute program length* and *effective program length* in linear GP. Correspondingly, we discern code growth of all instructions from growth of (structurally) effective code. This is referred to as *absolute growth* and *effective growth*.

10.2 Proposed Causes of Code Growth

Several theories have been proposed to explain the phenomenon of code bloat in genetic programming. Basically, three different causes of code growth can be named so far that do not contradict each other, but may coexist independently. All causes require the existence of fitness information, i.e., may not hold true on completely flat fitness landscapes. Thus, fitness may be regarded as a necessary precondition for code growth.

We discern two types of code that allow genetic programs to exceed the minimal size required for solving a problem: (1) intron code – which may be removed without changing the program behavior – and (2) semantically equivalent extensions (see Chapter 3). Only (semantically) effective program size depends *directly* on the fitness. At least to a certain extent, solutions have to increase their effective complexity to improve their fitness performance.

For the following considerations, we assume that all variation operators are designed and configured such that they are not explicitly biased towards creating longer offspring more frequently, at least not independent of fitness selection.

10.2.1 Protection Theory

The *protection theory* [16, 91, 10, 128] argues that code growth and, in particular, growth of noneffective code occurs as a protection against destructive variations. The *protection effect* is sometimes explained by a higher proportion of neutral variations (and a corresponding lower proportion of destructive variations) that results from a higher rate of noneffective code in programs.

A more general explanation for the protection effect and its influence on code growth may be found by considering the structural step size of variations, including both neutral and non-neutral variations. The destructive influence of a variation on the program structure strongly depends on its step size. If the maximum amount of code, that may be exchanged or deleted in one variation step, is large or unrestricted, evolution may reduce the impact on the effective code by developing a higher proportion of introns in programs. In this way, intron code controls the (relative) effective step size which depends on the ratio of effective and noneffective code in a program. Programs with a higher rate of noneffective code on average produce fitter offspring, i.e., offspring with a higher survival probability. It is argued that code grows because such offspring will be more likely reselected for reproduction and variation [91]. At any rate, a higher intron proportion in programs will increase the probability for variations to be neutral. This is even more so if the variation step size is small. Note that the effective step size is zero for neutral variations while the survival probability of offspring is definitely higher than after destructive variations.

10.2.2 Drift Theory

Another theory (*drift theory*) [70, 71] claims that code growth results from the structure of the search space or, more precisely, from the distribution of semantically identical solutions in the population. The same phenotype function may be represented by many structurally different programs. There are many more large genotypes than there are small ones with a certain fitness value, due to intron code and/or mathematically equivalent expressions. Therefore, genetic operators will, with a higher probability, create larger offspring that perform as well as their parents. Since the population of programs represents a sample of the search space, longer solutions will be also selected more frequently. Both effects will result in the population evolving in a random drift towards more complex regions of the search space.

This general drift theory may be criticized because it assumes that longer programs emerge due to a certain structure of the search space. It has to be noted, however, that not all programs of the search space are created equally likely and, thus, may not be composed of an arbitrarily large amount of introns. It will strongly depend on the variation operator applied and on the variation step size as we will see below. We have already demonstrated in Section 6.4 for effective mutation, that programs in the population do not have to become significantly larger than necessary. Hence, the part of the genotype space that is actually explored by a certain operator – starting from small initial programs – may be much smaller than the search space of all possible solutions.

10.2.3 Bias Theory

A third theory (*bias theory*) of code growth is based on the hypothesis of the existence of a *removal bias* in tree-based GP [125, 71, 128]. The change caused by removing a subtree can be expected to be the more destructive the larger the subtree. The effect of the replacing subtree on fitness, on the other hand, is independent of its size. As a result, the growing offspring from which the smaller subtree is removed (and into which the longer is inserted) will survive with a higher probability than its shrinking counterpart.

The size of exchanged subprograms, however, may not be the only reason for code growth. The lower fitness of the parent individual from which the larger subtree is extracted may simply be a result of the fact that the root of the subtree (crossover point) lies closer to the tree root where crossover more likely will be destructive. Vice versa, the smaller subtree will originate more likely from a region lower in the tree.

The removal bias theory presumes that there are no side effects induced by program functions in the problem environment. It is further important that both parents have, on average, the same size, since destructiveness of a removed subtree depends on the absolute program size. Finally, this theory relies strongly on the fact that variation operators affect only a single point in the program tree. We will see in Section 10.7 that such an implicit growth bias cannot be clearly identified in linear GP.

10.3 Influence of Variation Step Size

The maximum step size of a variation operator determines the potential amount of code growth that is possible in one variation step but it does not represent a direct cause. In general, we have to distinguish between *necessary preconditions* (indirect causes) for code growth and *driving forces* (direct causes) as introduced in the last section. A larger step size reduces the probability of neutral variations, but increases the probability that neutral code may emerge from non-neutral variations.

If we want to clearly identify a direct or indirect reason for code growth, it is important to design the experiment in such a way that other causes are disabled as much as possible. The protection effect (see Section 10.2.1) may be at least significantly lower if the step size of variation operators is reduced to a minimum and if program code is not *exchanged* between individuals. Both may be achieved for the imperative program structure of linear GP by mutations that insert *or* delete single random instructions only,[1] as described in Section 6.2. Under these conditions a protection effect may not occur in the form of a reduction of the effective step size, at least for all non-neutral variations that alter program length. The only remaining protection effect could result from reducing the *proportion* of destructive variations in favor of neutral variations. This is possible by increasing the number of introns in a program.

If the mutation step size is set constant to one, neutral instructions cannot be inserted or deleted *directly* along with a *non*-neutral variation, but only

---

[1]Code growth is not possible by exclusively applying *substitutions* of single instructions.

by a neutral variation. Among other things, this allows us to analyze destructive variations independently from their influence on the amount of intron code. Under such conditions, introns may only emerge from non-neutral variations by deactivation of depending instructions (apart from the location of the mutation). This is possible for introns on both the structural level and on the semantic level. The larger the amount of introns the more likely deactivation will become.

Instead, as occurs with segment variation, programs may grow faster and by a smaller number of variation steps if step sizes are larger or unrestricted. In particular, intron instructions may be inserted by variations, too, that are not neutral as a whole.

The high variability of the linear representation allows structural step sizes to be permanently minimal. The graph-based data flow and the existence of structurally noneffective code in linear genetic programs motivate this choice (see Chapter 3). Due to stronger constraints of the tree representation, small macro variations are difficult to achieve in regions of the tree near to the root. Similarly, introns hardly occur in nodes close to the root, but will be concentrated near leaves of the tree[128].

With minimal variations the drift effect will also be reduced because the difference between parent and offspring comprises only one instruction. By using only minimal steps the evolutionary process will drift less quickly towards more complex regions of search space. At least a drift of intron code will be not possible by non-neutral variations.

10.4   Neutral Variations

Most evolutionary computation approaches model the Darwinian process of natural selection and adaptation. In the Darwinian theory of evolution, organisms adapt to their environment through mutations of the genotype that spread in the population if they offer a fitness advantage. Natural selection is considered to be the dominating force for (molecular) evolution. In particular, the theory claims that most changes by mutation result in fitness changes. Most mutations are believed to be destructive and to quickly be sorted out from the population by selection. That is, a mutation is only believed to survive into the next generation if it improves fitness.

Contrary to this theory, Kimura's [61] neutral theory states that the majority of evolutionary changes on the molecular level are due to neutral or nearly neutral mutations. The neutral theory does not deny the existence of natural selection but assumes that only a small proportion of changes happens adaptively, i.e., follows a fitness gradient. The larger proportion of mutations is believed to stay silent on the phenotype level, i.e., to have no significant influence on survival or reproduction. Those neutral changes spread through populations by random genetic drift which is considered to be the main force of evolution. The orginal neutral theory has been generalized to include near-neutral variations [95, 96]. It has found support in experimental data [62] and is nowadays used as a null-hypothesis in experiments [31].

In linear GP we discern between two types of neutral variations. While *neutral noneffective variations* change the (structurally) noneffective code, *neutral effective variations* change the effective code (see Section 5.1). The first type of change may be avoided by making all genetic operations alter effective code. In Chapter 6 neutral instruction mutations have been identified as a motor of evolutionary progress. Best results were obtained by actively increasing the proportion of effective neutral mutations.

Neutral variations do not provide any gradient information to the evolutionary algorithm. That is, they reduce the probability for improving fitness by a gradient descent (*exploitation*). Instead, neutral variations allow evolution to more quickly overcome plateaus of the fitness landscape. The fitness landscape can be explored more widely and efficiently for potentially better suboptima (*exploration*). In doing so, neutral variations may be expected to prevent the evolutionary search from getting stuck in local suboptima (see also Section 5.4).

If destructive variations dominate the evolutionary process, it is hard for an individual to improve step-by-step and to spread within the population. More likely, it will decrease in fitness until it is replaced by a better individual. By neutral variations, instead, an individual may be altered without changing its ability to succeed in fitness selection. This offers evolution the possibility to develop solutions "silently", i.e., without exposing changes to fitness selection after every variation step. This intron code may become relevant when being reactivated later in the course of the evolutionary process (see Section 10.7.5). If the variation step size is large enough, intron manipulations may be carried out by non-neutral variations, too. However, the resulting individuals will survive with less likelihood because a larger amount of variations is destructive.

In [8] we first emphasized the relevance of neutral variations in genetic programming. In [12] we analyzed potential benefits of neutrality and neutral networks for evolutionary search in a Boolean problem space. Yu and Miller [143] found neutral variations advantageous for solving a Boolean problem after extra neutral code has been explicitly included into a graph representation of programs – similar to the structural introns existing *im-*

plicitly in linear GP (see Section 3.2). Lopez *et al.* [79] introduced unused code into tree-based GP by allowing non-executed subtrees to be part of the representation. This approach may be considered as an extended concept of explicit introns (see also Section 5.7.6).

10.5   Conditional Reproduction and Variation

We use a steady state evolutionary algorithm (see Section 2.3) and apply tournament selection with a minimum of two participants per tournament. Copies of the parent individuals are subjected to variations and may either replace the parents in the populations (no reproduction) or the tournament losers (reproduction). With tournament selection the reproduction rate determines the number of parent individuals surviving a variation step, i.e., that are accepted into the steady-state population together with the offspring. Under such a local selection scheme, it is not recommended to significantly restrict the reproduction rate. Even if diversity is better preserved by less individuals being overwritten, fitness convergence may suffer because better solutions spread slower in the population and can be lost with a higher probability. In particular, the loss of a new best-fit individual becomes possible if reproduction is not strictly applied. Due to the high complexity of genetic programs and the comparatively low rate of constructive variation (and thus improvements) during a GP run, information that has been lost may be hard to be regained in the following evolutionary steps.

Under which conditions can reproduction be skipped without risking to loose better solutions? When is reproduction absolutely necessary? Obviously, after noneffective variations the effective code has not changed and is already fully reproduced through the offspring individual. In this case, the variation includes a reproduction and additional copies of the parent individuals do not contribute to the preservation of information, but only to a loss of diversity. If reproduction happens only after effective variations, relevant information cannot get lost. This approach is referred to as *effective reproduction* and constitutes another way to preserve the effective diversity of a population, besides the explicit diversity selection which has been introduced in Chapter 9.

Noneffective code variations, by definition, are always neutral in terms of fitness change, but not all neutral events come about by variations of noneffective code. Since neutral variations do not necessarily preserve the structurally effective solution, skipping the reproduction step will make a difference. Recall that such variations may only be neutral on the particular fitness cases used but not necessarily in terms of all possible input data. This may reduce the generalization performance of programs.

An omission of the reproduction step after destructive variations is not motivated, since better individuals would be replaced by worse. Finally, reproduction after constructive variations should be retained because they are essential and the probability of such events is rather low.

In addition to reproduction of parent individuals, integration of offspring into the population may be restricted. Newly created individuals might be accepted only if they result from a certain type of variation. This *conditional acceptance* of variations implies that the reproduction step is omitted to keep the population content unchanged. Otherwise, parental information would be doubled, i.e., old information would be erased in the steady-state population without creating new information.

10.6   Experimental Setup

The different experiments documented in this chapter are conducted with the four benchmark problems that have already been introduced in Sections 5.8 and 6.3. Unless otherwise stated, the same system configuration is used here. Variants of this standard configuration will be described along with corresponding experiments in the following section.

10.7   Experiments

10.7.1   Conditional Instruction Mutations

The experiments documented in Tables 10.1 to 10.4 investigate the influence of different variation effects on both the complexity of (effective) programs and the prediction performance. Prediction errors are averaged over the best-of-run solutions. Absolute and effective program lengths are averaged over all programs created during runs. Figure 10.1 shows the generational development of average program length in the population. Due to the small step size of mutations used, the average length of *best* individuals develops almost identically (not documented).

In the no∗ experiments offspring are *not* inserted into the population if they result from a certain type of variation (destructive, neutral, noneffective). In addition, reproduction of parents is skipped. In other words, the variation is canceled without affecting the state of the population. Note that this is different from the control of neutrality discussed in Section 6.2.6 where variations are repeated until they are neutral. In all experiments the number of variations (and evaluations) that defines a

Table 10.1. *mexican hat*: Conditional acceptance of mutation effects and conditional reproduction using instruction mutations (mut, B1). Average results over 100 runs.

Config.	SSE		Length			Variations (%)		
	mean	*std.*	*abs.*	*eff.*	*%*	*constr.*	*neutral*	*noneff.*
mut	3.5	0.5	140	60	43	0.8	54	52
nodestr	3.3	0.5	139	61	44	0.2	53	52
noneutr	1.6	0.1	**38**	**28**	72	7.5	37	34
nononeff	1.5	0.1	**41**	**30**	74	4.8	41	32
effrepro	**1.5**	0.2	126	50	40	3.3	60	52

Table 10.2. *distance*: Conditional acceptance of mutation effects and conditional reproduction using instruction mutations (mut, B0). Average results over 100 runs.

Config.	SSE		Length			Variations (%)		
	mean	*std.*	*abs.*	*eff.*	*%*	*constr.*	*neutral*	*noneff.*
mut	6.5	0.3	78	32	41	0.5	63	63
nodestr	8.0	0.3	78	32	41	0.1	64	63
noneutr	6.0	0.3	**24**	**15**	63	6.3	48	47
nononeff	6.5	0.2	**25**	**16**	62	4.7	52	48
effrepro	**4.8**	0.3	56	25	44	4.1	61	58

generation remains the same (1,000). This means that both accepted and non-accepted variations are included in the calculation of prediction error, program lengths, and variation rates.

Standard instruction mutation (mut) is characterized by a more balanced emergence of neutral/noneffective operations and non-neutral/effective operations.

Destructive variations hardly contribute to evolutionary progress. For all test problems, prediction error changes only slightly compared to the standard approach if offspring from destructive variations are not accepted (nodestr), even though about 50 percent of all variations are rejected and the rate of constructive variations is much smaller, in particular for classification problems (see Tables 10.3 and 10.4). Obviously, the probability of selecting an individual that performs worse than its parent is so low that it hardly makes any difference if this individual is copied into the population or not. Due to a low survival rate of these offspring and due to the minimum mutation step size, destructive mutations do not influence code growth either.

The influence of neutral and constructive variations on code growth is in clear contrast to the influence of destructive variations. Obviously, survival probability of their offspring is higher. This facilitates both a

Table 10.3. *spiral*: Conditional acceptance of mutation effects and conditional reproduction using instruction mutations (mut, B1). Average results over 100 runs.

Config.	CE		Length			Variations (%)		
	mean	*std.*	*abs.*	*eff.*	*%*	*constr.*	*neutral*	*noneff.*
mut	13.6	0.6	128	64	50	0.3	50	42
nodestr	12.4	0.5	117	64	55	0.02	46	39
noneutr	20.0	0.6	**37**	**31**	82	5.0	32	20
nononeff	13.1	0.5	69	62	89	1.5	32	13
effrepro	**9.2**	0.4	117	83	71	1.1	45	25

Table 10.4. *three chains*: Conditional acceptance of mutation effects and conditional reproduction using instruction mutations (mut, B1). Average results over 100 runs.

Config.	CE		Length			Variations (%)		
	mean	*std.*	*abs.*	*eff.*	*%*	*constr.*	*neutral*	*noneff.*
mut	15.5	0.6	132	57	43	0.2	62	49
nodestr	16.4	0.7	124	53	43	0.03	62	49
noneutr	24.6	0.8	**34**	**28**	82	5.3	38	20
nononeff	12.9	0.7	80	71	88	1.0	45	13
effrepro	**12.4**	0.6	116	89	76	0.7	54	22

continuous further development of solutions and the growth of programs. It is important to note that both the absolute size and the effective size of programs are reduced the most by exclusion of neutral variation effects from the population (noneutr).[2]

Noneffective neutral variations create or modify noneffective instructions, i.e., structural introns. Accordingly, we may assume that mostly *effective neutral* variations are responsible for the emergence of semantic introns within the (structurally) effective part of program. However, effective neutral variations and semantic introns are harder to induce and, thus, occur with a lower frequency if the fitness function is continuous. This is reflected in the results for the two regression problems by similar rates of noneffective operations and neutral operations. For the discrete classification problems, instead, the proportion of neutral variations has been found to be significantly larger than the proportion of noneffective variations which means a higher rate of effective neutral variations. Note that branch instructions that have been used with both classification problems further promote the emergence of semantic introns.

---

[2]This is the case even if an explicit growth bias has been used with some problems (see Section 5.8).

In the **nononeff** experiments noneffective variations are rejected, i.e., only effective variations are accepted. In contrast to **noneutr**, this includes effective neutral variations. Semantic introns created by these variations may be responsible for the larger effective code that occurs with both classification problems in **nononeff** runs. With the two regression problems the average effective size is reduced (approximately by half) for both **noneutr** and **nononeff** because most neutral variations are noneffective. If we compare results after the same number of *effective* evaluations the **nononeff** approach corresponds to the **effmut** operator that calculates effective mutations algorithmically.

In both **noneutr** and **nononeff** runs the proportion of noneffective (intron) code is much lower, especially with the classification tasks. This clearly demonstrates that intron code in programs emerges mostly from neutral variations. Furthermore, the proportion of neutral variations and of noneffective variations is lower when we exclude the effects of such variations from the population. This may be taken as an indication that intron code increases the probability of neutral variation again.

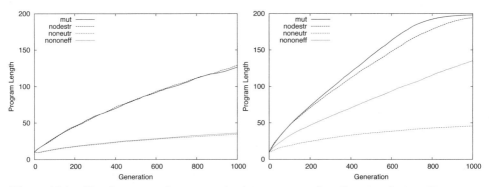

Figure 10.1. Development of average absolute program length using instruction mutations (**mut**) for *distance* (left) and *three chains* (right). (Similar developments for *mexican hat* and *spiral.*) Code growth significantly reduced without neutral variation effects. Average figures over 100 runs.

We may conclude that neutral variations – in contrast to destructive variations – strongly dominate code growth. Since mutation step sizes are small, constructive variations may only have a minor influence on code growth due to their low frequency. This is the case even though the proportion of constructive variations is much higher when not accepting neutral effects into the population (**noneutr**). Moreover, non-neutral variations may hardly be responsible for an unnecessary growth of code here because the variation step size is minimum. Then intron code cannot be created directly by such operations and *all* changes of a program are exposed to fitness selection.

Being able to induce small mutations at each position of the linear representation carries a special significance for our results. Indirect creation of intron instructions through deactivation seems to play a minor role only. The increasing robustness of effective code against deactivation of instructions renders those less frequent over the course of a run (see Section 9.7.2).

If one looks at prediction quality the noneutr experiments show a clear improvement on one of the two approximation problems (*mexican hat*) while a clear deterioration can be observed on both classification problems. The nononeff experiments, in turn, show performance never dropping below baseline results. Apparently, fitness is not negatively affected if only noneffective neutral variations are excluded. Thus, effective neutral variations may be more relevant than noneffective neutral variations.

We cannot automatically conclude from these results that neutral variations are more essential for solving classification problems only because they are discrete. At least small plateaus will exist on the fitness landscape with problems whose output range is continuous. Better performance may also result from the fact that programs grow larger by neutral changes and less likely go extinct by being overwritten. Recall that classification problems benefit less from a lower complexity of solutions than the two symbolic regressions, because the former make use of branch instructions.

10.7.2 Effective Reproduction

Reproduction after effective variations only (effrepro) is characterized by a clear gain in performance compared to the standard approach (mut) with about 50 percent noneffective variations (see Tables 10.1 to 10.4). Since the reproduction step is rather pointless if the effective code has not been altered (see Section 10.5), diversity of solutions may be better maintained without it. This is confirmed by a higher average fitness and standard deviation in the population (not documented). In contrast to nononeff, newly created individuals are always accepted and find their way into the population. Interestingly, the average prediction error is smaller than or equal to the error obtained in nononeff runs. This may be related to the (effective) program size that is less reduced by a lower reproduction rate of parents than by a lower acceptance rate of their offspring.

10.7.3   Conditional Segment Variations

This section documents the influence of different variation effects on code growth when using *unrestricted* segment operators in linear GP – including two-segment recombination (cross) and one-segment mutation (onesegmut). In Tables 10.5 to 10.8 either destructive variations (nodestr), neutral variations (noneutr) or both (noneutr+nodestr) have been prohibited. Again, both reproduction of parents and integration of offspring into the population are skipped, should the variation be of the corresponding type.

Table 10.5.   mexican hat: Conditional acceptance of variation effects using crossover (cross). Average results over 100 runs after 1,000 generations.

Config.	SSE		Length			Variations (%)		
	mean	*std.*	*abs.*	*eff.*	*%*	*constr.*	*neutral*	*noneff.*
cross	15.4	1.5	180	67	37	4.9	26	22
nodestr	12.4	1.4	177	68	38	0.5	23	22
noneutr	9.9	1.2	170	70	42	10.9	21	18
noneutr+nodestr	3.3	0.4	122	53	43	2.8	19	17

Table 10.6.   mexican hat: Conditional acceptance of variation effects using one-segment mutation (onesegmut). Average results over 100 runs after 1,000 generations.

Config.	SSE		Length			Variations (%)		
	mean	*std.*	*abs.*	*eff.*	*%*	*constr.*	*neutral*	*noneff.*
onesegmut	4.2	0.5	92	38	42	4.6	26	21
nodestr	5.3	0.6	99	43	43	0.2	20	19
noneutr	2.9	0.2	96	43	44	10.4	23	18
noneutr+nodestr	3.2	0.2	75	36	48	2.0	20	19

The step size of segment variations is restricted only by the program length. In contrast to instruction mutations, *non*-neutral (segment) variations may contribute to intron growth by inserting noneffective instructions along with effective ones. In general, the more instructions that can be inserted in one variation step, the less variations that are necessary to let programs bloat, provided that there is at least one cause of code growth valid for the applied genetic operator(s).

As already reported in Section 5.9.2, smaller solution sizes occur by using (one-)segment mutation instead of recombination in Tables 10.6 and 10.8. It will be argued in Section 10.8.2 that these results follow from the fact that randomly created segments restrict the formation and propagation of introns in the population.

Table 10.7. spiral: Conditional acceptance of variation effects using crossover (cross). Average results over 100 runs after 1,000 generations.

Config.	CE		Length			Variations (%)		
	mean	*std.*	*abs.*	*eff.*	*%*	*constr.*	*neutral*	*noneff.*
cross	26.1	0.7	185	102	55	3.6	23	14
nodestr	25.0	0.7	184	103	56	0.1	21	15
noneutr	27.6	0.6	174	106	61	8.7	25	12
noneutr+nodestr	26.1	0.5	101	57	56	1.1	23	13

Table 10.8. spiral: Conditional acceptance of variation effects using one-segment mutation (onesegmut). Average results over 100 runs after 1,000 generations.

Config.	CE		Length			Variations (%)		
	mean	*std.*	*abs.*	*eff.*	*%*	*constr.*	*neutral*	*noneff.*
onesegmut	21.2	0.6	126	65	51	2.4	27	19
nodestr	18.0	0.7	125	66	53	0.04	23	18
noneutr	27.8	0.6	63	36	56	7.2	29	17
noneutr+nodestr	31.4	0.5	37	21	59	0.7	25	19

Similar to the results found with instruction mutations in Section 10.7.1 code growth is hardly affected once destructive variations are not accepted (nodestr). In general, it seems to be very unlikely for a program solution to grow in a sequence of destructive operations without being overwritten.

As opposed to Section 10.7.1 programs grow here even if neutral offspring are not accepted into the population (noneutr). But still a significantly lower complexity has been found for the *spiral* classification when using one-segment mutations. While the fitness performance decreases for this problem, it improves clearly for *mexican hat*. In both problems the rate of constructive variation is more than doubled, compared to the standard approach. Mostly the constructive operations are responsible for growth of noneffective and effective code here. The difference in fitness between runs with and without neutral variations cannot stem from a difference in solution size, at least for *mexican hat*, as it may be the case for instruction mutations in Section 10.7.1.

If both neutral and destructive changes are prohibited (noneutr+nodestr) evolutionary progress and code growth are impacted only by constructive variations. Because the rate of constructive variations is even lower than in the comparative experiment, only a few new individuals are accepted into the population. Nevertheless, this is high enough to let programs grow. The maximum size limitation allows average program length to be more similar, at least in crossover experiments (see Tables 10.5 and 10.7).

Figure 10.2 reveals, however, more significant differences if the maximum limit is chosen so high (1,000 instructions) as to not affect the development of program length until a substantial number of generations (200 for *mexican hat* and 125 for *spiral*). Prohibiting neutral variation effects reduces code growth more than prohibiting destructive effects, although the latter events occur about three times as frequent. Indeed, destructive variation does not seem to have any influence on program growth for the *mexican hat* problem. Code growth is most restricted if neither destructive nor neutral crossover is accepted. The comparatively low number of constructive events alone is not sufficient to bloat programs even though segment length is not restricted.

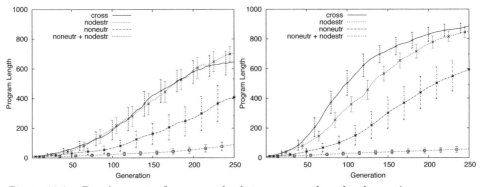

Figure 10.2. Development of average absolute program length when using crossover (**cross**) almost without restriction by the maximum program length (1,000 instructions). Code growth is reduced more without neutral variation effects than without destructive effects. Bars show standard deviation of program length in the population. Average figures over 30 runs for *mexican hat* (left) and *spiral* (right).

10.7.4   Semantic Diversity

We have seen above that the *average fitness of best solutions* changes only a little if destructive variations are not accepted. This is quite different for the *average fitness in the population* as a comparison between Figures 10.3 and 10.4 reveals. Normally, average fitness develops differently from best fitness and with a higher standard deviation if all offspring are included.[3] Typically, the difference between average fitness and best fitness is smaller for the discrete problem with its more narrow range of fitness values.

---

[3]Standard deviation applies to fitness values in the population, not to average fitness over multiple runs.

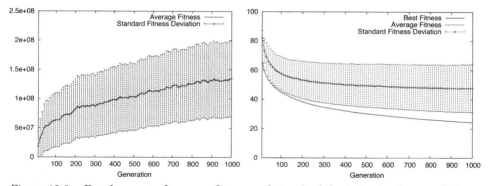

Figure 10.3. Development of average fitness and standard deviation in the population for *mexican hat* (left) and the *spiral* (right) using crossover (cross). Standard deviation is printed 5 times smaller for *mexican hat*. Average figures over 100 runs.

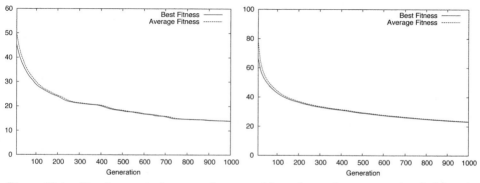

Figure 10.4. Development of average fitness and best fitness for *mexican hat* (left) and *spiral* (right). Very similar if destructive variations are canceled (nodestr). Standard deviation is below 1 (not printed). Average figures over 100 runs.

For both problems average fitness and best fitness are almost equal in Figure 10.4 if worse offspring are prohibited from entering the population (nodestr). Then most individuals share the same fitness value. A low standard deviation of fitness values is an indication for a low semantic diversity of programs in the population. Diversity of the effective code (structural diversity) may also be smaller, because only a few non-neutral (constructive) variations change effective code and most neutral variations only alter noneffective code. In contrast to a higher structural diversity (see Chapter 9), a higher semantic diversity seems to be less important.

The development of average fitness in noneutr runs does not behave differently from the development in normal runs (not shown).

10.7.5   Neutral Drift

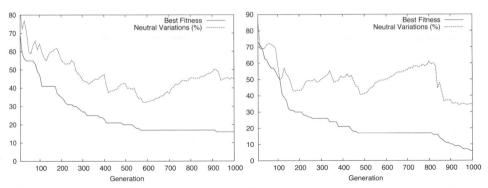

Figure 10.5.   spiral: Development of best fitness and the rate of neutral variation over two typical example runs using instruction mutations (mut, B0). Rate of neutral variations increases almost only on fitness plateaus (during stagnation periods of the best fitness).

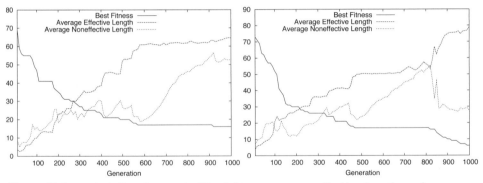

Figure 10.6.   spiral: Development of best fitness, average effective length, and average noneffective length over the same runs as in Figure 10.5. Neutral noneffective code grows continuously on fitness plateaus and shrinks on fitness gradients. Effective code grows stepwise. Length figures have been slightly shifted vertically for a better view.

Figures 10.5 and 10.6 show two characteristic example runs for the *spiral* problem using instruction mutations (mut). The development of the best fitness reflects approximately the progress in the population. Longer stagnation phases of the best fitness, as they occur especially with discrete problems, are correlated with periods of many neutral variations. Actually, the rate of neutral variations increases[4] continuously during such exploration phases, which promotes an increase of noneffective neutral code in the population individuals. One can see that both neutral code and

---

[4]The rate of neutral variation decreases over the *whole* run mostly by the influence of the maximum program length.

neutral variations show a slightly delayed (for a few generations) reaction to a new (best) fitness situation.

If a better (effective) solution occurs it spreads rapidly within a few generations. That is, the population follows (exploits) a newly detected positive fitness gradient. Interestingly, the amount of noneffective code drops again, together with the number of neutral variations during such a period. Almost simultaneously, the effective length increases which is reflected by a stepwise progression in Figure 10.6.

Such observations may be explained by code reactivations. After a period of neutral (and destructive) variations the "silently" developed neutral code is suddenly reactivated in a constructive way. During such *neutral walks* over plateaus of the fitness landscape the individual structure may be developed continuously by neutral changes.

The fact that reactivation of intron segments improves the (best) fitness, shows that introns do not only contribute to unnecessary code growth but are actually relevant for evolutionary progress and (indirectly) for the growth of effective code, too, and so are neutral variations. In particular, this demonstrates that the structurally noneffective code (created by noneffective neutral variations) is used for finding solutions, at least when applying random instruction mutations. Similar correlations as in Figures 10.5 and 10.6 may be expected for the development of *effective* neutral variations and semantic introns.

The above analysis of single runs has shown how neutral variations, code growth and fitness progress are interrelated. But what is the driving force that lets both neutral variations and neutral code increase during stagnation phases of the best fitness? Two possible theories may be put forward:

(1) Neutral variations fully preserve the semantics of a solution and, therefore, guarantee a high survival rate of offspring. Since the survival rate has been found to be very low after destructive variations and since the rate of constructive variations is generally low (see Section 10.7.1), individuals will mostly be selected that have resulted from a neutral variation.

Another important reason why neutral variations have a high impact on the growth of intron code is that the size of this code does not influence the program fitness directly. Especially structurally noneffective code emerges relatively easy in linear GP. Thus, introns may be argued to grow by random drift during the spreading of a population over plateaus of the fitness landscape.

As mentioned in Section 10.4, Kimura's [61] neutral theory considers a random genetic drift of neutral mutations as the main force of natural evolution. The *neutral theory* of code growth may thus regard a drift of intron code by neutral variations as the dominating force of code growth.

(2) By applying only deletions or insertions of single instructions, the possible influence of a protection effect in terms of a reduction of effective step size by more noneffective code is restricted as much as possible (see Section 10.3). However, protection may still occur such that a high proportion of neutral code reinforces the probability for neutral variations.

10.7.6   Crossover Step Size

For the following considerations the reader may recall that linear genetic programs as used in this book may be represented as an equivalent directed acyclic graph (see Section 3.3). Depending on the number of available program registers the graph structure of linear programs can be quite narrow compared to its length. When exchanging segments of instructions by linear crossover, such structures may be easily disrupted completely, meaning that all program paths are affected simultaneously. This leads us to believe that the influence of a segment on fitness depends only in part on its length. Linear crossover might not have a significantly larger destructive effect beyond a certain segment length.

In order to examine this idea we introduce the quantity of *relative fitness change* which is defined as the difference in fitness between parent and offspring (*absolute fitness change*), divided by the parental fitness:

$$\frac{\mathcal{F}_p - \mathcal{F}_o}{\mathcal{F}_p} \tag{10.1}$$

The average fitness change is usually negative since much more variation effects are destructive than constructive.[5]

Figure 10.7 confirms our assumption. In linear genetic programs the segment length (structural step size) is only proportional to the relative fitness change (semantic step size) up to a certain length. One can also see that the segment length beyond which average fitness stagnates is larger if more registers are provided.

In order to guarantee that average segment length remains the same over the entire run, one starts out with genetic programs of maximal size. In doing so, crossover will exchange equally long segments between two

---

[5]Recall here that the optimal fitness value $\mathcal{F}$ is always zero.

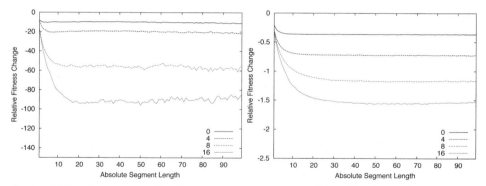

Figure 10.7. Average relative fitness change per segment length when using crossover (**cross**) and a constant program length of 200 instructions. Larger segments are not more destructive beyond a certain length depending on the number of calculation registers (0, 4, 8, and 16). Average figures over 30 runs for *mexican hat* (left) and *spiral* (right).

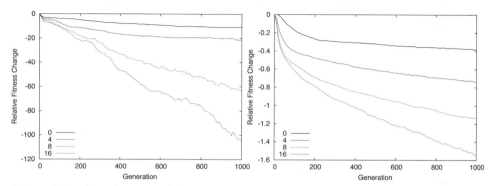

Figure 10.8. Development of the average relative fitness change when using crossover (**cross**) and a constant program length of 200 instructions. Crossover becomes relatively more destructive during a run. Average figures over 30 runs for *mexican hat* (left) and *spiral* (right).

individuals right from the beginning. Nevertheless, crossover will become more destructive over time. Figure 10.8 compares the development of relative fitness changes. The more the program fitness improves over the course of generations, the larger the relative destructive effect will be. The effect is more pronounced with more registers for calculation. We note in passing that very similar figures may be produced for two-segment mutations.

10.7.7 Implicit Bias: Linear Crossover

Let a variation operator be free from an *explicit bias* if there is no relevant code growth in the absence of fitness information. In other words, the same amount of code will be added, on average, to the population than is removed. While the exchange of subprograms during crossover may not increase average program size, subprogram mutation will have to be explicitly required to leave it unchanged. This has been realized in Section 5.7.5 by selecting the length of a randomly inserted segment in relation to the length of another randomly selected individual.

In turn, we refer to an *implicit bias* if program growth happens only in the presence of fitness and does not result simply from the variation operator. As noted in Section 10.2.3, removal bias has been argued to be a direct cause of code growth in tree-based genetic programming with subtree crossover. This implicit growth bias results from the fact that the deleted subtree may cause a fitness change that depends on the subtree size *in relation to* the program size. The fitness change caused by the inserted subtree, instead, is relatively independent from its size. One reason for this is the single connection point (edge) over which all subtrees may influence the result of the main program.

The situation is less clear when using crossover in linear GP. Several reasons may be found why the effect of an inserted instruction segment on fitness is *not* independent of its length. First, the more instructions are removed from or added to a linear program, the more content of (effective) registers will be changed. Recall from Section 3.3.1 that register manipulation corresponds to modification of edges in the graph representation of a linear genetic program. Thus, the longer an inserted instruction sequence is, the more variation points may be affected on the functional level.

Second, the available number of registers determines the maximal width of the (effective) DAG. The wider the program graphs are, the less program paths (variation points) will be modified. At least theoretically a removal bias becomes more likely under these conditions. However, since linear crossover operates on instruction level, it is rather unlikely – especially with many registers – that instruction segments form contiguous subgraphs.

Third, not all register manipulations will be effective, since not all instructions of an inserted or deleted segment usually contribute to the effective code. The *effective length* of crossover segments is approximately the same for insertions and deletions. It directly depends on the proportion of effective instructions in a program. More precisely, the number of effective registers at the variation point in the program context *and* the number of registers manipulated by the segment code determine how many segment instructions will be effective.

Soule and Heckendorn [128] have given experimental evidence for the removal bias theory in tree-based GP. We reproduce this experiment here for a linear program representation and linear crossover. The correlation between relative fitness change and relative segment length is calculated separately for inserted and deleted segments. *Relative segment length* denotes the absolute length of an inserted (deleted) segment as a percentage of the length of the destination (source) program.

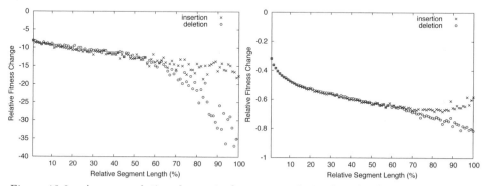

Figure 10.9. Average relative change in fitness per relative length of the inserted and the deleted crossover segments (cross). Average figures over 30 runs for *mexican hat* (left) and *spiral* (right).

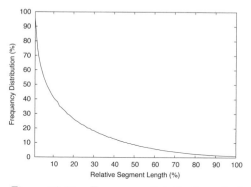

Figure 10.10. Frequency distribution of relative lengths of crossover segments (cross). Average figures over 30 runs for *mexican hat* (similar for *spiral*).

A removal bias may only be relevant for linear crossover if the length of the inserted segment and the deleted segment are allowed to be different. Due to the influence of the maximum length bound, however, this period may not last very long in the course of a run. Recall that the particular crossover implementation we use exchanges equally long segments should an offspring exceed the maximum size limit. Therefore, we allow a maximum program length (as well as a maximum segment length) of 1,000 instructions which guarantees that programs may grow almost unrestricted, at least during the 250 generations observed here (see Figure 10.2).

In Figure 10.9 a removal bias occurs only for relative segment lengths larger than 70%. For two reasons it may be questioned that such a bias has any relevant influence on code growth. First, programs resulting from larger destructive events may be selected for further variation with a very low probability and thus almost do not contribute to evolution at all (see Section 10.7.3). Second, such a large relative segment length does not occur very frequently as we learn from the frequency distribution in Figure 10.10.

10.7.8   Implicit Bias: Effective Instruction Mutation

In Section 6.4.3 we have seen how an explicit growth bias influences both code growth and prediction performance if instruction mutations are applied. Now we will investigate whether such mutations are implicitly biased, even if instructions are deleted or inserted with the same probability. Is deletion of a single instruction likely to be more destructive than insertion? If a randomly selected instruction is deleted, it depends on the proportion of (non-)effective instructions in a program whether the deletion is effective or not. If a random instruction is inserted at a particular program position, one can expect its destination register to be effective depending on the proportion of registers that are effective at that position. In a larger intron block the average number of effective registers is rather low. Thus, if an instruction is inserted in the context of other introns, the probability that the new instruction will be an intron can be expected to be high. Such interactions lead to similar proportions of semantic and structural variation effects for instruction deletions and instruction insertions (not documented).

Let us now consider effective instruction mutation as defined in Section 6.2.3. Deletion of an effective instruction node means the removal of several edges from the corresponding program graph – one for each operand register and at least one for the destination register – while each removed edge (register) may lead to the disconnection (deactivation) of other code. During insertion of an effective instruction, by comparison, only the choice of the destination register can be a source of deactivation. This would happen if another instruction which uses the same destination register becomes inactive. The operand registers, instead, add new register dependencies to other instructions, i.e., edges to the effective graph component. This may result in the reactivation of previously inactive code (see also

Section 6.2.4). But reactivation is less likely than deactivation, because the rate of inactive instructions is usually low with effective mutation.

Surprisingly, experimental results show that effective insertions lead to *larger* semantic variation step sizes, i.e., average fitness changes, than effective deletions (see Figure 10.11). Apparently, effective deletions are less destructive because the effective code stabilizes over a run, as demonstrated in Chapter 9. This imbalance leads to an *implicit shrink bias* or *insertion bias*, providing another argument for why the absolute size of programs remains small if effective code is created.

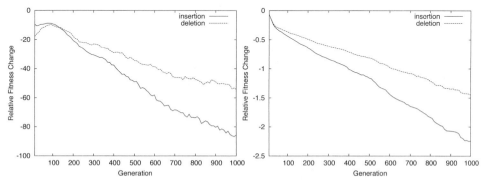

Figure 10.11. Development of the average relative fitness change for *mexican hat* (left) and *spiral* (right) when using effective instruction mutations (**effmut**). Insertions more destructive than deletions (implicit shrink bias). Average figures over 30 runs.

10.8 Control of Code Growth

This section shows different possibilities of how code growth may be controlled implicitly or explicitly in linear genetic programming. One can distinguish between control of code growth by variation or by selection. The following section summarizes results from Chapters 5 and 6 concerning the influence of different variation operators and variation parameters on code growth. In this section we will also analyze why code growth occurs to be so much more aggressive with segment recombination than with segment mutation.

10.8.1 Variation-Based Control

The absolute variation step size has been defined in Section 5.3 as the amount of code that is deleted and/or inserted during one variation step. Because a deletion and an insertion are always applied in combination during a crossover operation (**cross**) or a two-segment mutation (**segmut**), the speed of code growth depends on the maximum difference in size between the deleted and the inserted segment. Obviously, there is no code growth possible if this difference is zero. Another way to limit the length distance between parent and offspring in linear GP is to use a smaller maximum segment length that is independent of the program length.

A control of code growth by explicitly removing structural introns from the population (effcross) turned out to be insufficient for linear crossover. The protection effect leads to an increase of other (semantic) introns in this case. Depending on the problem and the configuration of the instruction set this replacement may, however, not allow programs to become similarly large. In addition, processing time will be increased since semantic introns cannot be detected and removed efficiently before fitness evaluation.

One-segment recombination (oneseg) as well as one-segment mutation (onesegmut) either insert *or* delete a segment with certain independent probabilities. Unlike two-segment variations there is no substitution of code. This allows the speed of code growth to be controlled by an explicit bias. For instance, a shrink bias may be induced either by allowing larger parts of code to be deleted, or by applying code deletions more frequently than code insertions. But only the latter variant does not increase the average variation step size.

Figure 10.12 compares code bloat for one-segment variations[6] with virtually no maximum limitation of program length. More precisely, the maximum limit of 1,000 instructions influences code growth only slightly over a period of 250 generations. In general, no influence may be expected until program length exceeds $\frac{l_{max}}{2}$ where l_{max} is maximum program length. Up until this point in time, selected segments are smaller than the remaining program memory. It is important to note that recombination leads to much faster and larger code bloat than mutation even if segment length and, thus, absolute step size is limited only by program length. We will come back to this phenomenon below. Using mutation instead of recombination forms one out of three methods favored here to limit the growth of (intron) code.

The relative difference in effective code (in Figure 10.12) is smaller since the size of this code depends more strongly on the problem fitness. Nevertheless, the difference is clear since the effective length indirectly depends on the absolute length (see Section 7.5). This is especially the case with only a few calculation registers. For the discrete *spiral* problem effective

---

[6]Similar observations have been made when comparing code growth of two-segment variations (not shown).

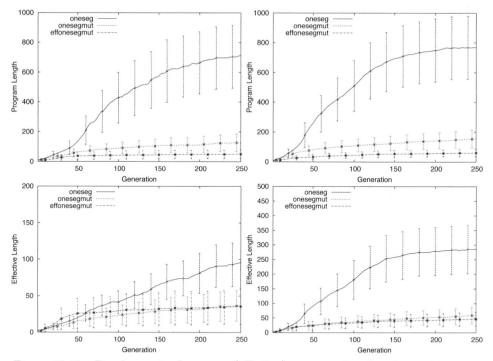

Figure 10.12. Development of average (effective) program length when using one-segment variations (**oneseg**, **onesegmut**, **effonesegmut**) with a maximum program length of 1,000 instructions. Programs significantly smaller with randomly created segments. Bars show standard deviation of program length within the population. Average figures over 30 runs for *mexican hat* (left) and *spiral* (right).

code grows larger also because the applied function set allows semantic introns to be created much more easily.

The difference in program size between recombination and segment mutation is smaller in Sections 5.9.1 and 5.9.2 due to a lower maximum bound of only 200 instructions, introduced to assure a comparison of prediction errors that is less depending on differences in program size.

A smaller absolute step size acts as another measure against code growth. By reducing mutation step size to one instruction (**mut**), evolution has no way to further reduce effective step size and destructive influence of deletions implicitly by producing more intron code. In this way, the evolutionary advantage of (structural or semantic) introns is suppressed.

It is interesting to see that the difference in average program size between unrestricted one-segment mutation (maximum step size) and one-instruction mutation (minimum step size) is smaller than it might have been expected (see Figure 10.13). This may be taken as another hint

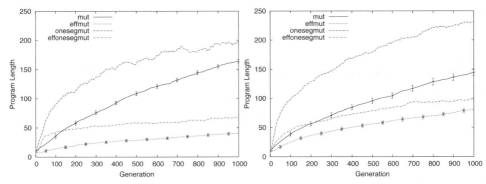

Figure 10.13. Development of average program length when using instruction mutations (mut, effmut) compared to segment mutations (onesegmut, effonesegmut) without a maximum limitation of program length. Programs significantly smaller if only effective instructions are created. Relatively small difference in program length between using minimum or maximum segment lengths, especially with effective mutations. Bars show standard deviation of program length within the population. Average figures over 30 runs for *mexican hat* (left) and *spiral* (right). 100 percent macro mutation without explicit length bias (B0).

that variation step size only indirectly influences code growth (see also Section 10.3). An influence by the maximum size (1,000 instructions) can be excluded for all mutation operators, simply because programs remain significantly smaller. Moreover, none of the operators are explicitly biased towards creating larger solutions, i.e., insertions and deletions are applied for 50 percent each. Recombination with a minimum segment length of one instruction produces program growth similar to instruction mutation (not shown). Thus, the relative difference in program growth between both variation types is much smaller compared to using segments of arbitrary length.

A *direct* insertion or variation of noneffective instructions is avoided by using effective mutations (effmut). Noneffective code (structural introns) may only result from an *indirect* deactivation of depending instructions. The avoidance of noneffective neutral variations, in general, leads to a significant reduction of noneffective code. In this way, effective mutation realizes an *implicit control of code growth* in linear GP [23, 11]. It also ensures that program size will depend more on fitness than on variation and that it will be closer to the minimum size required for solving the problem.

Alternatively, code growth is reduced if the direct creation of structural introns is disabled while the mutation step size remains unrestricted. This has been used with effective segment mutation (effonesegmut). In Figure 10.13 programs are not even half as large as when segments are created randomly (onesegmut). Avoiding direct insertion of (structural) intron code is a third way to reduce code growth.[7]

When operating with minimum step sizes *and* effective mutations (effmut), an explicit growth bias can be beneficial. That is to explicitly promote code growth by using more insertions than deletions of single instructions. Larger than minimum step sizes, instead, lead to a decrease in fitness and not necessarily to larger solutions. Noteworthy is that not only the proportion but also the size of effective code decreases if multiple instruction mutations (mut) are applied simultaneously at different points in the same individual (see Section 6.4.4).

Variation-based methods for controlling code growth in tree-based GP focus primarily on the crossver operator (see, e.g., in [72, 104, 129]).

10.8.2 Why Mutations Cause Less Bloat

An interesting question that arises when analyzing code growth in linear GP is why so much smaller programs occur with (segment) mutation than with recombination even if the segment length is not explicitly restricted. Instead, the *proportion* of (non)effective code in programs (and segments) remains similar over a run for both types of variations.

In the following paragraphs we summarize different hypotheses which may explain this phenomenon and support them by experimental evidence. In general, all causes given here represent preconditions for code growth rather than driving forces (see Section 10.2). Nevertheless, these conditions may significantly increase the influence of a driving force on the size of solutions.

(1) One explanation for stronger code growth by recombination is that recombination uses only material from the population. This facilitates a stabilization of (functional) program structure over a run in contrast to insertions of large random segments. We have seen in Section 9.7.2 that the effectiveness degree, i.e., the dependence degree of effective instructions, increases over the course of a run. In other words, the connectivity of nodes in the effective graph component increases. A formation of (several) larger graph components may be expected to some degree for noneffective instructions, too, which likely were effective at some point in evolution. If large random segments are inserted, instead, program structure might become more brittle because the dependence degree of instructions will

---

[7]Semantic intron formation increases the complexity of programs insufficiently here to protect (semantically) effective code.

generally be lower. As a result, depending program instructions are more likely to be deactivated or reactivated. Thus, both the *emergence* of large robust (intron) code and its *propagation* in the population is limited when using segment mutation.

These assumptions are at least in part confirmed by the results shown in Figure 10.14. For the *spiral* problem the dependence degree of effective instructions is significantly higher with (one-segment) recombination than with mutation.

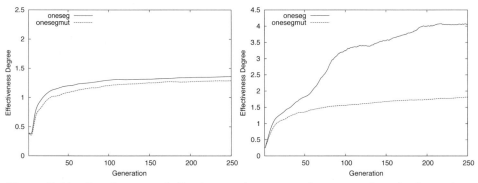

Figure 10.14. Development of effectiveness degree over the segment length when using recombination (**oneseg**) or mutation (**onesegmut**). Higher effectiveness possible with recombination. Average figures over 30 runs for *mexican hat* (left) and *spiral* (right).

On a structural level subtree mutation and recombination are more similar in their destructive effect in tree-based GP, since the indegree of tree nodes is always 1.

(2) The fitness of individuals in the population should be higher than the fitness of equally sized random programs. We may assume this to be true for arbitrarily large subprograms as well. Thus, a smaller fitness change, i.e., a smaller semantic step size, may be caused by segments originating from another individual than would be caused by segments created randomly.

Figure 10.15 compares the average fitness change between recombination and mutation. Especially for the *mexican hat* problem, mutated segments turn out to be much more destructive than recombined segments of equal size. This difference increases continuously with segment length. Since the diversity of population code is usually lower than that of random code, more similar segments may be exchanged by recombination than created by mutation. Interestingly, recombined segments cause smaller semantic step sizes than random segments even though their structural step sizes are larger, on average, as a result of larger program sizes.

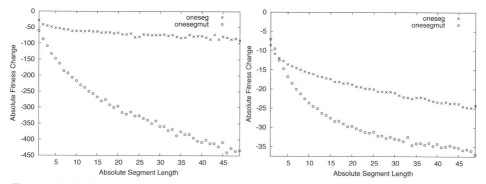

Figure 10.15. Development of fitness change over the segment length when using recombination (**oneseg**) or mutation (**onesegmut**). Mutation increasingly more destructive than recombination for larger segment lengths. Average figures over 30 runs for *mexican hat* (left) and *spiral* (right).

(3) The final possible cause that shall be mentioned here is the *duplication* of code in genetic programs. Code duplication may increase the amount of noneffective code. This is much more likely with recombination of existing genetic material from the population.

The existence and simple creation of structural introns facilitates these code extensions in linear GP. Local duplications of structurally noneffective instructions at the same position in the *effective* program, i.e., between two effective instructions, are always noneffective. Such copies can only modify (destination) registers that have no influence on the program output at that particular location.

Even duplications of effective code are not necessarily effective in linear genetic programs. Sequences of single identical instructions can be observed with only the last instruction being effective. The only condition to produce this effect is if the operand register(s) are different from the destination register.

The emergent phenomenon of code repetitions in genetic programs has been recently investigated with respect to the building block hypothesis and the use of different crossover operators [75–77, 137].

10.8.3   Selection-Based Control

The simplest form of growth control in genetic programming is to choose the maximum size limit of programs as small as necessary for representing successful solutions (see Section 7.5). The problem is, however, that the optimal size of a solution is not known in advance. A widespread approach to control program growth is referred to as *parsimony pressure*. In contrast to control of growth with variation operators a parsimony pressure is applied through selection. Usually this technique is implemented by integrating a size component into the fitness function: Larger programs are penalized by calculating a weighted sum of the two objectives, fitness and size [64].

The principle of Occam's Razor states that a shorter solution to a problem can be expected to be better and more generic than a longer solution. Parsimony pressure relies on the assumption that there is a positive correlation between shorter programs and better solutions. Because such a correlation may not be assumed for every problem and each configuration of GP (see also Section 7.5) parsimony pressure may not always be advantageous.

In the first place, the influence of parsimony pressure on the complexity and the evaluation time of linear genetic programs is interesting only for the effective code. Recall that all structural introns can be removed efficiently from a linear genetic program and, thus, do not cause computational costs (see Section 3.2.1) during a fitness calculation or in an application domain.

Parsimony pressure is less important for the performance of linear GP. First, more direct influence may be exerted on code growth through variation parameters than is possible in a tree representation of programs. The higher variability of the linear representation is responsible for this behavior, allowing single instructions to be deleted or inserted freely at all program positions. Second, the presence of noneffective code already imposes an *implicit* parsimony pressure on the effective code in genetic programming. This is especially interesting when using crossover in linear GP (see also Chapter 8) where structural introns may be detected efficiently.

In Chapter 9 and in [24] we introduced *two-level tournament selection* and pointed out its advantages compared to using a weighted sum for multi-objective optimizations. We argued that it may be used in particular for controlling program size. Luke and Panait [82] adopted this selection method for tree-based GP and compared it against limiting the maximum tree depth. For other selection-based methods against code bloat the reader may consult, e.g., [55, 56, 101].

10.8.4   Effective Complexity Selection

The separation of linear genetic programs into active and inactive code on a structural level offers the possibility for *code-specific* complexity and growth control. This is realized by using our two-level selection method from Section 9.4. First, a certain number of individuals (here always three) is selected by fitness and, second, among those only the two shortest programs are allowed to participate in variation. In order to limit code growth we may put a specific selection pressure on individuals by choosing the smallest *effective, noneffective,* or *absolute* program. Selection pressure is controlled solely by a selection probability that determines how often the complexity selection is applied.

Code-specific parsimony pressure has been proposed by Soule *et al.* [124] as a mean to restrict the growth of tree programs without restricting their effective code. Introns were identified in the form of non-executed subtrees resulting from nested branches whose contradicting conditions were relatively easy to identify. Recall that detection of introns in tree-based GP is not easy in general because it strongly depends on program functions.

Table 10.9. *mexican hat*: Second-level selection for effective, noneffective, and absolute complexity using selection rates 100%, 50%, 25% and crossover (cross). Average results over 100 runs after 1,000 generations.

Code	Selection (%)	SSE		Length			Variations (%)		
		mean	*std.*	*abs.*	*eff.*	%	*constr.*	*neutral*	*noneff.*
—	—	15.4	1.5	180	67	37	4.9	26	22
abs.	25	11.1	1.4	153	59	39	5.3	25	22
abs.	50	**9.6**	1.4	78	37	47	5.6	29	24
abs.	100	30.7	2.2	8	5	62	5.0	38	24
eff.	25	12.9	1.5	183	58	32	4.5	28	26
eff.	50	**12.2**	1.4	184	47	26	3.5	34	31
eff.	100	14.9	1.4	181	27	15	1.7	51	50
noneff.	25	10.9	1.4	149	64	43	5.7	24	21
noneff.	50	**9.4**	1.3	95	54	57	6.5	24	19
noneff.	100	19.3	2.1	51	45	88	7.0	26	16

Experimental results in Tables 10.9 and 10.10 show for two test problems, *mexican hat* and *spiral,* that noneffective complexity selection is more successful than effective complexity selection when using unrestricted linear crossover. *Mexican hat* benefits slightly more from the latter variant, probably due to a stronger correlation between shorter programs and better solutions. This behavior is different from the *spiral* problem which is not helped much by effective complexity selection. By imposing a specific pressure on the effective size, the actual solution size is penalized more specifically while the growth of noneffective code is almost not affected. Thus, a smaller proportion of effective instructions is maintained in programs which reduces the effective crossover step size. The proportion of noneffective and neutral variations is increased only slightly, though, because of the large absolute step size.

In both test cases a moderate penalty for noneffective complexity has a positive influence on prediction performance, even if effective step size is larger with a larger proportion of effective code. In Table 10.9 absolute length is relatively more reduced than effective length with higher selection pressure. In Table 10.10, instead, the effective size increases while the absolute size remains virtually unaffected. While in the first case performance decreases, in the latter case the loss of structural introns is compensated by semantic introns. A similar effect has been observed by totally removing noneffective code during effective crossover (see Section 5.9.1).

Table 10.10.   *spiral*: Second-level selection for effective, noneffective, and absolute complexity using selection rates 100%, 50%, 25% and crossover (**cross**). Average results over 100 runs after 1,000 generations.

Code	Selection (%)	CE		Length			Variations (%)		
		mean	*std.*	*abs.*	*eff.*	*%*	*constr.*	*neutral*	*noneff.*
—	—	26.1	0.7	185	102	55	3.6	23	14
abs.	25	22.7	0.7	167	102	61	4.1	21	12
abs.	50	**20.9**	0.7	132	92	69	4.8	19	10
abs.	100	32.4	1.0	30	25	83	6.3	18	10
eff.	25	26.5	0.7	188	78	42	3.2	26	21
eff.	50	**26.0**	0.6	185	66	36	2.9	29	24
eff.	100	27.3	0.7	184	43	24	1.7	40	37
noneff.	25	**22.3**	0.7	179	134	75	4.1	20	8
noneff.	50	22.6	0.7	172	160	93	4.1	19	3
noneff.	100	23.1	0.7	182	181	99	3.5	20	1

Code-specific complexity selection also allows investigation into how much selection pressure on absolute length benefits from a reduction of effective code or noneffective code. If a general pressure works better than any code-specific pressure, the specific forms might complement each other. Unfortunately, prediction performance with an absolute complexity control has not been found to be different from the results obtained with noneffective complexity selection, at least for moderate selection probabilities of 25 and 50 percent. Only for the *spiral* problem is there a small improvement. However, since an absolute complexity selection produces smaller effective programs, it better suppresses the emergence of semantic introns (in the structurally effective code) with crossover.

We learned in Section 5.7.6 that a more reliable and stronger reduction of crossover step size on effective code may be obtained by using explicit introns. These replace most implicit noneffective code and, thus, reduce possible side effects of reactivations. As a result, smaller effective solutions are possible. Note that explicit introns constitute another method for controlling the growth of effective code by means of selection.

As indicated in Section 9.4, one advantage of a two-level selection process over penalizing program length by a weighted term in the fitness function is that the primary selection by fitness is less compromised. Moreover, when coding multiple objectives into the fitness value the selection pressure is stronger at the end than at the beginning of a run where programs are small. This generates further difficulties for finding an appropriate weighting of the fitness components. Complexity selection, instead, puts a more uniform pressure on individuals that compares their relative differences in length only.

10.9 Summary and Conclusion

This chapter studied the phenomena of code growth and neutral variations in linear genetic programming. Different reasons for code growth were investigated for the linear GP approach. In particular, we analyzed the influence of different variation effects on program size for different linear genetic operators. Again we summarize some important conclusions:

☐ Neutral variations were identified as an indirect but major cause of code growth and the emergence of introns. Almost no code growth occurred if neutral variations were not accepted *and* if the structural step size of variations was reduced to a minimum. Both conditions ensure that intron instructions are not created directly at the variation point. In general, the importance of neutral variations is emphasized as a driver of evolutionary progress and code growth.

☐ The influence of non-neutral – especially destructive – variations on code growth has been found surprisingly low, even if variation step sizes are larger.

☐ The conditional reproduction of parent individuals after effective variations only better preserves the (effective) diversity of solutions. This technique, named effective reproduction, achieved a clear gain in performance with instruction mutations.

☐ A relevant influence of implicit length biases on the growth of linear genetic programs has not been found in general. While the removal bias theory could not be confirmed for linear crossover, an implicit shrink bias was detected with effective instruction mutations.

☐ Different methods for controlling code growth by variation or selection proposed in this and other chapters of the book were discussed. The two-level selection method from Chapter 9 was applied for a selective control of effective or noneffective program complexity.

☐ Recombination has been found to increase the size of programs much more dramatically than (segment) mutation in linear GP, especially if program size and variation step size are kept unrestricted for both macro operators. Several possible reasons were analyzed as explanation for this phenomenon. We also demonstrated that code growth is affected only slightly by the step size of mutation, in clear contrast to recombination.

The following measures have shown to reduce growth of code in linear GP, independent of their influence on performance.

☐ Use of macro mutation instead of recombination

☐ Reduction of variation step size

☐ Avoidance of neutral variations

☐ Avoidance of direct generation of neutral code

☐ Implicit or explicit shrink bias in variation operators

☐ (Effective) complexity selection

Chapter 11

EVOLUTION OF PROGRAM TEAMS

This chapter applies linear GP to the evolution of cooperative teams to several prediction problems. Different linear methods for combining outputs of the team programs are compared. These include hybrid approaches where (1) a neural network is used to optimize the weights of programs in a team for a common decision and (2) a real-numbered vector (the representation of evolution strategies) of weights is evolved in tandem with each team. The cooperative team approach results in an improved training and generalization performance compared to the standard GP method.

11.1   Introduction

Two main approaches can be distinguished concerning the combination of individual solutions in genetic programming: Either the individuals (genetic programs) can be evolved independently in different runs and combined *after* evolution, or a certain number of individuals can be *co-evolved* in parallel as a *team*. The focus of this chapter is on the latter approach.

Team evolution is strongly motivated by natural evolution. Many predators, e.g., lions, have learned to hunt pray most successfully in a pack. By doing so, they have developed cooperative behavior that offers them a much better chance to survive than they would have as single hunters. In GP we expect the parallel evolution of team programs to solve certain tasks more efficiently than the usual evolution of individuals. Individual members of a team may solve an overall task in *cooperation* by specializing to a certain degree on subtasks.

Post-evolutionary combination, instead, suffers from the drawback that a successful combination of programs is only detected by chance. It might require many runs to develop a sufficient number of individual solutions and numerous trials to find a good combination. Coevolution of k programs, instead, will turn out to be more efficient in time than k independent runs. Teams with highly cooperative and specialized members are hard to find by chance, especially since they usually require only a certain adaptation of their members to the training data. Most combinations of best-of-run individuals – since too much adapted to a problem – may reduce noise but may hardly develop cooperation.

Team solutions require multiple decisions of their members to be merged into one *collective decision*. Several methods to combine the outputs of team programs are compared in this chapter. The coevolutionary team approach not only allows the combined error to be minimized but also an optimal *composition* of programs to be found. In general, the optimal team composition is different from simply taking individual programs that are already quite perfect predictors for themselves. Moreover, the diversity of the individual decisions of a team may become an object of optimization.

In this chapter we also present a combination of GP and neural networks (NN) – the weighting of multiple team programs by a linear neural network. The neural optimization of weights may result in an improved performance compared to standard combination methods. Recall that the name *linear GP* refers to the linear structure of the genetic programs. It does not mean that the method itself is linear, i.e., may solve linearly separable problems only, as this is the case for linear NN. On the contrary, prediction models developed by GP are usually highly non-linear.

In another hybrid approach the representations of linear GP and evolution strategies (ES) [110, 119] are coevolved in that a vector of programs (team) and a vector of program weights form one individual and undergo evolution and fitness calculation simultaneously.

11.2   Team Evolution

Haynes *et al.* [47] introduced the idea of team evolution into the field of genetic programming. Since then evolution of teams has been investigated mostly in connection with cooperating agents solving multi-agent control problems. Luke and Spector [80] tested the teamwork of homogeneous and heterogeneous agent teams in a predator/prey domain and showed that a heterogeneous approach is superior. In contrast to heterogeneous teams, homogeneous teams are composed of completely identical agents and can be evolved with the standard GP approach. Haynes and Sen

[48] tested a similar problem with different recombination operators for heterogeneous teams.

Soule [126] applied teams to another non-control problem – a parity problem – by using majority voting to combine the the Boolean outputs of members. He [127] later documented specialization in teams for a linear regression problem and found better performance with teams when using a special voting method but not with averaging.

In this chapter the team approach is applied to three different prediction problems, two classification tasks and one approximation task. In data mining the generalization ability of predictive models is the most important criterion. In contrast to control tasks only heterogeneous teams are of interest here, because for prediction tasks there is nothing to be gained from the combination of the outputs of completely identical programs that would constitute homogeneous teams.

11.2.1 Team Representation

In general, teams of individuals can be implemented in different ways. First, a certain number of individuals can be selected randomly from the population and evaluated in combination as a team. The problem with this approach is known as the *credit assignment problem*: The combined fitness value of the team has to be shared and distributed among team members.

Second, team members can be evolved in separate subpopulations which provide a more specialized development. In this case, the composition and evaluation of teams might be separated from the evolution of their members by simply taking the best individuals from each deme in each generation and by combining them. This procedure, however, raises another problem: An optimal team is not necessarily composed of best individuals for each team position. Specialization and coordination of the team individuals is not a matter of evolution then. These phenomena might only emerge accidentally.

The third approach, favored here, is to use an explicit team representation that is considered one individual by the evolutionary algorithm [48]. The population is subdivided into fixed, equal-sized groups of individuals. Each program is assigned a fixed position index in its team (program vector). The members of a team undergo a coevolutionary process because they are always selected, evaluated and varied simultaneously. This eliminates the credit assignment problem and renders the composition of teams an object of evolution.

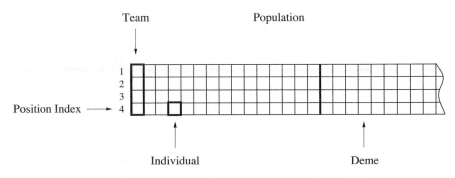

Figure 11.1. Population subdivided into teams and demes.

Figure 11.1 shows the partitioning of the total population used in the experiments described below. First, the population is subdivided into *demes* [130] which, in turn, are subdivided into *teams* of individual programs. Exchange of genetic information between demes has not been realized by migration of whole teams. Instead, teams (tournament winners) are selected for recombination occasionally from *different* demes while their offspring inherit code from both demes (*interdemetic recombination*). Demes are used because they better preserve the diversity of a population. This, in turn, reduces the probability of the evolutionary process to get stuck in a local minimum (see also Chapter 4).

The coevolutionary approach prohibits teams of arbitrary size because the complexity of the search space and the training time, respectively, would grow exponentially with the number of coevolved programs. On the other hand, the team size has to be large enough to cause an improved prediction compared to the traditional approach, i.e., team size one. Our experimental experience with this trade-off suggests that moderate numbers of team members are adequate (see Section 11.5).

11.2.2   Team Operators

Team representations require special genetic operators, notably for recombination. Genetic operations on teams, in general, reduce to the respective operations on their members. Researchers [48] found that a moderate number of crossover points works better than recombining either one or every team position per operation. This is due to the trade-off between a sufficient variation, i.e., speed of the evolutionary process, and the destructive effect of changing too many team members at the same time.

For recombination the participating individuals of the two parent teams can be chosen of arbitrary or equal position. If recombination between team positions is forbidden completely, the members of a team evolve independently in isolated *member demes*. Luke and Spector [80] showed that team recombination restricted in this way can outperform free recombination for a control problem. Isolated or semi-isolated coevolution of team members is argued to promote specialization in behavior. A possible alternative to random selection might be genetic operators that modify team members depending on their respective individual fitness. Members may be sorted by error and the probability of an individual becoming a subject of crossover or mutation would depend on its error rank. By doing so, worse individuals would be varied more often than better ones. Improving the fitness of worse members might have a better chance to improve the overall fitness of the team. However, we will see below that there is not necessarily a positive correlation between a better member fitness and a better team fitness. Also note that this technique does not allow member errors to differ much in a team which might have a negative effect on specialization, too.

11.3   Combination of Multiple Predictors

In principle, this chapter integrates two research topics, the evolution of teams discussed above and the combination of multiple predictors, i.e., classifiers or regressors. In contrast to teams of agents, teams whose members solve a prediction problem require the aggregation of the members' outputs to produce a common decision.

In the neural network community different approaches have been investigated to deal with the combination of multiple decisions in neural network *ensembles* [45, 103, 68]. Usually, neural networks are combined after training and are hence already quite perfect in solving a classification or approximation problem on their own. The ensemble members are not trained in combination and the composition of the ensemble does not undergo an optimization process. In [141] neural networks are evolved and a subset of the final population is combined afterwards. Different combination methods – including averaging and majority voting – are compared while a genetic algorithm is used to search for a near optimal ensemble composition.

For genetic programming Zhang *et al.* [144] applied a weighted majority algorithm in classification to combine the Boolean outputs of a selected subpopulation of genetic programs after evolution. This approach resulted in an improvement of generalization performance, i.e., more robustness compared to standard GP and simple majority voting, especially in the case of sparse and noisy training data.

The decisions of different *types* of classifiers including neural networks and genetic programs are combined by an averaging technique in [123]. The result is an improved prediction quality of thyroid normal and thyroid carcinoma classes that has been achieved in this medical application. Langdon *et al.* [73, 74] combine the outputs of multiple NN classifiers by genetic programming for a drug discovery application.

11.3.1   Making Multiple Decisions Differ

In principle, all members in a team of predictors are intended to solve the same complete task. The problem is not artificially subdivided among members and there are no subproblems explicitly assigned to specific team positions. In many real-world applications such subdivision would not be possible because the problem structure is completely unknown. We are interested in teams where *specialization*, i.e., a partitioning of the solution, emerges from the evolutionary process itself.

Specialization strongly depends on the heterogeneity of teams. Heterogeneity is achieved by evolving members that produce slightly diverging outputs for the same input situation. Nothing will be gained from the combination of outputs of identical predictors (homologous teams). Note that this is in contrast to agent teams that solve a control task where each agent program usually has side effects on the problem environment.

In genetic programming the inherent noise of the evolutionary algorithm already provides a certain heterogeneity for team members. Additionally, it can be advantageous to restrict recombination between *different* team positions [80]. This may be particularly important if a team member does not "see" the full problem and is facing a different subtask than the other members.

Otherwise, *interpositional recombination* allows innovative code to spread to other positions in a team. Moreover, a moderate exchange of genetic information between member demes helps to better preserve diversity of the overall team population. We will see later that for teams of predictors an interpositional exchange of code does not necessarily reduce specialization potential and quality of results.

Besides restricted recombination there are more specific techniques to increase heterogeneity in teams and, thus, to promote the evolution of specialization:

One possible approach is to force the individuals of a team to disagree on decisions and to specialize in different domains of the training data. This can be achieved by training each member position with (slightly) different training data sets. This technique requires the individual errors of the members to be integrated into the fitness function (see Section 11.4.2). Note that only member outputs of equal input situations can be used to calculate the combined error of the team.

Different training subsets for team members can be derived from the full data set that is used to determine the training error of the team. For instance, small non-overlapping subsets may be left out as in *cross validation*, a method used to improve the generalization capabilities of neural networks over multiple runs. The subsets may be sampled either at the beginning of a run or resampled after a certain number of generations. The latter technique (*stochastic sampling*) introduces some additional noise into the sampling process. This may allow smaller and more different subsets to be used since it guarantees that every team position over time is confronted with every training example.

Finally, different function sets can be chosen for different team positions to promote specialization as well. If recombination between different positions is allowed the team crossover operator has to be adapted such that only individual members built from the same function set are allowed to recombine.

11.3.2 Combination Methods

The problem that arises with the evolution of team predictors lies in the combination of the outputs of the individual members during fitness evaluation of a team. All *combination methods* tested here compute the resulting team output from a *linear* combination of its members' outputs. (1) A non-linear combination of already non-linear predictors (genetic programs) will not necessarily result in a better performance. (2) A non-linear combinator might solve too much of the prediction problem itself. Figure 11.2 illustrates the general principle of the approach.

Moreover, only basic combination methods are documented and compared in this chapter. Even if there are hybridizations of the methods possible, e.g., EVOL/OPT or EVOL/MV (weighted majority voting), the concurrent application of two combinations is not necessarily more powerful. We noticed that more complicated combination schemes are rather difficult to handle for the evolutionary algorithm. These might be more reasonable with a post-evolutionary combination of (independent) predictors. Most of the methods – except WTA (see Section 11.3.8) – can be applied to parallel as well as to sequentially evolved programs.

For classification problems there exist two major possibilities to combine the outputs of multiple predictors: Either the raw output values or the classification decisions can be aggregated. In the latter case the team members act as full (pre)classifiers themselves. The drawback of that method is that the mapping of the continuous outputs to discrete class identifiers *before* they are combined reduces the information content that each individual might contribute to the common team decision. Therefore, we decided for the former and combined raw outputs – except for majority voting that requires class decisions implicitly.

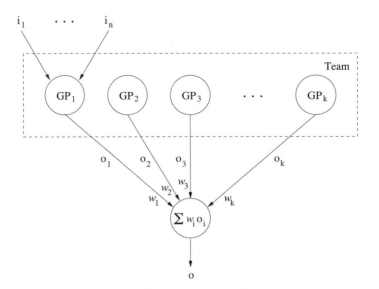

Figure 11.2. Linear combination of genetic programs.

Some of the combination methods are only applicable to classification tasks and are based on one of the following two *classification methods*:

□ *Interval classification* (INT). Each output class of the problem definition corresponds to a certain interval of the full value range of the (single) program output. In particular, for classification problems with two output classes, the continuous program output is mapped to class output 0 or 1 – depending on a classification threshold of 0.5. More generally, the class identifier is selected which is closest to the program output.

□ *Winner-takes-all classification* (WTA). Here for *each* output class exactly one program output (output register) is necessary. The output with the highest value determines the class decision of the individual.

The following combination methods are introduced for problems with two output classes while a generalization to more output classes is not complicated. One should also note that none of the methods presented here produce relevant extra computational costs.

11.3.3   Averaging (AV)

There are different variants of combinations possible to compute a weighted sum of the outputs of programs in a team. The simplest form is to use uniform weights for all members, i.e., the *simple average* of k outputs as team output. In this way the influence of each individual on the team decision is exactly the same. The evolutionary algorithm has to adapt the team members to the fixed weighting only.

$$o_{team} = \frac{1}{k} \sum_{i=1}^{k} o_{ind_i} \tag{11.1}$$

11.3.4   Weighting by Error (ERR)

A more sophisticated method is to use the fitness information of each team member for the computation of its weight. By doing so, better individuals get a higher influence on the team output than worse.

$$w_i = 1/e^{\beta E(gp_i)} \tag{11.2}$$

$E(gp_i)$ is the individual error explained in Equation 11.8. β is a positive scaling factor to control the relation of weight sizes. The error-based weighting gives lower weights to worse team members and higher weights to better ones. Weights should be normalized so that they are all positive and sum to one:

$$w_i = \left\| \frac{w_i}{\sum\limits_{j=1}^{k} w_j} \right\| \tag{11.3}$$

With this approach, evolution decides over the weights of a program member by manipulating its error value. In our experiments the individual weights are adjusted during training with the help of fitness information. Using data different from the training data may reduce overtraining of teams and increases their generalization performance, but causes additional computation time.

In general, error-based weighting has not been found to be consistently better than a simple average of outputs. The reason might be that the quality of a single member solution must not be directly related to the fitness of the whole team. If the combined programs had been evolved in independent runs, deriving the member weights from this independent fitness might be a better choice. In such a case stronger dependencies between programs – that usually emerge during team evolution by specialization – cannot be expected.

11.3.5   Coevolution of Weights (EVOL)

In this approach team and member weights are evolved in tandem (see Figure 11.3). The real-valued vector of weights is selected together with the vector of programs. During each fitness evaluation the weight vector is varied by a certain number of mutations. Only mutations improving fitness are allowed to change the current state of weighting, a method typical for an (1+1)-ES [119]. The mutation operator updates single weight values by applying normally distributed random changes with a constant standard deviation (*mutation step size*) of 0.02. The initial weights are randomly selected from range $[0, 1]$.

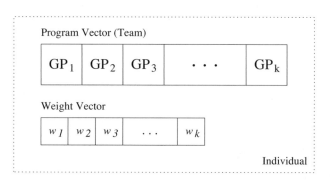

Figure 11.3.   Coevolution of program team and vector of weights as individual.

Alternatively, a complete (1+1)-ES run might be initiated to optimize the weighting of each team during fitness calculation. This, of course, would significantly increase the computational costs depending on the run length. It also might not be advantageous since teams adapt to a given weighting situation. With EVOL optimization of the weighting is happening in coevolution with the members, not during each team evaluation. Thus, the coevolutionary aspect that allows team solutions to adapt to different weighting situations is the more important one. Even if the diversity of the population decreases at the end of a GP run improvements are still possible by changing the influence of single team members.

11.3.6   Majority Voting (MV)

A special form of linear combination is *majority voting* which operates on *class* outputs. In other words, the continuous outputs of team programs are transformed into discrete class decisions *before* they are combined.

Let us assume that there are exactly two output classes. Let O_c denote the subset of team members that predict class $c \in 0, 1$:

$$O_c := \{i | o_{ind_i} = c, i = 1, .., k\} \tag{11.4}$$

The class which most of the individuals predict for a given fitness case is selected as team output:

$$o_{team} = \begin{cases} 0 & : & |O_1| < |O_0| \\ 1 & : & |O_1| \geq |O_0| \end{cases} \tag{11.5}$$

Clear decisions by majority voting are enforced for two output classes if the number of members is uneven. Otherwise, the team decision needs to be explicitly defined for an equal number of votes (class 1 here).

11.3.7 Weighted Voting (WV)

Another voting method, *weighted voting*, is introduced here for the winner-takes-all classification where each team program returns exactly one output value for each of m output classes. For all classes c these values are summed to form the respective outputs of the team:

$$\forall c \in \{0, .., m\} : o_{team,c} = \sum_{i=1}^{k} o_{ind_i,c} \tag{11.6}$$

The class with the highest output value defines the response class of the team as illustrated in Figure 11.4.

With this combination method each team individual contributes a continuous "weight" for each class instead of a clear decision for one class. If discrete class outputs would be used, the method would correspond to majority voting. Here weighting comes from the member programs themselves. When using interval classification instead of WTA classification each program might compute its own weight in a separate (second) output variable.

11.3.8 Winner-Takes-All (WTA)

We discern two different *winner-takes-all combination* methods: The first method selects the individual with the *clearest class decision* to determine the output of a team. With interval classification the member output that is closest to one of the class numbers (0 or 1) is identified as the clearest decision. The winner may also be seen as the individual with the highest *confidence* in its decision. Specialization may emerge if different members of the team win this contest for different fitness cases.

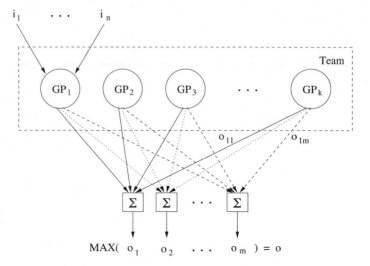

Figure 11.4. Combination of genetic programs by weighted voting.

If separate outputs are used instead of output intervals (WTA *classifi-cation*) the clearest decision might be defined as the largest difference between the highest output and the second highest output of a team member.

The second and simpler WTA combination (referred to as WTA2) just chooses the *minimum output* as team output.[1] This selection happens *before* the continuous outputs are transformed into class decisions and is valid for interval classification. For WTA classification the member with the lowest sum of outputs could be chosen. This variant is also possible for regression problems.

Of course, it is not a feasible alternative to select the member whose output is closest to the desired output during training. In such a case a decision on unknown (unlabeled) data would not be possible.

11.3.9   Weight Optimization (OPT)

The final approach tested uses a *linear* neural network[2] to find an op-timal weighting of the teams' individuals. The learning method applied is RPROP [111], a backpropagation variant about as fast as Quickprop which requires less adjustment of parameters. Data are processed first by

---

[1]This is determined by definition and could be the maximum output as well.
[2]Hidden layers of nodes are not defined.

the programs of a team before the neural network combines their results (see also Figure 11.2). Only a single neuron weights the connections to the genetic programs whose outputs represent the input layer of the linear neural network. Outputs of programs are computed once for all data inputs before the neural learning is done. In [138] a predictor is trained using the outputs of multiple other predictors as inputs.

We apply weighting by average (AV) and use the neural network only for optimizing the weights of the currently *best* team (outside of the population). This saves computation time and decouples the process of finding an optimal weighting from the process of breeding team individuals. The linear network structure assures that there is only a weighting of program outputs by the neural network and that the actual, non-linear problem is solved exclusively by the genetic programs.

11.4 Experimental Setup

11.4.1 Benchmark Problems

We examine the team approach using the different combination methods with two classification problems and one regression problem. The *heart* problem is composed of four data sets from the UCI Machine Learning Repository [88] and differs from the data set described in Section 4.2 in the coding of inputs (13 integer values here) and in a higher number of examples (720 here).

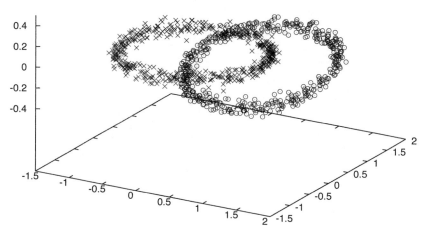

Figure 11.5. *two chains* problem.

Two chains denotes a popular machine learning problem, similar to *three chains* used in Chapter 6. Two chained "rings" representing two different classes of data points (500 each) have to be separated. The rings "touch" each other at two regions without intersection (see Figure 11.5).

The *three functions* problem tests the ability of teams to approximate three different functions simultaneously which are a sine, a logarithm and a half circle (see Figure 11.6). 200 data points were sampled for each function within an input range of $[0, 2\pi]$. A function index will be passed to the genetic programs as an additional input, in order to distinguish among the three functions.

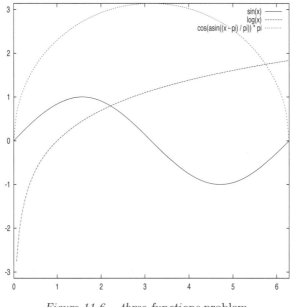

Figure 11.6.   three functions problem.

As done before, data samples of all problems were subdivided randomly into three sets: training set (50%), validation set (25%) and test set (25%). Each time a new best team occurs its error is calculated using the validation set in order to check its generalization ability *during* training. From all best teams emerging over a run the one with minimum validation error is selected and tested on the test set once *after* the training is complete.

11.4.2 Team and Member Fitness

The *fitness* $\mathcal{F}$ of a team might integrate two major goals: the overall error of the team $E(team)$ and, optionally, the errors of program members $E(gp_j)$ to be minimized.

$$\mathcal{F}(team) = E(team) + \delta \cdot \frac{1}{m} \sum_{j=1}^{m} E(gp_j) \qquad (11.7)$$

In our experiments the combined team and member errors are calculated for the training data. Provided that outputs of team members are saved, member errors should be computed virtually without additional overhead. The influence of the average member error on team fitness is controlled by a multiplicative parameter δ.

In Equation 11.7 E denotes the error of a predictor gp that is computed as the sum of square distances (SSE) between the predicted output(s) $gp(\vec{i_k})$ and the desired output(s) $\vec{o_k}$ over n examples $(\vec{i_k}, \vec{o_k})$:

$$E(gp) = \sum_{k=1}^{n} (gp(\vec{i_k}) - \vec{o_k})^2 + w \cdot CE = SSE + w \cdot CE \qquad (11.8)$$

The *classification error* (CE) is calculated as the number of incorrectly classified examples in Equation 11.8. The influence of the classification error is controlled by a weight factor w. For classification problems w has been set to 2 in order to favor classification quality, otherwise it has been set to 0.

11.4.3 Parameter Settings

Table 11.1 lists the parameter settings used for all experiments. Population size is 3,000 teams while each team is composed of the same number of individual members. The population has been chosen to be sufficiently large to preserve diversity of the more complex team solutions. The total *number of members per team* and the *number of members varied* during crossover and mutation are the most important parameters when investigating the evolution of teams. Team members are always varied simultaneously by crossover *and* mutation.

The number of generations is limited to 1,000, both for GP teams and for standard GP. Note that team members are far less subject to change – one or two per team – than stand-alone individuals. While this may reduce the speed of progress of single team members it does not hold back the fitness progress of the whole team.

Table 11.1. General parameter settings.

Parameter	Setting
Number of generations	1,000
Number of demes	6
Number of teams (population size)	3,000
Number of team members (team size)	4
Number of varied members	1–2
Maximum member length	128
Maximum initial length	32
Crossover rate	100%
Interdemetic crossover	3%
Mutation rate	100%
Instruction set	$\{+, -, \times, /, x^y\}$
Constants	$\{0,..,99\}$

11.5   Experiments

We document the results of applying different team approaches to the three problems of Section 11.4.1. Prediction accuracies and code size are compared for team configurations and a standard GP approach.

The team approach, in general, has been found to produce better results than standard GP for all three prediction tasks. Mainly problems that can be divided into simpler subproblems benefit from a team evolution because in such a case team members can specialize and solve the overall task more successfully in cooperation.

Second, team solutions can be expected to be less brittle and more general in the presence of noisy training data. Due to their collective decision making the effect of noise will be reduced significantly. This can be seen already for combinations of stand-alone solutions.

If nearly optimal solutions already occur with a standard GP approach teams cannot be expected to do much better. In this case the additional computational overhead of more complex team solutions will outweigh possible advantages.

11.5.1   Prediction Accuracy

Table 11.2 summarizes some basic characteristics of our different team approaches. Outputs of team members are continuous, except for majority voting (MV) where program outputs have to be mapped to discrete class identifiers first. The weighted voting approach (WV) is based on a WTA classification method. All other methods use interval classification.

Table 11.2. Configuration of the different team approaches.

Method	Combination	Classification	Outputs
GP	—	INT	cont
TeamGP	AV	INT	cont
	OPT	INT	cont
	ERR	INT	cont
	EVOL	INT	cont
	MV	INT	class
	WV	WTA	cont
	WTA	INT	cont
	WTA2	INT	cont

The following tables compare best results of standard GP with different team approaches. Minimum training and validation error are determined among best solutions of a run. The solution with minimum validation error is applied to unknown data at the end of a run to compute a test error. All figures denote average results from series of 60 test runs. In order to avoid unequal initial conditions each test series has been performed with the same set of 60 random seeds.

The classification rates for the *two chains* problem in Table 11.3 show that already the standard team approach (AV) reaches approximately an eight-fold improvement in training performance over standard GP. Most interesting are the results of the winner-takes-all combination that select a *single* member program to decide for the team on a certain input situation. Both team variants (WTA and WTA2) nearly always find the optimum (0% CE) for training and validation data. With standard GP the optimum solution has not been found even once during 60 trials. This is a strong indication for a high specialization of team members, and clearly demonstrates that highly coordinated behavior emerges from the parallel evolution of programs. This cannot be achieved by a combination of standard GP programs which have been evolved independently. Cooperative team evolution is much more sophisticated than just testing random compositions of programs. In fact, the different members in a team have adapted to each other during the coevolutionary process.

Among the team approaches which combine outputs of *several* individual members, WV turned out to be about as powerful as MV or EVOL. This is remarkable because the WV method requires twice as many output values – two instead of one output per member – to be coordinated. Furthermore, optimization of weights is done by the member programs themselves within this variant.

Table 11.3. *two chains*: Classification error (CE) in percent, averaged over 60 runs. Standard error in parentheses.

Method	Training CE (%)	Member CE (%)	Validation CE (%)	Test CE (%)
GP	3.67 (0.25)	—	5.07 (0.30)	5.69 (0.37)
AV	0.44 (0.08)	25.8 (1.96)	0.82 (0.12)	2.08 (0.14)
OPT	0.36 (0.07)	32.1 (0.71)	0.69 (0.09)	1.96 (0.15)
ERR	1.31 (0.15)	20.9 (1.49)	1.91 (0.20)	2.73 (0.18)
EVOL	0.33 (0.07)	28.0 (2.09)	0.71 (0.16)	2.00 (0.17)
MV	0.37 (0.08)	25.7 (1.51)	1.48 (0.17)	2.17 (0.19)
WV	0.39 (0.09)	27.7 (1.98)	0.76 (0.14)	1.91 (0.18)
WTA	0.02 (0.01)	59.2 (2.27)	**0.00** (0.00)	**0.33** (0.18)
WTA2	**0.00** (0.00)	64.3 (1.53)	0.00 (0.00)	0.65 (0.29)

Table 11.4 shows the prediction results for the *heart* problem. This application demonstrates not only the ability of teams in real data-mining but also in noisy problem environments, since many data attributes are missing or are unknown. The difference in prediction error between GP and TeamGP is about 2 percent which is significant in the respective real problem domain. The problem structure does not offer many possibilities for specialization. Especially in the case of winner-takes-all approaches, we can see that they do not generalize significantly better here than the standard approach. The main benefit of the other combination methods seems to be that they improve fitness and generalization from noisy data by a collective decision making of *more than one* team member.

Table 11.4. *heart*: Classification error (CE) in percent, averaged over 60 runs. Standard error in parentheses.

Method	Training CE (%)	Member CE (%)	Validation CE (%)	Test CE (%)
GP	13.6 (0.16)	—	14.5 (0.17)	19.0 (0.36)
AV	11.5 (0.15)	28.1 (2.18)	13.4 (0.18)	18.2 (0.30)
OPT	11.5 (0.17)	32.0 (2.03)	12.8 (0.18)	**17.5** (0.26)
ERR	11.9 (0.12)	28.6 (1.79)	12.9 (0.13)	18.0 (0.25)
EVOL	11.4 (0.13)	32.9 (2.39)	**12.7** (0.13)	18.1 (0.28)
MV	**10.9** (0.13)	24.6 (1.34)	13.6 (0.16)	17.5 (0.23)
WV	11.5 (0.11)	32.4 (2.41)	12.9 (0.15)	17.9 (0.24)
WTA	11.9 (0.17)	60.5 (2.44)	14.5 (0.22)	18.5 (0.31)
WTA2	12.9 (0.16)	61.5 (2.27)	14.9 (0.26)	19.2 (0.32)

Experimental results for the *three functions* problem are given in Table 11.5. Note that not all team variants are applicable to a regression problem. The regression task at hand has been solved most successfully by EVOL teams. This combination variant allows different weighting situations to be coevolved with the program teams and results in smaller prediction errors compared to uniform weights (AV). TeamGP in general (except for WTA2) is found to be about four times better in training and generalization than the standard GP approach. Note that the average member error can become extremely high compared to the respective team error for this problem.

Table 11.5. three functions: Mean square error (MSE × 100), averaged over 60 runs. Standard error in parentheses.

Method	Training MSE	Member MSE	Validation MSE	Test MSE
GP	16.9 (0.90)	—	16.2 (0.98)	16.6 (0.99)
AV	4.7 (0.27)	738 (50)	3.9 (0.22)	4.3 (0.25)
OPT	4.4 (0.30)	913 (69)	3.7 (0.27)	3.8 (0.27)
ERR	4.6 (0.33)	6340838 (4030041)	3.9 (0.30)	4.0 (0.30)
EVOL	**3.2** (0.27)	33135 (11041)	**2.6** (0.22)	**2.7** (0.24)
WTA2	11.0 (0.68)	154762629 (9025326)	9.8 (0.68)	10.1 (0.68)

Some general conclusions can be drawn from the three applications:

Teams of predictors have proven to give superior results for known data as well as for unknown data. On the one hand, specialization of team members can be considered responsible. On the other hand, improved generalization performance of teams may result from an increased robustness of team solutions against noise in the data space. This, in turn, is mainly due to the combination of multiple predictors that absorbs larger errors or wrong decisions made by single members.

Comparing the different team configurations among each other further shows that different combination methods dominate for different problems. A general ranking of methods cannot be produced. It is worth trying several variants when dealing with the evolution of multiple predictors.

Some methods that allow various weighting situations outperformed the standard team approach using uniform weights (AV). Among those methods the parallel evolution of weights together with the team programs (EVOL) turned out to be the most successful. Optimizing weights by using a neural network (OPT), instead, is done independent of evolution (see Section 11.3.9). Because the individuals in best teams are already quite adapted to a fixed (equal) weighting, optimization may not lead to the same significant improvements.

For all three examples the average member error was highest with winner-takes-all combinations. This is not surprising since only one member is selected at a time to make a final decision for the whole team while outputs of the other members may be arbitrary. Apparently, specialization potential is highest with these combinations. For all applications we can observe that the performance of team members is significantly worse than the performance of stand-alone GP individuals.

11.5.2   Code Size

The computational costs of team evolution (as compared to individual evolution) can be paid, at least in part, by the savings obtained from the following two effects:

☐ Only the (structurally) effective code needs to be executed.

☐ The average effective code size of team members is significantly smaller than the effective size of stand-alone individual solutions.

As explained in Chapter 3 the structurally noneffective code does not need to be executed and, thus, does not cause any computational costs no matter how complex it might become during the evolutionary process. Here we concentrate on the second effect by comparing effective code size for different team configurations and standard GP. Recall that there is no selection pressure on noneffective code and structurally noneffective code emerges easily with linear crossover. As a result, absolute solution size typically grows almost unbound and quickly reaches the maximum size limit (number of members × 128 instructions).

Table 11.6. two chains: Absolute and effective code size of teams with 4 members and standard GP in instructions. Effective code of teams about twice as large as standard individuals on average. WTA solutions are smaller than standard individuals.

Method	Code Size	Effective Size	Introns (%)
GP	128	45	64.8
AV	347	86	75.2
OPT	332	76	77.1
ERR	320	78	75.6
EVOL	294	67	77.2
MV	451	99	78.0
WV	448	124	72.3
WTA	92	**33**	64.1
WTA2	98	33	66.3

For the three applications, Tables 11.6 to 11.8 show effective and absolute code size of best solutions. All teams hold the same number of members (4). The WV combination based on winner-takes-all classification produces the largest teams. It seems that multiple outputs calculated by WV members increase their complexity. WTA teams are found to be smallest in code size. Actually, they are not much larger than a single standard individual in effective size and might even become smaller (see Table 11.6). This can be seen as another indication for the high specialization potential of the members in these teams. Among the other variants teams with non-uniform weights, like EVOL, are often smaller than standard teams (AV).

Table 11.7. heart: Absolute and effective code size of teams with 4 members and standard GP in instructions. Effective code of teams not even 50 percent larger than standard individuals on average.

Method	Code Size	Effective Size	Introns (%)
GP	128	38	70.3
AV	488	56	88.5
OPT	485	48	90.1
ERR	479	46	90.3
EVOL	481	**44**	90.9
MV	497	56	88.7
WV	504	68	86.5
WTA	479	57	88.1
WTA2	405	48	88.1

The proportion of noneffective code is comparably high for all team approaches. The intron proportion for standard GP is lower mostly because of the restriction of maximum size.

One reason for reduced growth of (effective) team members can be seen in the *lower variation probability* compared to standard GP individuals. We will see in the following section that it is not recommended to vary too many members simultaneously during a team operation. Best team prediction is obtained by varying only one member. Then the probability for crossover at a certain team position is reduced by a factor equal to the number of members. One might expect that member programs will grow faster the more members are varied. That this is not true, however, will be demonstrated in Section 11.5.4. Members with best prediction accuracy and largest effective length occur with the *lowest* variation rate.

As a result, there must be a reason other than variation speed for the relatively small effective size of teams. We have already seen in the last section that teams perform better than standard individuals after a sufficient number of generations. In order to make team solutions more efficient there must be *cooperation* going on between team members which allows them to specialize in certain subtasks. Because these subtasks can

Table 11.8. three function: Absolute and effective code size of teams with 4 members and standard GP in instructions.

Method	Code Size	Effective Size	Introns (%)
GP	128	58	54.7
AV	435	131	69.9
OPT	432	125	71.1
ERR	465	136	70.8
EVOL	456	123	73.0
WTA2	354	**76**	78.5

be expected to be less difficult than the main problem, subsolutions may be less complex than a full one-program solution. Therefore, a positive correlation between smaller (effective) member size and higher degree of specialization may be assumed.

11.5.3 Number of Team Members

We restrict the following analysis to the standard team approach (AV). Results are, however, representative for most other combination variants.

To find out the optimum number of team members, it is important that each team member is varied with a probability of 50 percent. Otherwise, if only one member would be changed at a time, the variation speed of members would be directly reduced with their number.

Table 11.9 compares the classification errors for the *two chains* problem and different numbers of team members ranging from one (standard GP) to eight. Using teams with many more individuals would be computationally unacceptable even if only effective instructions are executed. Both prediction performance and generalization performance increase with the number of members. But starting from a team size of about 4 members significant improvements no longer occur.

The connection between the number of members and the average code size of a member (in number of instructions) is shown in Table 11.10. Maximum code size for each member is 128 instructions. Absolute size and effective size per member decrease up to team size 4. Beyond 4 members, both sizes stay almost the same. This directly corresponds to the development in prediction quality from Table 11.9.[3]

---

[3]The amount of genetic material of the whole team increases with the number of members.

Table 11.9. *two chains*: Classification error (CE) in percent for different number of team members, averaged over 60 runs. Standard error in parentheses. Half of the team members are varied.

#Members	Training CE (%)	Member CE (%)	Validation CE (%)	Test CE (%)
1	3.33 (0.31)	3.3 (0.31)	4.70 (0.35)	5.59 (0.39)
2	1.33 (0.21)	16.5 (1.23)	2.34 (0.33)	3.31 (0.31)
3	0.89 (0.17)	23.1 (1.89)	1.59 (0.27)	2.64 (0.28)
4	0.37 (0.06)	27.4 (1.91)	0.69 (0.12)	1.84 (0.20)
5	0.36 (0.08)	32.8 (1.53)	0.47 (0.12)	1.90 (0.17)
6	0.38 (0.08)	32.6 (2.01)	0.58 (0.11)	1.76 (0.16)
7	0.30 (0.06)	30.2 (2.35)	0.48 (0.10)	1.78 (0.16)
8	0.39 (0.09)	34.1 (2.32)	0.48 (0.09)	1.76 (0.11)

Table 11.10. *two chains*: Average member size in instructions for different numbers of team members. Half of the team members are varied.

#Members	Member Size	Effective Size	Introns (%)
1	128	46	64.0
2	126	36	71.4
3	98	25	74.5
4	94	20	78.7
5	82	19	76.8
6	85	21	75.3
7	75	18	76.0
8	73	18	75.3

The reason for the reduction in effective member size can be seen in a distribution of the problem task among team individuals whereby the subtask each member has to fulfill gets smaller and easier. A second indication can be seen in Table 11.9, where average member error (on the basis of the full training set) increases respectively. Probably, beyond a certain number of individuals a task cannot be split any further. As a result, members keep to a certain effective size and prediction quality. Finally, there is only so small a complexity of programs that can fulfill a certain function.

The proportion of effective (and intron) code is not significantly affected, even though genetic operators change half of the members simultaneously in larger teams.

11.5.4   Number of Varied Members

All results so far have been produced by varying only a moderate number of team members simultaneously. To justify this choice, the number of members varied ranges from 1 to 4 in Table 11.11 while team size remains fixed. Both prediction and generalization performance are best if only one individual is varied at a time.

Table 11.11.   three functions: Mean square error (MSE × 100) with different numbers of varied members, averaged over 60 runs. Standard error in parentheses. Number of team members is 4.

#Varied Members	Training MSE	Member MSE	Validation MSE	Test MSE
1	4.1 (0.37)	903 (92)	3.4 (0.30)	3.7 (0.36)
2	5.4 (0.47)	730 (73)	4.8 (0.45)	4.9 (0.47)
3	6.5 (0.44)	538 (50)	5.5 (0.38)	6.3 (0.48)
4	8.3 (0.66)	421 (53)	7.1 (0.61)	7.6 (0.70)

Table 11.12.   three functions: Code size of team in instructions for different numbers of varied members. Number of team members is 4.

#Varied Members	Code Size	Effective Size	Introns (%)
1	440	148	66.4
2	424	125	70.5
3	388	113	70.9
4	320	99	69.1

Table 11.12 demonstrates the correlation between the number of team members varied and the code size of teams. Interestingly, effective and absolute code size decrease with variation strength. Although the variation probability per member is lowest if only one member is varied during a team operation, the effective code is largest. Simultaneously, the overall prediction accuracy of teams increases while average member error is highest with the lowest level of variation in Table 11.11.

One reason for these findings might be that smaller steps in variation allow more directed improvements of a solution than larger steps. Obviously, the effect of variation on the whole team is larger if more members are affected. In particular, single team individuals may specialize more strongly within the collective. By doing so, their errors in relation to a solution of the overall task as well as their complexity increase. As already observed in Section 11.5.1 higher member errors correspond to a higher degree in specialization.

Another reason might be that it is easier for smaller team solutions to survive during evolution. Lower (effective) complexity is the dominating protection against destruction here. The intron proportion is not affected significantly, i.e., the proportion of effective and noneffective code remains relatively constant in programs. Similar results have been found in Section 6.4.4 where a smaller variation step size, i.e., number of mutation points, produced better and larger effective programs.

11.5.5 Interpositional Recombination

In the preceding experiments recombination was restricted to happen between program members at the same position in both teams (*intra*positional recombination). It has been argued in Section 11.3.1 that in teams of multiple predictors – where by definition each member solves the same problem – allowing recombination between different member positions (*inter*positional recombination) could be beneficial. Only by interpositional recombination, member code can be moved from one position to another.

Table 11.13. *two chains*: Classification error (CE) in percent, averaged over 60 runs, with restricted (reprinted from Table 11.3) and unrestricted recombination. Standard error in parentheses.

Recombination	Training MSE	Member MSE	Validation MSE	Test MSE
free	0.34 (0.05)	25.7 (1.42)	0.65 (0.10)	1.82 (0.11)
restricted	0.44 (0.08)	25.8 (1.96)	0.82 (0.12)	2.08 (0.14)

Table 11.14. *three functions*: Mean square error (MSE × 100), averaged over 60 runs, with restricted (reprinted from Table 11.5) and unrestricted recombination. Standard error in parentheses.

Recombination	Training MSE	Member MSE	Validation MSE	Test MSE
free	4.4 (0.27)	682 (44)	3.7 (0.23)	3.8 (0.23)
restricted	4.7 (0.27)	738 (50)	3.9 (0.22)	4.3 (0.25)

Tables 11.13 and 11.14 show results for restricted and unrestricted recombination. Free (interpositional) recombination performs slightly better than restricted recombination with the problems tested. Thus, intrapositional recombination might be less relevant when dealing with teams of predictors. At least, it does not seem to have any positive influence.

11.5.6 Member Fitness

Finally, we investigate the effect of including ($\delta = 1$) or not including ($\delta = 0$) the average member error in the fitness function (Equation 11.7). Results in Tables 11.15 and 11.16 document that the average fitness of

team members is significantly better without the inclusion. This reduces
the specialization potential of members because the cooperating individuals are restricted to be good predictors on their own. As a result, the
quality of team prediction decreases significantly if individual errors are
included.

Table 11.15. *two chains*: Classification error (CE) in percent, averaged over 60 runs,
with and without including member fitness in Equation 11.7. Standard error in parentheses.

δ	Training MSE	Member MSE	Validation MSE	Test MSE
0	0.44 (0.08)	25.8 (1.96)	0.82 (0.12)	2.08 (0.14)
1	1.91 (0.21)	12.4 (0.61)	3.00 (0.25)	3.92 (0.28)

Table 11.16. *three functions*: Mean square error (MSE $\times$ 100), averaged over 60 runs,
with and without including member fitness. Standard error in parentheses.

δ	Training MSE	Member MSE	Validation MSE	Test MSE
0	4.7 (0.27)	738 (50)	3.9 (0.22)	4.3 (0.25)
1	19.4 (0.49)	34.6 (1.6)	18.0 (0.49)	18.1 (0.51)

If, on the other hand, individual errors are not included in the fitness
function there is no direct relation between fitness of a single member
and the quality of the common team solution. This allows the errors of
members to differ quite strongly within a team and to be significantly
larger than the team error.

11.6 Combination of Multiple Program Outputs

There is another interesting method of team evolution in linear GP. In the
standard case, a single register content is defined as the output of a linear
program. The program response, however, can be derived from more than
one register. Multiple outputs of a *single* program may be interpreted as
multiple predictions and can be combined by using the same methods as
proposed for team solutions in this chapter.

The aggregation of several program outputs may be supposed to promote
internal parallelism of calculations as well as a specialization of subprograms. But it has to be noted that a linear program may already combine
multiple calculation paths, i.e., the content of multiple registers in its
regular working.

Depending on the number of registers complementary subsolutions can
be computed by using relatively independent sets of registers in the same
program. Then subprograms would represent almost disconnected com-

ponents of the data flow graph. A complete separation like between team members, however, is rather unlikely, even if the number of registers is high compared to the number of inputs.

11.7 Summary and Conclusion

The results of this chapter can be summarized as follows:

☐ The team approach was applied successfully to several prediction problems and has been found to reduce both training error and generalization error significantly compared to the individual approach. This was already achieved by using standard averaging to combine outputs of team programs.

☐ Several linear combination methods were compared while different methods turned out to be the most successful ones. Two benchmark problems were presented on which either a winner-takes-all combination (WTA) or the coevolution of variable member weights (EVOL) performed notably better than other approaches.

☐ The average effective complexity of teams with four members was only about two times larger than stand-alone solutions. With some combination methods, team solutions have been found that are even smaller. Thus, the evolution of program teams is quite efficient because (structurally) noneffective instructions are not executed.

☐ A high degree of specialization and cooperation has been observed such that team members showed a much lower prediction performance and a smaller (effective) size than individuals. Beyond a certain optimum number of team members, however, both features did not change any more. One explanation could be that the overall problem task cannot be further divided into smaller subtasks.

☐ By including the prediction errors of members in the fitness function of teams, their specialization potential was reduced drastically. While the average member performance increased the overall team performance decreased.

☐ Best team solutions emerged with no more than one team member being varied at a time. Interestingly, teams seemed to be smaller and less specialized if several members were varied simultaneously.

☐ Intrapositional recombination of members has not been found to be more powerful than interpositional recombination for teams of predictors.

Epilogue

What have we achieved and where do we go from here?

This book has discussed linear genetic programming, a variant of GP that employs sequences of imperative instructions as genetic material. We focused on properties and behaviors of the linear representation and argued that it has a number of advantages over tree-based GP. We also pointed out extended similarities with its biological counterpart – the DNA sequence – that have so far not been appreciated sufficiently in the literature. For example, the fact that non-coding subsequences can be kept in the code and manipulated silently, i.e., without being activated, is pretty much analogous to what happens in real genomes.

Thinking in terms of data flow and register connections allowed us to accelerate artificial evolution in linear GP by considerable factors, on the basis of both absolute runtime and number of generations. It also allowed us to considerably increase the efficiency of evolutionary search operators. This led to an induction of more powerful solutions while at the same time keeping solution size and code growth under control.

We used a variety of benchmark problems to produce empirical results that were able to shed light on fundamental questions in GP and linear GP, in particular. We ventured to explain non-trivial phenomena and to develop powerful techniques, all with an eye to their implications on the practice of GP. As an empirical text, the book is heavily based on experimental data. These were generated through thousands of GP runs, comprising millions of program evaluations done with billions of CPU cycles.

Naturally, this book cannot have the last word on linear GP. If it has helped to promote the popularity of the approach and has opened avenues for further inquiry, it has served a good purpose. We sincerely hope to have conveyed the message and convinced the reader to give this method a try.

As we have already emphasized in the preface to this book, we hope readers have enjoyed immersing themselves into genetic programming reality. There are so many aspects of GP still under-explored, and so many questions not answered, and so many not even asked yet, that research on code evolution will go on for many years to come. Perhaps some of you will have conceived of an idea during reading this text. It is now time for you to take action and implement this idea in an actual GP setting, coming up with interesting answers and perhaps even more interesting questions.

References

[1] R. Allen and K. Kennedy, *Optimizing Compilers for Modern Architectures*. Morgan Kaufmann, San Francisco, CA, 2002.

[2] L. Altenberg, *Emergent Phenomena in Genetic Programming*. In A.V. Sebald and L.J. Fogel (eds.) *Proceedings of the Third Annual Conference on Evolutionary Programming*, pp. 233–241, World Scientific, 1994.

[3] L. Altenberg, *The Evolution of Evolvability in Genetic Programming*. In K.E. Kinnear (ed.) *Advances in Genetic Programming*, ch. 3, pp. 47–74, MIT Press, Cambridge, MA, 1994.

[4] D. Andre and J.R. Koza, *Parallel Genetic Programming: A Scalable Implementation Using The Transputer Network Architecture*. In P.J. Angeline and K.E. Kinnear (eds.) *Advances in Genetic Programming II*, ch. 16, pp. 317–337, MIT Press, Cambridge, MA, 1996.

[5] P.J. Angeline and J.B. Pollack, *The Evolutionary Induction of Subroutines*. In *Proceedings of the Fourteenth Conference of the Cognitive Science Society*, pp. 236–241, Lawrence Erlbaum, NJ, 1992.

[6] P.J. Angeline, *Subtree Crossover: Building Block Engine or Macro Mutation*. In J.R. Koza, K. Deb, M. Dorigo, D.B. Fogel, M. Garzon, H. Iba, and R.L. Riolo (eds.) *Proceedings of the Second Annual Conference on Genetic Programming (GP'97)*, pp. 9–17, Morgan Kaufmann, San Francisco, CA, 1997.

[7] W. Banzhaf, *Genetic Programming for Pedestrians*. In S. Forrest (ed.) *Proceedings of the Fifth International Conference on Genetic Algorithms (ICGA'93)*, p. 628, Morgan Kaufmann, San Francisco, CA, 1993.

[8] W. Banzhaf, *Genotype-Phenotype-Mapping and Neutral Variation: A Case Study in genetic programming*. In Y. Davidor, H.-P. Schwefel, and R. Männer (eds.) *Parallel Problem Solving from Nature (PPSN) III*, pp. 322–332, Springer, Berlin, 1994.

[9] W. Banzhaf, P. Nordin, R. Keller, and F. Francone, *Genetic Programming – An Introduction. On the Automatic Evolution of Computer Programs and its Application*. dpunkt/Morgan Kaufmann, Heidelberg/San Francisco, 1998.

[10] W. Banzhaf and W.B. Langdon, *Some Considerations on the Reason for Bloat.* Genetic Programming and Evolvable Machines, vol. 3(1), pp. 81–91, 2002.

[11] W. Banzhaf, M. Brameier, M. Stautner, and K. Weinert, *Genetic Programming and its Application in Machining Technology.* In H.-P. Schwefel, I. Wegener, and K. Weinert (eds.) *Advances in Computational Intelligence – Theory and Practice,* Natural Computing Series, ch.7, pp. 194–242, Springer, Berlin, 2003.

[12] W. Banzhaf and A. Leier, *Evolution on Neutral Networks in Genetic Programming.* In T. Yu, R.L. Riolo, and B. Worzel (eds.) *Genetic Programming Theory and Practice III,* ch. 14, pp. 207–221, Springer, 2005.

[13] R. Baumgart-Schmitt, A. Wenzel, H. Danker-Hopfe, and W.M. Herrmann, *Genetic Programming Approach for the Optimal Selection of Combinations of Neural Networks to Classify Sleep Stages by Quisi.* Methods and Findings in Experimental and Clinical Pharmacology, vol. 24, pp. 27–32, 2002.

[14] W.G. Baxt, *Applications of Artificial Neural Networks to Clinical Medicine.* Lancet, vol. 346, pp. 1135–1138, 1995.

[15] C.J. Biesheuvel, I. Siccama, D.E. Grobbee, and K.G.M. Moons, *Genetic Programming Outperformed Multivariable Logistic Regression in Diagnosing Pulmonary Embolism.* Journal of Clinical Epidemiology, vol. 57, pp. 551–560, 2004.

[16] T. Blickle and L. Thiele, *Genetic Programming and Redundancy.* In J. Hopf (ed.) *Genetic Algorithms within the Framework of Evolutionary Computation (Workshop at KI'94),* Technical Report No. MPI-I-94-241, pp. 33–38, Max-Planck-Institut für Informatik, 1994.

[17] T. Blickle and L. Thiele, *A Comparison of Selection Schemes Used in Genetic Algorithms.* Technical Report 11/2, TIK Institute, ETH, Swiss Federal Institute of Technology, 1995.

[18] C.C. Bojarczuk, H.S. Lopes, and A.A. Freitas, *Genetic Programming for Knowledge Discovery in Chest-Pain Diagnosis.* IEEE Engineering in Medicine and Biology Magazine, 19(4), pp. 38–44, 2000.

[19] C.C. Bojarczuk, H.S. Lopes, A.A. Freitas, and E.L. Michalkiewicz, *A Constrained-Syntax Genetic Programming System for Discovering Classification Rules: Application to Medical Data Sets.* Artificial Intelligence in Medicine, vol. 30(1), pp. 27–48, 2004.

[20] M. Brameier, W. Kantschik, P. Dittrich, and W. Banzhaf, *SYSGP - A C++ Library of Different GP Variants.* Technical Report CI-98/48, Collaborative Research Center 531, University of Dortmund, 1998.

[21] M. Brameier and W. Banzhaf, *A Comparison of Linear Genetic Programming and Neural Networks in Medical Data Mining.* IEEE Transactions on Evolutionary Computation, vol. 5(1), pp. 17–26, 2001.

[22] M. Brameier and W. Banzhaf, *Evolving Teams of Predictors with Linear Genetic Programming.* Genetic Programming and Evolvable Machines, vol. 2(4), pp. 381–407, 2001.

[23] M. Brameier and W. Banzhaf, *Effective Linear Program Induction.* Technical Report CI-108/01, Collaborative Research Center 531, University of Dortmund, 2001.

[24] M. Brameier and W. Banzhaf, *Explicit Control of Diversity and Effective Variation Distance in Linear Genetic Programming.* In J.A. Foster, E. Lutton, J. Miller, C. Ryan, and A.G.B. Tettamanzi (eds.) *Proceedings of the Fifth European Conference on Genetic Programming (EuroGP 2002)*, LNCS, vol. 2278, pp. 37–49, Springer, Berlin, 2002.

[25] M. Brameier and W. Banzhaf, *Neutral Variations Cause Bloat in Linear GP.* In C. Ryan, T. Soule, M. Keijzer, E. Tsang, R. Poli, and E. Costa (eds.) *Proceedings of the Sixth European Conference on Genetic Programming (EuroGP 2003)*, LNCS, vol. 2610, pp. 286–296, Springer, Berlin, 2003.

[26] E.K. Burke, S. Gustafson, G. Kendall, and N. Krasnogor, *Is Increased Diversity in Genetic Programming Beneficial? – An Analysis of the Effects on Performance.* In R. Sarker, R. Reynolds, H. Abbass, K.C. Tan, B. McKay, D. Essam, and T. Gedeon (eds.) *Proceedings of the Congress on Evolutionary Computation (CEC 2003)*, pp. 1398–1405, IEEE Press, 2003.

[27] E.K. Burke, S. Gustafson, and G. Kendall, *Diversity in Genetic Programming: An Analysis of Measures and Correlation with Fitness.* IEEE Transactions on Evolutionary Computation, vol. 8(1), pp. 47–62, 2004.

[28] P.A. Castillo, J. Gonzles, J.J. Merelo, A. Prieto, V. Rivas, and G. Romero, *SA-Prop: Optimization of Multilayer Perceptron Parameters using Simulated Annealing.* In *Proceedings of the International Work-Conference on Artificial and Natural Neural Networks (IWANN'99)*, LNCS, vol. 1606, pp. 661–670, Springer, Berlin, 1999.

[29] K. Chellapilla, *Evolving Computer Programs without Subtree Crossover.* IEEE Transactions on Evolutionary Computation, vol. 1(3), pp. 209–216, 1998.

[30] N.L. Cramer, *A Representation for the Adaptive Generation of Simple Sequential Programs.* In J. Grefenstette (ed.) *Proceedings of the First International Conference on Genetic Algorithms (ICGA'85)*, pp. 183–187, 1985.

[31] J.F. Crow, *Thomas H. Jukes.*, Genetics, vol. 154, pp. 955–956, 2000.

[32] L.J. Dekker, W. Boogerd, G. Stockhammer, J.C. Dalebout, I. Siccama, P.P. Zheng, J.M. Bonfrer, J.J. Verschuuren, G. Jenster, M.M. Verbeek, T.M. Luider, and P.A.S. Smitt, *MALDI-TOF Mass Spectrometry Analysis of Cerebrospinal Fluid Tryptic Peptide Profiles to Diagnose Leptomeningeal Metastases in Patients with Breast Cancer.* Molecular & Cellular Proteomics, vol. 4(9), pp. 1341–1349, 2005.

[33] S. Droste and D. Wiesmann, *Metric Based Evolutionary Algorithms.* In R. Poli, W. Banzhaf, W.B. Langdon, J.F. Miller, P. Nordin, and T.C. Fogarty (eds.) *Proceedings of the Third European Conference on Genetic Programming (EuroGP 2000)*, LNCS, vol. 1802, pp. 29–43, Springer, Berlin, 2000.

[34] A. Ekart and S. Nemeth, *Maintaining the Diversity of Genetic Programs.* In J.A. Foster, E. Lutton, J. Miller, C. Ryan, and A. Tettamanzi (eds.) *Proceedings of the Fifth European Conference on Genetic Programming (EuroGP 2002)*, LNCS, vol. 2278, pp. 162–171, Springer, Berlin, 2002.

[35] C. Estebanez, J.M. Valls, R. Aler, and I.M. Galvan, *A First Attempt at Constructing Genetic Programming Expressions for EEG Classification.* In W. Duch, J. Kacprzyk, E. Oja, and S. Zadrozny (eds.), *Proceedings of Fifteenth International Conference on Artificial Neural Networks: Biological Inspirations (ICANN 2005)*, LNCS, vol. 3696, pp. 665–670, Springer, Berlin, 2005.

[36] R.W. Floyd and R. Beigel, *The Language of Machines: An Introduction to Computability and Formal Languages.* Computer Science Press, New York, 1994.

[37] L.J. Fogel, A.J. Owens, and M.J. Walsh, *Artificial Intelligence through Simulated Evolution.* Wiley, New York, 1996.

[38] D.B. Fogel, *Evolutionary Computation: Towards a New Philosophy of Machine Intelligence.*, Wiley, New York, 1995.

[39] R. Friedberg, *A Learning Machine: Part I.* IBM Journal of Research and Development, vol. 2, pp. 2–13, 1958.

[40] R. Friedberg, B. Dunham, and J. North, *A Learning Machine: Part II.* IBM Journal of Research and Development, vol. 3, pp. 282–287, 1959.

[41] D. Goldberg, *Genetic Algorithms in Search, Optimization, and Machine Learning.* Addison-Wesley, Reading, MA, 1989.

[42] H.F. Gray, R.J. Maxwell, I. Martinez-Perez, C. Arus, and S. Cerdan, *Genetic Programming for Classification of Brain Tumors from Nuclear Magnetic Resonance Biopsy Spectra.* In J.R. Koza, D.E. Goldberg, D.B. Fogel, and Rick L. Riolo (eds.) *Proceedings of the First Annual Conference on Genetic Programming (GP'96)*, p. 424, MIT Press, Cambridge, MA, 1996.

[43] J.J. Grefenstette, *Predictive Models Using Fitness Distributions of Genetic Operators.* In L.D. Whitley and M.D. Vose (eds.) *Foundations of Genetic Algorithms 3*, pp. 139–161, Morgan Kaufmann, San Francisco, CA, 1995.

[44] D. Gusfield, *Algorithms on Strings, Trees and Sequences: Computer Science and Computational Biology*, Cambridge University Press, 1997.

[45] L.K. Hansen and P. Salamon, *Neural Network Ensembles.* IEEE Transactions on Pattern Analysis and Machine Intelligence, vol. 12(10), pp. 993–1001, 1990.

[46] K. Harries and P. Smith, *Exploring Alternative Operators and Search Strategies in Genetic Programming.* In J.R. Koza, K. Deb, M. Dorigo, D.B. Fogel, M. Garzon, H. Ibam, and R.L. Riolo (eds.) *Proceedings of the Second Annual Conference on Genetic Programming (GP'97)*, pp. 147–155, Morgan Kaufmann, San Francisco, CA, 1997.

[47] T. Haynes, S. Sen, D. Schoenefeld, and R. Wainwright, *Evolving a Team.* In E.V. Siegel and J.R. Koza (eds.), *Working Notes for the AAAI Symposium on Genetic Programming*, pp. 23–30, MIT Press, Cambridge, MA, 1995.

[48] T. Haynes and S. Sen, *Crossover Operators for Evolving a Team*. In J.R. Koza, K. Deb, M. Dorigo, D.B. Fogel, M. Garzon, H. Iba, and R.L. Riolo (eds.) *Proceedings of the Second Annual Conference on Genetic Programming (GP'97)*, pp. 162–167, Morgan Kaufmann, San Francisco, CA, 1997.

[49] M.I. Heywood and A.N. Zincir-Heywood, *Dynamic Page-Based Crossover in Linear Genetic Programming*. IEEE Transactions on Systems, Man and Cybernetics, vol. 32B(3), pp. 380–388, 2002.

[50] J. Holland, *Adaption in Natural and Artificial Systems*. University of Michigan Press, Ann Arbor, MI, 1975.

[51] J.H. Hong and S.B. Cho, *Cancer Prediction Using Diversity-Based Ensemble Genetic Programming*. In V. Torra, Y. Narukawa, and S. Miyamoto (eds.) *Proceedings of the Second International Conference on Modeling Decisions for Artificial Intelligence (MDAI 2005)*, LNCS, vol. 3558, pp. 294–304, 2005.

[52] C. Igel and K. Chellapilla, *Investigating the Influence of Depth and Degree of Genotypic Change on Fitness in Genetic Programming*. In W. Banzhaf, J. Daida, A.E. Eiben, M.H. Garzon, V. Honavar, M. Jakiela, and R.E. Smith (eds.) *Proceedings of the Genetic and Evolutionary Computation Conference (GECCO'99)*, pp. 1061–1068, Morgan Kaufmann, San Francisco, CA, 1999.

[53] C. Igel and K. Chellapilla, *Fitness Distributions: Tools for Designing Efficient Evolutionary Computations*. In L. Spector, W.B. Langdon, U.-M. O'Reilly, and P.J. Angeline (eds.) *Advances in Genetic Programming III*, ch. 9, pp. 191–216, MIT Press, Cambridge, MA, 1999.

[54] T. Jones and S. Forrest, *Fitness Distance Correlation as a Measure of Problem Difficulty for Genetic Algorithms*. In L.J. Eshelmann (ed.), *Proceedings of the Sixth International Conference on Genetic Algorithms (ICGA'95)*, pp. 184–192, Morgan Kaufmann, San Francisco, CA, 1995.

[55] E.D. de Jong, R.A. Watson, and J.B. Pollack, *Reducing Bloat and Promoting Diversity using Multi-Objective Methods*. In L. Spector, E.D. Goodman, A. Wu, W.B. Langdon, H.M. Voigt, M. Gen, S. Sen, M. Dorigo, S. Pezeshk, M.H. Garzon, and E. Burke (eds.) *Proceedings of the Genetic and Evolutionary Computation Conference (GECCO 2001)*, pp. 11–18, Morgan Kaufmann, San Francisco, CA, 2001.

[56] E.D. de Jong and J.B. Pollack, *Multi-Objective Methods for Tree Size Control*. Genetic Programming and Evolvable Machines, vol. 4(3), pp. 211–233, 2003.

[57] W. Kantschik and W. Banzhaf, *Linear-Graph GP – A New GP Structure*. In J.A. Foster, E. Lutton, J. Miller, C. Ryan, and A.G.B. Tettamanzi (eds.) *Proceedings of the Fifth European Conference on Genetic Programming (EuroGP 2002)*, LNCS, vol. 2278, pp. 83–92, Springer, Berlin, 2002.

[58] M. Keijzer, *Improving Symbolic Regression with Interval Arithmetic and Linear Scaling*. In C. Ryan, T. Soule, M. Keijzer, E. Tsang, R. Poli, and E. Costa (eds.) *Proceedings of the Sixth European Conference on Genetic Programming (EuroGP 2003)*, LNCS, vol. 2610, pp. 70–82, Springer, Berlin, 2003.

[59] R. Keller and W. Banzhaf, *Explicit Maintenance of Genetic Diversity on Genospaces*, Internal Report, University of Dortmund, 1995.

[60] M. Kimura and G.H. Weiss, *The Stepping Stone Model of Population Structure and the Decrease of Genetic Correlation with Distance*. Genetics, vol. 49, pp. 313–326, 1964.

[61] M. Kimura, *The Neutral Theory of Molecular Evolution*. Cambridge University Press, 1983.

[62] M. Kimura, *Some Recent Data Supporting the Neutral Theory*. In M. Kimura and N. Takahata (eds.) *New Aspects of the Genetics of Molecular Evolution*, pp. 3–14, Springer, Berlin, 1991.

[63] J.R. Koza, *Hierarchical Genetic Algorithms Operating on Populations of Computer Programs*. In N.S. Sridharan (ed.) *Proceedings of the Eleventh International Joint Conference on Artificial Intelligence (IJCAI'89)*, vol. 1, pp. 768–774, Morgan Kaufmann, San Francisco, CA, 1989.

[64] J.R. Koza, *Genetic Programming: On the Programming of Computer Programs by Natural Selection*. MIT Press, Cambridge, MA, 1992.

[65] J.R. Koza, *Genetic Programming II: Automatic Discovery of Reusable Programs*. MIT Press, Cambridge, MA, 1994.

[66] J.R. Koza, F.H. Bennett III, D. Andre, and M.A. Keane *Genetic Programming III: Darwinian Invention and Problem Solving*. Morgan Kaufmann, San Francisco, CA, 1999.

[67] J.R. Koza, M.A. Keane, M.J. Streeter, W. Mydlowec, J. Yu, and G. Lanza, *Genetic Programming IV: Routine Human-Competitive Machine Intelligence*. Springer, 2003.

[68] A. Krogh and J. Vedelsby, *Neural Network Ensembles, Cross Validation, and Active Learning*. In G. Tesauro, D.S. Touretzky, and T.K. Leen (eds.) *Advances in Neural Information Processing Systems*, vol. 7, pp. 231–238, MIT Press, Cambridge, MA, 1995.

[69] H.C. Kuo, H.K. Chang, and Y.Z. Wang *Symbiotic Evolution-Based Design of Fuzzy-Neural Diagnostic System for Common Acute Abdominal Pain*. Expert Systems with Applications, vol. 27(3), pp. 391–401, 2004.

[70] W.B. Langdon and R. Poli, *Fitness Causes Bloat*. In P.K. Chawdhry, R. Roy, and R.K. Pant (eds.) *Soft Computing in Engineering Design and Manufacturing*, pp. 13–22, Springer, 1997.

[71] W.B. Langdon, T. Soule, R. Poli, and J.A. Foster, *The Evolution of Size and Shape*. In L. Spector, W.B. Langdon, U.-M. O'Reilly, and P.J. Angeline (eds.) *Advances in Genetic Programming III*, ch. 8, pp. 163–190, MIT Press, Cambridge, MA, 1999.

[72] W.B. Langdon, *Size Fair and Homologous Tree Genetic Programming Crossovers*. Genetic Programming and Evolvable Machines, vol. 1(1/2), pp. 95–119, 2000.

[73] W.B. Langdon, S.J. Barrett, and B.F. Buxton, *Genetic Programming for Combining Neural Networks for Drug Discovery*. In R. Roy, M. Köppen, S. Ovaska, T. Furuhashi, and F. Hoffmann (eds.) *Soft Computing and Industry Recent Applications*, pp. 597–608, Springer, Berlin, 2002.

[74] W.B. Langdon, S.J. Barrett, and B.F. Buxton, *Combining Decision Trees and Neural Networks for Drug Discovery*. In J.A. Foster, E. Lutton, J. Miller, C. Ryan, and A.G.B. Tettamanzi (eds.) *Proceedings of the Fifth European Conference on Genetic Programming (EuroGP 2002)*, LNCS, vol. 2278, pp. 60–70, Springer, Berlin, 2002.

[75] W.B. Langdon and W. Banzhaf, *Repeated Patterns in Tree Genetic Programming*. In M. Keijzer, A. Tettamanzi, P. Collet, J. van Hemert, and M. Tomassini (eds.) *Proceedings of the Eighth European Conference on Genetic Programming (EuroGP 2005)*, LNCS, vol. 3447, pp. 190–202, Springer, Berlin, 2005.

[76] W.B. Langdon and W. Banzhaf, *Repeated Sequences in Linear Genetic Programming Genomes*. Complex Systems, vol. 15(4), pp. 285–306, 2005.

[77] W.B. Langdon and W. Banzhaf, *Repeated Patterns in Genetic Programming*. Natural Computing, vol. 5, 2006, forthcoming.

[78] P.J.G. Lisboa, *A Review of Evidence of Health Benefit from Artificial Neural Networks in Medical Intervention*. Neural Networks, vol. 15, pp. 11–39, 2002.

[79] E.G. Lopez, K. Rodriguez Vazquez, and R. Poli, *Beneficial Aspects of Neutrality in GP*. In F. Rothlauf (ed.) *Late Breaking Papers at the Genetic and Evolutionary Computation Conference (GECCO 2005)*, 2005.

[80] S. Luke and L. Spector, *Evolving Teamwork and Coordination with Genetic Programming*. In J.R. Koza, D.E. Goldberg, D.B. Fogel, and Rick L. Riolo (eds.) *Proceedings of the First Annual Conference on Genetic Programming (GP'96)*, pp. 150–156, MIT Press, Cambridge, MA, 1996.

[81] S. Luke and L. Spector, *A Revised Comparison of Crossover and Mutation in Genetic Programming*. In J.R. Koza, W. Banzhaf, K. Chellapilla, K. Deb, M. Dorigo, D.B. Fogel, M.H. Garzon, D.E. Goldberg, H. Iba, and Rick Riolo (eds.) *Proceedings of the Third Annual Conference on Genetic Programming (GP'98)*, pp. 208–213, Morgan Kaufmann, San Francisco, CA, 1998.

[82] S. Luke and L. Panait, *Fighting Bloat with Nonparametric Parsimony Pressure*. In J.J. Merelo-Guervos, P. Adamidis, H.-G. Beyer, J.L. Fernandez-Villacanas, and H.-P. Schwefel (eds.) *Parallel Problem Solving from Nature (PPSN) VII*, LNCS, vol. 2439, pp. 411–421, Springer, Berlin, 2002.

[83] B. Manderick, M. de Weger, and P. Spiessens, *The Genetic Algorithm and the Structure of the Fitness Landscape*. In R. Belew and L. Booker (eds.) *Proceedings of the Fourth International Conference on Genetic Algorithms (ICGA'91)*, pp. 143–150, Morgan Kaufmann, San Francisco, CA, 1991.

[84] T. Mitchell, *Machine Learning*. McGraw-Hill, New York, 1996.

[85] P. Monsieurs and E. Flerackers, *Reducing Population Size While Maintaining Diversity*. In C. Ryan, T. Soule, M. Keijzer, E. Tsang, R. Poli, and E. Costa

(eds.) *Proceedings of the Sixth European Conference on Genetic Programming (EuroGP 2003)*, LNCS, vol. 2610, pp. 142–152, Springer, Berlin, 2003.

[86] J.H. Moore, J.S. Parker, N.J. Olsen and T.M. Aune, *Symbolic Discriminant Analysis of Microarray Data in Autoimmune Disease.* Genetic Epidemiology, vol. 23(1), pp. 57–69, 2002.

[87] G. Navarro and M. Raffinot, *Flexible Pattern Matching in Strings – Practical Online Search Algorithms for Texts and Biological Sequences*, Cambridge University Press, 2002.

[88] D.J. Newman, S. Hettich, C.L. Blake and C.J. Merz, *UCI Repository of Machine Learning Databases*, University of California, Department of Information and Computer Science, <http://www.ics.uci.edu/~mlearn/MLRepository.html>.

[89] P.S. Ngan, M.L. Wong, K.S. Leung, and J.C.Y. Cheng, *Using Grammar Based Genetic Programming for Data Mining of Medical Knowledge.* In J. Koza, W. Banzhaf, K. Chellapilla, K. Deb, M. Dorigo, D.B. Fogel, M.H. Garzon, D.E. Goldberg, H. Iba, and R.L. Riolo (eds.) *Proceedings of the Third Annual Conference on Genetic Programming (GP'98)*, Morgan Kaufmann, San Francisco, CA, 1998.

[90] P. Nordin, *A Compiling Genetic Programming System that Directly Manipulates the Machine-Code.* In K.E. Kinnear (ed.) *Advances in Genetic Programming*, ch. 14, pp. 311–331, MIT Press, Cambridge, MA, 1994.

[91] P. Nordin and W. Banzhaf, *Complexity Compression and Evolution.* In L.J. Eshelman (ed.) *Proceedings of the Sixth International Conference on Genetic Algorithms (ICGA'95)*, pp. 310–317, Morgan Kaufmann, San Francisco, CA, 1995.

[92] P. Nordin, F. Francone, and W. Banzhaf, *Explicit Defined Introns and Destructive Crossover in Genetic Programming.* In P. Angeline and K.E. Kinnear (eds.) *Advances in Genetic Programming II*, ch. 6, pp. 111–134, MIT Press, Cambridge, MA, 1996.

[93] P.J. Nordin, *Evolutionary Program Induction of Binary Machine Code and its Applications.* PhD thesis, University of Dortmund, Department of Computer Science, 1997.

[94] P. Nordin, W. Banzhaf, and F. Francone, *Efficient Evolution of Machine Code for CISC Architectures using Blocks and Homologous Crossover. Advances in Genetic Programming III*, ch. 12, pp. 275–299, MIT Press, Cambridge, MA, 1999.

[95] T. Ohta, *The Nearly Neutral Theory of Molecular Evolution.* Annual Review of Ecology and Systematics, vol. 23, pp. 263–286, 1992.

[96] T. Ohta, *Near-Neutrality in Evolution of Genes and Gene Regulation.* Proceedings of the National Academy of Sciences (PNAS), vol. 99, pp. 16134–16137, 2002.

[97] M. Oltean, C. Grosan, and M. Oltean, *Encoding Multiple Solutions in a Linear Genetic Programming Chromosome.* In M. Bubak, G.D. van Albada, P.M.A. Sloot, and J. Dongarra (eds.) *Proceedings of the Fourth International Conference on Computational Science (ICCS 2004)*, LNCS, vol. 3038, pp. 1281–1288, Springer, Berlin, 2004.

[98] U.-M. O'Reilly and F. Oppacher, *Program Search with a Hierarchical Variable Length Representation: Genetic Programming, Simulated Annealing, and Hill Climbing.* In Y. Davidor, H.-P. Schwefel, and R. Männer (eds.) *Parallel Problem Solving from Nature (PPSN) III*, pp. 397–406, Springer, Berlin, 1994.

[99] U.-M. O'Reilly and F. Oppacher, *A Comparative Analysis of GP.* In P.J. Angeline and K.E. Kinnear (eds.) *Advances in Genetic Programming II*, ch. 2, pp. 23–44, MIT Press, Cambridge, MA, 1996.

[100] U.-M. O'Reilly, *Using a Distance Metric on Genetic Programs to Understand Genetic Operators.* In J.R. Koza (ed.) *Late Breaking Papers at the Genetic Programming Conference (GP'97)*, 1997.

[101] L. Panait and S. Luke, *Alternative Bloat Control Methods.* In K. Deb, R. Poli, W. Banzhaf, H.-G. Beyer, E. Burke, P. Darwen, D. Dasgupta, D. Floreano, J. Foster, M. Harman, O. Holland, P.L. Lanzi, L. Spector, A.Tettamanzi, D. Thierens, and A. Tyrrell (eds.) *Proceedings of the Genetic and Evolutionary Computation Conference (GECCO 2004)*, LNCS, vol. 3103, pp. 630–641, Springer, Berlin, 2004.

[102] C.A. Pena-Reyes and M. Sipper *Evolutionary Computation in Medicine: An Overview.* Artificial Intelligence in Medicine, vol. 19(1), pp. 1–23, 2000.

[103] M.P. Perrone and L.N. Cooper, *When Networks Disagree: Ensemble Methods for Neural Networks.* In R.J. Mammone (ed.) *Neural Network for Speech and Image Processing*, pp. 126–142, Chapman-Hall, London, 1993.

[104] M.D. Platel, M. Clergue, and P. Collard, *Homology Gives Size Control in Genetic Programming.* In R. Sarker, R. Reynolds, H. Abbass, K.C. Tan, B. McKay, D. Essam, and T. Gedeon (eds.) *Proceedings of the Congress on Evolutionary Computation (CEC 2003)*, pp. 281–288, IEEE Press, 2003.

[105] M.D. Platel, M. Clergue, and P. Collard, *Maximum Homologous Crossover for Linear Genetic Programming.* In C. Ryan, T. Soule, M. Keijzer, E. Tsang, R. Poli, and E. Costa (eds.) *Proceedings of the Sixth European Conference on Genetic Programming (EuroGP 2003)*, LNCS, vol. 2610, pp. 194–203, Springer, Berlin, 2003.

[106] M. Podbregar, M. Kovacic, A. Podbregar-Mars, and M. Brezocnik, *Predicting Defibrillation Success by Genetic Programming in Patients with Out-of-Hospital Cardiac Arrest.* Resucitation, vol. 57(2), pp. 153–159, 2003.

[107] R. Poli, *Exact Schema Theory for Genetic Programming and Variable-Length Genetic Algorithms with One-Point Crossover.* Genetic Programming and Evolvable Machines, vol. 2, pp. 123–163, 2001.

[108] R. Poli, N.F. McPhee, and J.E. Rowe, *Exact Schema Theory and Markov Chain Models for Genetic Programming and Variable-length Genetic Algorithms with Homologous Crossover.* Genetic Programming and Evolvable Machines, vol. 5, pp. 31–70, 2004.

[109] L. Prechelt, Proben1 – *A Set of Neural Network Benchmark Problems and Benchmarking Rules.* Technical Report 21/94, University of Karlsruhe, 1994.

[110] I. Rechenberg, *Evolutionsstrategie '94.* Frommann-Holzboog, 1994.

[111] M. Riedmiller and H. Braun, *A Direct Adaptive Method for Faster Backpropagation Learning: The RPROP Algorithm.* In *Proceedings of the International Conference on Neural Networks (ICNN'93)*, pp. 586–591, San Francisco, CA, 1993.

[112] B.D. Ripley, *Neural Networks and Related Methods for Classification.* Journal of the Royal Statistical Society: Series B (Methodological), vol. 56, pp. 409–456, 1994.

[113] B.D. Ripley and R.M. Ripley, *Neural Networks as Statistical Methods in Survival Analysis.* In R. Dybowski and V. Grant (eds.) *Artificial Neural Networks: Prospects for Medicine*, Landes Biosciences Publishers, Texas, 1997.

[114] C. Robert, C.D. Arreto, J. Azerad, and J.F. Gaudy, *Bibliometric Overview of the Utilization of Artificial Neural Networks in Medicine and Biology.* Scientometrics, vol. 59, pp. 117–130, 2004.

[115] S.C. Roberts, D. Howard, and J.R. Koza, *Evolving Modules in Genetic Programming by Subtree Encapsulation.* In J.F. Miller, M. Tomassini, P.L. Lanzi, C. Ryan, A.G.B. Tettamanzi, and W.B. Langdon (eds.) *Proceedings of the Fourth European Conference on Genetic Programming (EuroGP 2001)*, LNCS, vol. 2038, pp. 160–175, Springer, Berlin, 2001.

[116] J.P. Rosca and D.H. Ballard, *Causality in Genetic Programming.* In L.J. Eshelmann (ed.), *Proceedings of the Sixth International Conference on Genetic Algorithms (ICGA'95)*, pp. 256–263, Morgan Kaufmann, San Francisco, CA, 1995.

[117] J.P. Rosca, *Generality Versus Size in Genetic Programming.* In J.R. Koza, D.E. Goldberg, D.B. Fogel, and R.L. Riolo (eds.) *Proceedings of the First Annual Conference on Genetic Programming (GP'96)*, pp. 381–387, MIT Press, Cambridge, MA, 1996.

[118] D. Sankoff and J.B. Kruskal (eds.) *Time Warps, String Edits, and Macromolecules: The Theory and Practice of Sequence Comparison*, Addison-Wesley, Reading, MA, 1983.

[119] H.-P. Schwefel, *Evolution and Optimum Seeking.* Wiley, New York, 1995.

[120] H.-P. Schwefel, I. Wegener, and K. Weinert (eds.) *Advances in Computational Intelligence – Theory and Practice*, Natural Computing Series, Springer, Berlin, 2003.

[121] B. Sendhoff, M. Kreutz, and W. von Seelen, *A Condition for the Genotype-Phenotype Mapping: Causality.* In T. Bäck (ed.) *Proceedings of the Seventh International Conference on Genetic Algorithms (ICGA'97)*, pp. 73–80, Morgan Kaufmann, San Francisco, CA, 1997.

[122] P.W.H. Smith and K. Harries, *Code Growth, Explicitly Defined Introns, and Alternative Selection Schemes.* Evolutionary Computation, vol. 6(4), pp. 339–360, 1998.

[123] R.L. Somorjai, A.E. Nikulin, N. Pizzi, D. Jackson, G. Scarth, B. Dolenko, H. Gordon, P. Russell, C.L. Lean, L. Delbridge, C.E. Mountford, and I.C.P. Smith, *Computerized Consensus Diagnosis – A Classification Strategy for the Robust Analysis of MR Spectra. 1. Application to H-1 Spectra of Thyroid Neoplasma.* Magnetic Resonance in Medicine, vol. 33, pp. 257–263, 1995.

[124] T. Soule, J.A. Foster, and J. Dickinson, *Code Growth in Genetic Programming.* In J.R. Koza, D.E. Goldberg, D.B. Fogel, and R.L. Riolo (eds.) *Proceedings of the First Annual Conference on Genetic Programming (GP'96),* pp. 215–223, MIT Press, Cambridge, MA, 1996.

[125] T. Soule and J.A. Foster, *Removal Bias: A New Cause of Code Growth in Tree-based Evolutionary Programming.* In *Proceedings of the International Conference on Evolutionary Computation (ICEC'98),* pp. 781–786, IEEE Press, New York, 1998.

[126] T. Soule, *Voting Teams: A Cooperative Approach to Non-Typical Problems using Genetic Programming.* In W. Banzhaf, J. Daida, A.E. Eiben, M.H. Garzon, V. Honavar, M. Jakiela, and R.E. Smith (eds.) *Proceedings of the Genetic and Evolutionary Computation Conference (GECCO'99),* pp. 916–922, Morgan Kaufmann, San Francisco, CA, 1999.

[127] T. Soule, *Heterogeneity and Specialization in Evolving Teams.* In D. Whitley, D. Goldberg, E. Cantu-Paz, L. Spector, I. Parmee, and H.-G. Beyer (eds.) *Proceedings of the Genetic and Evolutionary Computation Conference (GECCO 2000),* pp. 778–785, Morgan Kaufmann, San Francisco, CA, 2000.

[128] T. Soule and R.B. Heckendorn, *An Analysis of the Causes of Code Growth in Genetic Programming.* Genetic Programming and Evolvable Machines, vol. 3(3), pp. 283–309, 2002.

[129] J. Stevens, R.B. Heckendorn, and T. Soule, *Exploiting Disruption Aversion to Control Code Bloat.* In H.-G. Beyer, U.-M. O'Reilly, D.V. Arnold, W. Banzhaf, C. Blum, E.W. Bonabeau, E. Cantu-Paz, D. Dasgupta, K. Deb, J.A. Foster, E.D. de Jong, H. Lipson, X. Llora, S. Mancoridis, M. Pelikan, G.R. Raidl, T. Soule, A.M. Tyrrell, J.P. Watson, and E. Zitzler (eds.) *Proceedings of the Genetic and Evolutionary Computation Conference (GECCO 2005),* pp. 1605–1612, ACM Press, 2005.

[130] W.A. Tackett, *Recombination, Selection and the Genetic Construction of Computer Programs.* PhD thesis, University of Southern California, Department of Electrical Engineering Systems, 1994.

[131] K.C. Tan, Q. Yu, C.M. Heng, and T.H. Lee, *Evolutionary Computing for Knowledge Discovery in Medical Diagnosis.* Artificial Intelligence in Medicine, vol. 27(2), pp. 129–154, 2003.

[132] K.C. Tan, Q. Yu, C.M. Heng, and T.H. Lee, *A Distributed Evolutionary Classifier for Knowledge Discovery in Data Mining.* IEEE Transactions on Systems, Man and Cybernetics, vol. 35C(2), pp. 131–142, 2005.

[133] R. Tanese, *Distributed Genetic Algorithms.* In J.D. Schaffer (ed.) *Proceedings of the Third International Conference on Genetic Algorithms (ICGA'89),* pp. 434–439, Morgan Kaufmann, San Francisco, CA, 1989.

[134] A. Teller, *Turing Completeness in the Language of Genetic Programming with Indexed Memory.* In *Proceedings of the World Congress on Computational Intelligence (WCCI'94)*, vol. 1, pp. 136–141, IEEE Press, New York, 1994.

[135] A. Teller, *PADO: A New Learning Architecture for Object Recognition.* In K. Ikeuchi and M. Veloso (eds.) *Symbolic Visual Learning*, pp. 81–116, Oxford University Press, 1996.

[136] J.D. Watson, N.H. Hopkins, J.W. Roberts, J.A. Steitz, and A.M. Weiner, *Molecular Biology of the Gene.* Benjamin/Cummings Publishing Company, 1987.

[137] G.C. Wilson and M.I. Heywood, *Context-Based Repeated Sequences in Linear Genetic Programming.* In M. Keijzer, A. Tettamanzi, P. Collet, J. van Hemert, and M. Tomassini (eds.) *Proceedings of the Eighth European Conference on Genetic Programming (EuroGP 2005)*, LNCS, vol. 3447, pp. 240–249, Springer, Berlin, 2005.

[138] D.H. Wolpert, *Stacked Generalization.* Neural Networks, vol. 5(2), pp. 241–260, 1992.

[139] D.H. Wolpert and W.G. Macready, *No Free Lunch Theorem for Optimization.* IEEE Transactions on Evolutionary Computation, vol. 1(1), pp. 67–82, 1997.

[140] S. Wright, *Isolation by Distance.* Genetics, vol. 28, pp. 114–138, 1943.

[141] X. Yao and Y. Liu, *Making Use of Population Information in Evolutionary Artificial Neural Networks.* IEEE Transactions on Systems, Man and Cybernetics, vol. 28B(3), pp. 417–425, 1998.

[142] T. Yu, *Hierarchical Processing for Evolving Recursive and Modular Programs using Higher Order Functions and Lambda Abstractions.* Genetic Programming and Evolvable Machines, vol. 2(4), pp. 345–380, 2001.

[143] T. Yu and J. Miller, *Neutrality and the Evolvability of Boolean Function Landscapes.* In J.F. Miller, M. Tomassini, P.L. Lanzi, C. Ryan, A.G.B. Tettamanzi, and W.B. Langdon (eds.) *Proceedings of the Fourth European Conference on Genetic Programming (EuroGP 2001)*, LNCS, vol. 2038, pp. 204–217, Springer, Berlin, 2001.

[144] B.-T. Zhang and J.-G. Joung, *Enhancing Robustness of Genetic Programming at the Species Level.* In J.R. Koza, D.E. Goldberg, D.B. Fogel, and R.L. Riolo (eds.) *Proceedings of the First Annual Conference on Genetic Programming (GP'96)*, pp. 336–342, MIT Press, Cambridge, MA, 1996.

[145] P. Zohar, M. Kovacic, and M. Brezocnik, *Prediction of Maintenance of Sinus Rhythm after Electrical Cardioversion of Atrial Fibrillation by Non-deterministic Modelling.* Europace, vol. 7(5), pp. 500–507, 2005.

Index

Printed in the United States of America.